Women, Celebrity and Cultures of Ageing

Women, Celebrity and Cultures of Ageing

Freeze Frame

Edited by

Deborah Jermyn
University of Roehampton, UK

and

Su Holmes
University of East Anglia, UK

First published 2015 by
PALGRAVE MACMILLAN

Palgrave Macmillan in the UK is an imprint of Macmillan Publishers Limited, registered in England, company number 785998, of Houndmills, Basingstoke, Hampshire RG21 6XS.

Palgrave Macmillan in the US is a division of St Martin's Press LLC, 175 Fifth Avenue, New York, NY 10010.

Palgrave Macmillan is the global academic imprint of the above companies and has companies and representatives throughout the world.

Palgrave® and Macmillan® are registered trademarks in the United States, the United Kingdom, Europe and other countries.

ISBN 978-1-349-58090-3   ISBN 978-1-137-49512-9 (eBook)
DOI 10.1057/9781137495129

This book is printed on paper suitable for recycling and made from fully managed and sustained forest sources. Logging, pulping and manufacturing processes are expected to conform to the environmental regulations of the country of origin.

A catalogue record for this book is available from the British Library.

A catalog record for this book is available from the Library of Congress.

Deborah dedicates this book to Su and to all the girlfriends who share her burgeoning affection for velour, and to Matt (how about we get old together?)

Su dedicates this book to Debs, who has offered her another unique experience of co-writing and co-editing, and to Tabitha, who as yet knows nothing of being old.

Contents

List of Figures   ix

Acknowledgements   x

Notes on Contributors   xi

Introduction: A Timely Intervention – Unravelling the
Gender/Age/Celebrity Matrix   1
Deborah Jermyn and Su Holmes

1 Here, There and Nowhere: Ageing, Gender and Celebrity
   Studies   11
   Su Holmes and Deborah Jermyn

2 Reconfiguring Elinor Glyn: Ageing Female Experience and
   the Origins of the 'It Girl'   25
   Karen Randell and Alexis Weedon

3 Bette Davis: Acting and Not Acting Her Age   43
   Martin Shingler

4 Moms Mabley and Whoopi Goldberg: Age, Comedy and
   Celebrity   59
   Sadie Wearing

5 *'Je joue le rôle d'une petite vieille, rondouillarde et bavarde, qui
   raconte sa vie…'* ['I am playing the role of a little old lady,
   pleasantly plump and talkative, who is telling the story
   of her life…']: The Significance of Agnès Varda's Old Lady
   Onscreen   77
   Rona Murray

6 Ageing Grace/Fully: Grace Jones and the Queering of the
   Diva Myth   97
   Nathalie Weidhase

7 From the Woman Who 'Had It All' to the Tragic, Ageing
   Spinster: The Shifting Star Persona of Jennifer Aniston   112
   Susan Berridge

8   'Don't Wear Beige – It Might Kill You': The Politics of
    Ageing and Visibility in *Fabulous Fashionistas*   127
    Deborah Jermyn

9   The Best Exotic Graceful Ager: Dame Judi Dench and
    Older Female Celebrity   146
    Melanie Williams

10 'I'm Not Past My Sell By Date Yet!': Sarah Jane's Adventures
    in Postfeminist Rejuvenation and the Later-Life Celebrity
    of Elisabeth Sladen   162
    Hannah Hamad

11 'Call the Celebrity': Voicing the Experience of Women and
    Ageing through the Distinctive Vocal Presence of Vanessa
    Redgrave   178
    Ros Jennings and Eva Krainitzki

Index   197

List of Figures

2.1 Elinor Glyn in *It* (Clarence G. Badger, 1927)   31
2.2 Page from *Cosmopolitan* (1927) showing adverts alongside Glyn's story, 'It'   34
5.1 Screen shot of Varda in *Les plages d'Agnès* [The Beaches of Agnès] (2008)   80
5.2 Jamel Debbouze and Agnès Varda trade remarks on *Le Grand Journal* (2013)   84
5.3 Varda observes her ageing skin. *Les glaneurs et la glaneuse* (2000)   89
8.1 Sue Bourne in a media masterclass screening of *Fabulous Fashionistas* at University of Roehampton (2014)   131
8.2 Sue Kreitzman's window display at Selfridges featuring a Sue-styled mannequin, London (2015)   133
8.3 'Don't wear beige' – Sue's celebrated adage fashioned into a Tatty Devine pendant and for sale in Selfridges, London   134

Acknowledgements

We would like to thank Felicity Plester and Sneha Kamat Bhavnani at Palgrave Macmillan, and the generous anonymous reviewers who first read our proposal, for their support; our contributors and colleagues at the Universities of Roehampton and East Anglia; Janet McCabe for her invaluable input at the start of this project; and Tom Junod at *Esquire* for writing such an insultingly patronising article, 'In Praise of 42-Year Old Women', that we are forever committed to crushing his position.

Some of the chapters collected here began life at the 'Acting Their Age: Women, Ageing and the Movies' conference held at Newcastle University in May 2012, and we are grateful to Rebecca Knight for organising such an enjoyable and memorable event that enabled so many of us interested in the themes of this book to come together.

Notes on Contributors

Susan Berridge is Lecturer in Film and Media at the University of Leeds. Her research focuses on representations of age, gender, sexuality and sexual violence in popular culture. She has published on these themes in journals including *Feminist Media Studies, Journal of British Cinema and Television* and *New Review of Film and Television Studies*. Susan is also the co-editor of the Commentary and Criticism section of *Feminist Media Studies*.

Hannah Hamad is Lecturer in Film Studies at King's College London. She joined the department in January 2013, where she teaches in the areas of film history, the cultural politics of contemporary Hollywood cinema, fathers in film, and research and scholarship in Film Studies. She is the author of *Postfeminism and Paternity in Contemporary US Film: Framing Fatherhood* (2014) as well as numerous articles on postfeminist cultures of popular film and television, Hollywood stardom, contemporary celebrity culture, and UK cultures of reality TV. She is also a member of the editorial board of the journals *Celebrity Studies* and *Television and New Media*.

Su Holmes is a reader in Television at the University of East Anglia. She is the author of *British TV and Film Culture in the 1950s* (2005), *Entertaining TV: The BBC and Popular Programme Culture in the 1950s* (2008) and *The Quiz Show* (2008). She is also the co-editor of *Understanding Reality TV* (2004), *Framing Celebrity* (2006), *Stardom and Celebrity: A Reader* (2007), and *In the Limelight and Under the Microscope: Forms and Functions of Female Celebrity* (2011). She is now working on feminist approaches to eating disorders, as well as historical research into British children's television.

Ros Jennings is Director of the Centre for Women, Ageing and Media (WAM) and Head of Postgraduate Research at the University of Gloucestershire. She is a founder member of the European Network in Ageing Studies (ENAS), author of the *WAM Manifesto* (2012) and contributor to the UK *Charter against Ageism and Sexism in the Media* (launched 3 October 2013). She is co-editor with Abigail Gardner (2013) of *Rock On: Women, Ageing and Popular Music* and leader of the annual WAM International Summer School. Her research interests are older women and popular culture (in particular, popular music, television and film).

Deborah Jermyn is a reader in Film and Television at the University of Roehampton. Her work, with a recent focus on representations of older in contemporary media, has been been widely published, including articles in *CineAction, Critical Studies in Television* and *Celebrity Studies*. She is editor of *Female Celebrity and Ageing: Back in the Spotlight* (2013) and her books include *Sex and the City* (2009) and *Prime Suspect* (2010). Her current projects include a monograph on director Nancy Meyers.

Eva Krainitzki is a part-time lecturer at the School of Media and a research fellow at the Centre for Women, Ageing and Media (WAM) at the University of Gloucestershire. After graduating with a Master's from the University of Lisbon, she joined WAM as a funded doctoral researcher. She holds a PhD with a thesis on the intersection of ageing and lesbian identities in contemporary narrative film. Eva has published on Judi Dench's star image and the Bond film in the *Journal of Aging Studies*, 2014, and the portrayal of lesbian characters in film in the *Journal of Lesbian Studies*, 2015. Her research interests are ageing, lesbian images and popular culture (film and television).

Rona Murray is a PhD candidate at Lancaster University, researching into contemporary women's authorship in film and television. For a number of years she has worked independently and with National Media Museum (Bradford) to programme and present films directed by women and has recently taken on the role of Resources Officer for the Women's Film and Television History Network. Her article on Kathryn Bigelow appeared in *Networking Knowledge*, and she is currently writing on Agnès Varda's short films.

Karen Randell is Professor of Film and Culture at the University of Bedfordshire. Her research interests are trauma and war, and her publications include *The War Body on Screen* (2008), *Re-framing 9/11: Film, Popular Culture and 'The War on Terror'* (2010), *The Dark Side of Love: From Euro-Horror to American Cinema* (Palgrave Macmillan, 2011) and *The Cinema of Terry Gilliam: It's a Mad World* (2013).

Martin Shingler is Senior Lecturer in Radio & Film at the University of Sunderland. He is the author of *Star Studies: A Critical Guide* (2012) and the co-editor of the BFI *Film Star* book series. He's published 14 essays on the work of Hollywood actress Bette Davis and is currently writing a book for Palgrave Macmillan entitled *When Warners Brought Broadway to Hollywood, 1923–39*.

Sadie Wearing is Lecturer in Gender Theory, Culture and Media at the London School of Economics. Her research interests are in ageing, gender and culture and feminist and gender theory. She has published extensively on ageing in relation to popular culture and literature in both contemporary and historical contexts. She is the author with Niall Richardson of *Gender in the Media* (Palgrave Macmillan, 2014) and co-editor of *The Sage Handbook of Feminist Theory* (2014). She is a member of the editorial collective for *Feminist Review*.

Alexis Weedon is UNESCO Professor of New Media Forms of the Book at the University of Bedfordshire. Her research interests are in publishing, book history and cross-media adaptation. Her publications include *Victorian Publishing: The Economics of Book Production for a Mass Market* (2003), the five-volume *History of the Book in the West* (2010) and with V.L. Barnett *Elinor Glyn in Hollywood, Author, Filmmaker and Businesswoman*. In 1995, she co-founded *Convergence: The International Journal of Research into New Media Technologies* with Julia Knight.

Nathalie Weidhase is a PhD student at the University of Roehampton, where she researches postfeminist representations of femininity in popular music. Her research interests include (postfeminist) popular culture, feminist theory, and gender and digital media. Her research has appeared in the journal *Celebrity Studies*.

Melanie Williams is Senior Lecturer in Film and Television Studies at the University of East Anglia. She specialises in research on British cinema and is the author of *David Lean* (2014) and *Prisoners of Gender: Women in the Films of J. Lee Thompson* (2009), and co-editor of *Shane Meadows: Critical Essays* (2013), *Ealing Revisited* (2012), *Mamma Mia! The Movie: Exploring a Cultural Phenomenon* (2012) and *British Women's Cinema* (2009). She is currently working on a study of female British film stars and is co-investigator on the AHRC-funded project 'Transformation and Tradition in British Cinema of the 1960s: Industry, Creativity, and National Branding'.

Introduction: A Timely Intervention – Unravelling the Gender/Age/Celebrity Matrix

Deborah Jermyn and Su Holmes

Hallowe'en. The favourite holiday of the year for those of us with a weakness for fancy dress and costume parties. Over the years in the celebrity world, supermodel Heidi Klum has become known for her legendary Hallowe'en parties and extravagant costumes, from the 'Forbidden Fruit' in 2006 (an elaborate apple ensemble complete with evil serpent) to Cleopatra, Queen of the Nile, in 2012. In 2013, her party was scheduled to be held at Marquee in New York City. All eyes were on the entrance to see what kind of imaginative affair Klum would concoct this time.

But what is this? A vintage Rolls Royce has pulled up. Out steps a frail looking old lady. She walks with a cane, her sturdy beige handbag swung over the other arm. Her wispy white hair is pulled back, but still, she is unrecognisable. Who is the old lady?

The old lady is Heidi Klum in fancy dress costume.

What does Klum's choice of 'costume' in 2013 tell us about the status of 'elderly women' in contemporary culture, and indeed about contemporary celebrity, and its discursive constructions of 'old' age? When did looking old become not merely something that millions of people worldwide get on with every day and instead become something worthy of a circus sideshow, a spectacle, something to point at, stand aghast at, laugh at? What is most particularly compelling about the costume here specifically, of course, is the wearer. A supermodel – Heidi Klum, celebrated as one of the most beautiful women in the world and recognised internationally, too, for her success as host of *Project Runway* (Lifetime, US, 2004–) – has rendered herself the antithesis of all she stands for as a celebrity. There is nothing glamourous in this anonymous figure before us. It speaks of none of the desire that

1

celebrity prompts, no head-turning beauty resides here – this is just another old lady. As *Us Weekly* magazine noted:

> The 40-year-old German stunner completely transformed herself for the big event, with ultra-realistic age spots on her body and raised varicose veins running up her famously long legs. Gone were her trademark blonde tresses; in their place was a stringy, white wig.
>
> Klum's face was unrecognizable, too. Her normally taut skin appeared to sag, and there were wrinkles all over her forehead, chin, and neck. She wore a pearl necklace, printed top, and a houndstooth suit, and she had a black cane to help her walk. (Takeda, 2013)

What is most striking when pondering this account is how utterly unremarkable the description is. We read of age spots and varicose veins, white hair and wrinkles, physical frailty; in other words, the signifiers of advanced age. Unlike the fantastical 'Forbidden Fruit' and Cleopatra, if one wants to gawp at a 'costume' like this, one surely only has to take a trip to one's local high street. Klum's costume underlines how in a youth-obsessed culture the everyday lives and appearances of older people remain 'Other' – and its appearance specifically on Halloween marks the notion, too, of ageing being *scary*, the stuff of horror films and frightening folklore. Unsurprisingly, some outraged reactions to Klum's choice of outfit followed. *The Guardian's* Invisible Woman columnist, for example, pondered her incensed response to photos of Klum, observing:

> [I] began to wonder whether she was trying to subvert the whole supermodel eternal youth myth. Perhaps she was saying something profound about all of us heading the same way. Something like 'age is compulsory' or perhaps 'life is terminal'. But after reading her comments on Twitter, such as 'Little old me' – I decided I was crediting her with too much existential angst.
>
> No, it is quite simply that making herself into an old woman for an evening is meant to be funny – not ironic, not an indication of the inner terror of a young and beautiful woman, not witty or making a point, it is purely to ridicule the old. (Invisible Woman, 2013)

For Klum, of course, and as Takeda (2013) notes above, all this was the substance of a breathtaking transformation, a clever trick played on the assembled onlookers and admirers; for what could be more unexpected, more freakish, more astonishing, than a model being an old woman? Fashion and celebrity, however, are fickle fields indeed. So, let us fast-forward just a few months to 2014, when it began to seem like Klum may not have been just simply crass – perhaps she was an *innovator*. For at the age of 68, that spring, Charlotte Rampling is announced as the forthcoming face of NARS cosmetics. This is closely followed by news that Jessica Lange, aged 64, will front the new Marc Jacobs Beauty campaign. Note the significance here of the fact that these are not 'anti-ageing' brands or products, but regular (indeed rather aspirational) make-up lines. As women in their 60s, of course, Rampling and Lange demonstrate once more how subjective the terms 'old' and 'older' are; certainly, they are not the 'crones' that Klum was emulating in her costume. But their modelling contracts were greeted with curiosity and approval and appear to have helped open eyes and doors for the use of older models elsewhere.

At the time of writing early in 2015, then, much media debate has been prompted by the recent appointment of celebrated 80-year-old writer Joan Didion as the face of Céline – and, not only that, in a campaign where she still looks like Joan Didion (i.e., not sporting the polished, and no doubt airbrushed, professional finesse of actors Rampling and Lange in their adverts). Elsewhere, at 93, style arbiter Iris Apfel found herself in demand fronting two spring 2015 campaigns, for jewellery designer Alexis Bittar as well as Kate Spade. There were inevitably some concerns voiced that old age was being exploited here as a mere trend and would prove just another 'fashion fad', to be dropped in a season's time. And it would be sweeping indeed to claim these campaigns as evidence of a new and greater diversity in these industries, since all these women are white, speak of class privilege and are in possession of the kinds of trim bodies deemed aspirational by our culture whatever a woman's age.[1] But so, too, were the campaigns cautiously welcomed in some quarters, as perhaps indicative of a growing awareness of the need to expand representation across age ranges in the fashion and celebrity industries, not least to take into account the tastes of a breadth of differently aged consumers purchasing these goods and brands. In Molly Mulshine's words: 'Looking at an 80-year old who is confident, self-possessed and stylish not only makes you long for whatever she's wearing but also for her state of mind ... That seems so much more bankable than yet another fashion spread featuring an anonymous, gazelle-like child in women's clothing' (Mulshine, 2015).

Bookended in this way, these two snapshots of women, ageing and celebrity seemingly tell very different stories about how this matrix is configured in contemporary culture. As Deborah Jermyn noted in a special issue of *Celebrity Studies* on women, celebrity and ageing in 2012, ours is 'a culture where the representation of ageing and "older" female celebrities is by turns seemingly hopeful and newly affirming one moment and destructive and retrograde the next' (Jermyn, 2012: 10). Indeed, one of the reasons Klum's costume seemed so mortifying at one level was because of how hopelessly *out of step* it seemed with an apparent growing awareness of ageism (and the sexism frequently imbricated in this) in a zeitgeist which has become highly attuned to the fact of our ageing population (see Holmes and Jermyn's essay in Chapter 1 of this collection). The clash of values seemingly at stake in these stories of ageing female celebrity – where Klum shows old age is impossible to reconcile with the notion of female celebrity, and Didion et al. show the older woman celebrity need not fade away into invisibility but instead may still embody style and desirability – speaks volumes about the cultural moment we are in and the 'problem' that ageing women constitute for it. It is precisely this contradictory dialectic – and the discursive and representational terrain in between – which this volume seeks to interrogate, as we argue that celebrity has become *the* central lens in popular culture through which to interrogate questions of ageing and gender.

We open, then, with a chapter by Su Holmes and Deborah Jermyn that sets out the scholarly and disciplinary context for what follows in the collection. They chart the myriad ways in which, despite being a central structural framework within the gendered discourses of celebrity culture, ageing has remained largely neglected by Celebrity Studies, thus becoming simultaneously, as their title suggests, 'Here, there and nowhere'. In exploring the ways in which we now appear to be in the midst of a proliferating body of work with regard to the study of gender and ageing, the essay seeks to examine the recent growth of scholarship in this regard, whilst also arguing for the necessity of new avenues for future research.

'Reconfiguring Elinor Glyn: Ageing Female Experience and the Origins of the "It Girl"' (Chapter 2) is the first of our essays to look at historical precursors for understanding ageing female celebrity. Karen Randell and Alexis Weedon continue the emphasis on the elision of the 'older' woman by examining the ways in which, despite being a considerably influential figure in 1920s popular culture, Glyn has until very recently been marginalised in histories of the period which privilege the youth-centred nature of the flapper era. Focusing on Glyn's Hollywood status in the 1920s, the chapter examines her pervasive and intertextual celebrity, and the ways in which she functioned as an authority on sexual etiquette, marriage and the 'passion of love' for a younger female audience. Exploring Glyn's construction 'as a mature and sexually experienced woman, able to advise young women in Britain and America' on matters of the heart, Randell and Weedon offer a historical – and more literal – example of the intersection between celebrity, pedagogy and age and show how Glyn's famed notion of the desirability of 'It' – still very much with us in the proclaimed 'It Girls' of today – was never envisaged as predicated on youth, or gender for that matter.

In Chapter 3, Martin Shingler continues the focus on the often fraught intersection between age, femininity, stardom and longevity. As he explores in 'Bette Davis: Acting and Not Acting Her Age', Davis was an actress who did not shy away from depicting old age – an approach that he sees as key to her durability as a screen performer – even opting to play more mature characters before she was considered 'old'. Indeed, Davis was often understood as an actress who offered more challenging representations of femininity than generally seen on the Hollywood screen and here Shingler demonstrates how these images were 'inescapably interwoven' with discourses of ageing. As he notes, the 'very persistence of [Davis'] ... image and performances over many decades, not just as an "old star" but as an enduringly and atypically visible ageing *woman* star, in itself unsettled one of the gendered inequities at the heart of Hollywood'.

Reflecting the intention of the collection to extend work on the relationship between celebrity, ageing and femininity, which has overwhelmingly focused on *white* women as the key touchstone in these debates, Sadie Wearing's essay (Chapter 4) examines the role that age and ageing play in the construction and circulation of two black female comics, Jackie 'Moms' Mabley and Whoopi Goldberg. Focusing in particular on Goldberg's documentary *Whoopi Goldberg Presents Moms Mabley* (2013), the chapter uses the film to explore the ways in which gender, ethnicity and ageing intersect across the images of both women. Ultimately, Wearing argues that whilst a history of racialised representation shapes the discourses on ageing femininity available to Goldberg and Mabley (who as an African-American stand-up comedienne and vaudeville veteran enjoyed an unusual degree of fame as a black woman performer prior to her death in 1975), 'they both refuse to conform to the conventional meanings attached to these and ... use their comedy as a space to redefine and comment upon cultural expectations of age and femininity'.

Like Bette Davis in some respects, the filmmaker Agnès Varda (widely known as the 'mother of the French New Wave') has enjoyed career longevity and success in an industry which privileges the careers of men, whilst over the years ageing has also been explicitly and self-consciously incorporated as a key element of her persona on screen. In Chapter 5, Rona Murray finds that within the context of French popular culture, Varda's particular form of celebrity has been vital to her pursuit of her *'cinema d'auteur-témoin'* ('cinema of author as witness'), and increasingly so as she moves into her third – and fourth – age, having started her filmmaking career in the 1950s. While her public persona was established on television through her work as part of the French New Wave, it has grown and developed over time to take on an increasingly personal dimension. Murray finds that Varda has long been curious about the ageing process in her films, but her lasting celebrity has enabled her as an artist to explore the meaning and experience of old age as a woman on screen. Her later works, and the public's response to them, attest to the power and importance of the dual aspects of her public persona – of 'Agnès' (the woman) and of 'Varda' (the artist).

As with Varda, narratives of motherhood and the maternal come to the fore again in our next essay, unexpectedly perhaps given the subject's reputation as a 'diva'. Nathalie Weidhase's work in Chapter 6 on singer/actress/model Grace Jones interrogates the ways in which Jones' comeback album *Hurricane* (2008) – especially in terms of its lyrical content – dramatises discourses on female ageing that function to 'queer' the concepts of gender, race and sexuality. Similarly to Wearing, Weidhase demonstrates how racialised discourses attend the construction and circulation of Jones' image, and that media attention to her supposedly 'ageless' (black) body detracted from critical attention to the actual content of her musical comeback. However, Weidhase argues that Jones' particular performances of ageing femininity – and especially her '"queering" of the diva myth' – function to trouble and disrupt such traditional representational paradigms.

By comparison, in Chapter 7, Susan Berridge's analysis of Jennifer Anniston's shifting image emphasises the ways in which media discourses function to contain, regulate and discipline female celebrity images in relation to (the postfeminist notion of) 'the "time crisis" which measures success through the attainment of particular life goals such as marriage and motherhood'. The trajectory Aniston's stardom has travelled exemplifies the way that women stars are made age-accountable by the media in ways their male counterparts are not. Examining the coverage of Aniston in US and UK celebrity gossip and entertainment magazines – particularly in the period after her split from actor Brad Pitt in 2005 – Berridge explores the ways in which Aniston's image has moved between a model of aspirational femininity to a 'high-profile' exemplar of 'temporal failure', a rhetoric which is deeply unforgiving to those who fail to conform to an image of maternal familialism within an 'appropriate' biological time frame.

There is no such sense of 'temporal failure' to be found among the subjects of Sue Bourne's, 2013 documentary, *Fabulous Fashionistas*. Broadcast in the UK on Channel Four's respected *Cutting Edge* series, Bourne's film about six style-conscious women with an average age of 80 was met with much enthusiasm and was widely embraced for offering such an unusually vibrant account of the lives of older women. Consequently, some of the subjects have become recognisable cultural commentators and public figures in the UK, speaking out against ageism, taking up modelling and in effect becoming minor celebrities. But a feminist critique begs the question as to whether there is something simultaneously regressive in the film, which lends itself to a neo-liberal address at times, in that it is the women's wardrobes that provided them with this platform. In Chapter 8, drawing on interviews with the director and two of the film's subjects, Jermyn explores how the seemingly glib 'Fashionista' title was really only ever 'a McGuffin to talk about ageing and life' (Kreitzman, 2015) and finds that instead Bourne demonstrates the potential of fashion (or rather style) to offer avenues for 'creativity, escapism and self-expression' in a film which strikingly extends the mainstream lexicon of ageing femininities.

Melanie Williams then focuses on the image of the 80-year-old esteemed British actress Dame Judi Dench, whose image – despite its longevity – has been passed over for analysis in favour of younger ('mature') examples such as Helen Mirren. In Chapter 9, she examines how Dench's image manages to negotiate discourses of respectability (she is a Dame and has been proclaimed a 'national treasure') as well as the more 'demotic' promise of being 'badass' and transgressive. Indeed, in discussing how Dench is seen to embody the (classed) ideal of the 'graceful ager' (Dolan and Tincknell, 2012: xi), whilst simultaneously challenging gendered expectations of 'old age', we are again presented with the fact that, although often proscriptive, punitive and regulatory, the discursive construction of older female celebrity is neither uniform nor simplistic.

As with Berridge's essay on Aniston, Hannah Hamad's discussion, in Chapter 10, of actress Elisabeth Sladen, who played Sarah Jane Smith in *Doctor Who* and the spin-off series, *The Sarah Jane Adventures*, explores the ways in which ageing women are subject to a form of policing by the media in a postfeminist context. At the same time, given that she experienced a remarkable resurgence in her celebrity and career during her 60s (reprising her role in *Doctor Who* in 2006, and starring in the spin-off from 2007–2011), Sladen also stands – like Elinor Glyn – as someone who disrupts normative expectations regarding the often prescribed temporal trajectory of the female celebrity career. As in Jermyn's essay, Hamad further observes how, despite existing as the unavoidable endpoint of the ageing process, death often remains largely absent from cultural work on representations of age, examining how Sladen's mediated narrative of ageing had to incorporate her untimely death in 2011 into its possibilities and parameters. Indeed, as Hamad asserts, 'rather than giving truth to the postfeminist lie that female ageing can be reversed, evaded or halted, Sladen's death enabled her embodied negotiation of this discourse in the face of her imminent end to be celebrated as a triumph of a well-lived femininity'.

Finally, in Chapter 11's '"Call the Celebrity": Voicing the Experience of Women and Ageing through the Distinctive Vocal Presence of Vanessa Redgrave', Ros Jennings and Eva Krainitzki consider a crucial – but often overlooked – signifier of ageing: the celebrity voice. Focusing on the historical British television series *Call the Midwife* (BBC, 2012–), the chapter explores how the use of Vanessa Redgrave's voice-over contributes to the programme's complex and fluid construction of femininity and ageing, facilitating 'a rare example of female subjectivity that is built on a continuum of ages rather than firm or oppositional divisions between young and old'.

Whilst the concept of a continuum of ageing offers a fluid temporality for thinking about the relations between femininity, age and female celebrity, the title of this book – *Freeze Frame* – suggests a fragment of suspended time, which is nevertheless caught and wrested from the ephemeral. Indeed, on one level, the 'frozen frame' speaks of how women celebrities often remain captured in time and perhaps haunted by images of their younger selves that remain in regular circulation, the moment of their 'heyday', pictures which are rolled out routinely, as cautionary tales showing what they once were contrasted with what they became (see, for example, Ginette Vincendeau's work on Brigitte Bardot's unruly ageing, (2013: 128–130)), or as rare exemplars of women who have 'aged well'. At another level, this title speaks of the pre-eminent option open to these women to try and stay 'in the celebrity game' – namely to 'freeze' the ageing process via cosmetic surgery and other invasive procedures, interventions which have become increasingly normalised for ordinary women (and men) too. But such anti-ageing measures are not without risk – nothing invites more disdain than the 'frozen' expressions on women celebrities that result from too much Botox and fillers, or too many face lifts. As Kirsty Fairclough (2012) has shown, the 'hyper-scrutiny' women celebrities are subjected to in contemporary culture sets an impossible standard, where 'undetectable' surgery is to be revered but the signs of too much 'work' on stars such as Nicole Kidman are contemptuously condemned. While this book focuses on celebrity, then, such is the (ubiquitous) operation of celebrity discourse that the contexts described in these essays sketch out 'cultures of ageing' that millions of women must negotiate at some time or another: be that via the projected lifestyles and narratives of the models that advertise the clothes they buy, the women that star in the films they watch, or the celebrities held up for ridicule or reverence in the newspapers they read. And it is for this reason, as we call for here, that scholars, critics and campaigners alike must continue to look towards understanding and interrogating how and why age matters in the representation of the female life course. As Lynn Segal provocatively reminds us, 'Old age is no longer the condition that dare not speak its name, but we have a long way to go before we can joke that it is the identity that refuses to be silent' (2013: 38) – whatever Heidi Klum might think.

Note

1. In this respect Dolce and Gabbana's SS15 campaign, featuring three ordinary and anonymous, corpulent 'old ladies' in widow's mourning garb (sporting colourful flamenco-style D&G accessories) might be deemed to have taken the 'trend' for ageing models a step further again, though notably the actual clothing range was still modelled by young, slender women.

References

Dolan, J. and Tincknell, E. (2012) (eds) *Aging Femininities: Troubling Representations* (Cambridge: Cambridge Scholars Press).

Fairclough, K. (2012) 'Nothing Less Than Perfect: Female Celebrity, Ageing and Hyper-scrutiny in the Gossip Industry', *Celebrity Studies*, 3(1), pp. 90–103.

Jermyn, D. (2012) '"Get a Life, Ladies. Your Old One Is Not Coming Back": Ageing, Ageism and the Lifespan of Female Celebrity', *Celebrity Studies*, 3(1), pp. 1–12.

Kreitzman, S. (2015) personal interview with Deborah Jermyn, London, 13 February.

Mulshine, M. (2015) 'In With the Old: Why the Timing Is Perfect For Models Over 60', *The Observer*, 2 March, available at: http://observer.com/2015/02/style-advanced-style-spring-campaigns/ [accessed 20 April 2015)

Segal, L. (2013) *The Pleasures and The Perils of Ageing: Out of Time* (London: Verso).

Takeda, A. (2013) 'Heidi Klum Reveals Incredible Halloween Costume, Is Completely Unrecognizable as an Old Lady: Picture', *Us Weekly*, 31 October, available at http://www.usmagazine.com/celebrity-news/news/heidi-klum-reveals-2013-halloween-costume-is-completely-unrecognizable-as-an-old-lady-picture-20133110 [accessed 16 February 2015].

The Invisible Woman (2013) 'Heidi Klum's "Old Woman" Halloween Costume Isn't Funny', *The Guardian*, 1 November, available at http://www.theguardian.com/commentisfree/2013/nov/01/heidi-klum-halloween-costume-old-woman [accessed 16 February 2015].

Vincendeau, G. (2013) *Brigitte Bardot* (Basingstoke: Palgrave Macmillan).

1
Here, There and Nowhere: Ageing, Gender and Celebrity Studies

Su Holmes and Deborah Jermyn

In December 2014, the 68-year-old former Tory MP and Junior Health Minister Edwina Currie was the sixth celebrity to be voted out of the jungle in the UK version of *I'm a Celebrity... Get Me Out of Here!* (ITV, 2004–). When asked in her exit interview whether she had enjoyed her time in the competition and whether it had been what she expected, part of her response noted in passing that she had been 'prepared to do it... *for the extension... and [having] older women on TV and all that sort of stuff'* (tx, 2014, author emphasis). On one level, her comment seemed to point to the fact that in recent years, a cultural discourse recognising the invisibility and inequity endured by older women in the media has been widely adopted, even 'mainstreamed' (see Jermyn, 2013). At the same time, the way in which Currie expressed this recognition so fleetingly and knowingly before moving on with her answer might have been said to have implied a certain wry disdain, as if she was paying lip service to an already tired or 'PC' presumption. Currie can long have been said to hold a contradictory relationship with feminism; rising in the 1980s to become one of the most visible women in British politics at a time when such women were even rarer on the ground than they are now – and thus seeming to reap the rewards of feminism's second-wave activism – she has nevertheless insisted in quite aggressively dismissive terms that she has never been a feminist herself (e.g., Currie, 2009). Similarly, in this exchange she seemed both to be visibly taking/making a stand for (here, older) women, before promptly undercutting their significance. This was a moment which exemplified how the critical, cultural discourse surrounding the media treatment of older women has achieved a recognised level of visibility, then, whilst also suggesting the difficulty of legitimating this discourse in lasting ways. Indeed, whilst Currie certainly offered a stoic and formidable representation of the older

11

woman whilst in the jungle – for example, undertaking gruesome 'bush tucker trials' with brio – her wider framing and representation in the text often functioned to delegitimise her voice and presence. Furthermore, the 'laddish' banter of the presenting duo, Ant and Dec, repeatedly performed revulsion at her 'inappropriate' flirtation with younger male campmates, and they even referred to her as 'an old Currie' (i.e., an unappetising 'old curry' now past its best) in one particular link.

We open this chapter with this example for the way in which it neatly crystallises so many of the issues, challenges and contradictions at stake in the relationship between female celebrity and discourses of ageing. The scope of what follows here, both within this chapter and the book as a whole, is necessarily interdisciplinary and aims to speak to such arenas as Feminist Gerontology, wider social sciences work on ageing and Feminist Media Studies, as well as Star and Celebrity Studies. We write here primarily, however, as scholars of the latter. This chapter will thus chart the myriad ways in which ageing is a central structural framework within the gendered discourses of celebrity culture, and yet has remained, until very recently, largely neglected by Celebrity Studies. Indeed, we seek to examine how gender has been crucial to Celebrity Studies for some time, but how – like much of Feminist Media Studies more widely – it has often elided questions of age; in other words, making the age/gender dyad seem simultaneously here, there and nowhere.

Age strikes back... the 'new' visibility of ageing scholarship

The very presence of this book speaks to the fact that we are in the midst of a proliferating body of work with regard to the discussion and study of ageing. This, of course, is not by any means to claim that the field is 'new'. As Josie Dolan and Estella Tincknell observe, 'feminist pioneers' Simone de Beauvoir (1971) and Germaine Greer (1991) long since produced landmark work in marking out a feminist conceptualisation of gender and ageing (albeit 20 years apart), drawing attention to the ways in which post-menopausal women are made 'culturally and socially invisible' (Dolan and Tincknell, 2012: ix), and constituting part of a small but significant 'canon' to which we would add Susan Sontag and her milestone essay 'The Double Standard of Ageing' (1972). Subsequently, other crucial interventions in debates about women and ageing were offered by Kathleen Woodward in *Figuring Age: Women, Bodies and Generations* (1999) and Margaret Morganroth Gullette in *Declining to Decline: Cultural Combat and the Politics of the Midlife* (1997) and *Aged by Culture* (2004). But broadly, and despite the increasing move toward intersectionality within feminism and thus to recognition of political difference within the category of 'woman', ageing has remained all too absent across Media and Cultural Studies. Until – perhaps – now. This newer work might be seen to have been prompted by a range of particular social, cultural and intellectual contexts. First, as is now widely and recurrently recognised, we are living in an era of a rapidly ageing population. One recent UK research project announced that 1 in 3 children born today will live to be 100 years old (ESRC, 2014). The social, environmental and cultural implications of this demographic shift are enormous, and scholars from a range of disciplines have become increasingly driven to grasp how these will be felt and how they might be anticipated. This is an interest perhaps prompted not just by a desire to understand how best to address and engage with the growing numbers of 'seniors' already making up the population, but by the recognition that *we are* the ageing population; this is not a social shift somehow external to us that we are conceptualising entirely from the outside. Rather the provisions, attitudes and recognition we facilitate today will serve *us* in the future.

Secondly, within the British context at least, there have been a number of recent high-profile media cases in which female TV presenters and newsreaders, including *Strictly Come Dancing* (BBC, 2004–) judge Arlene Phillips and *Countryfile* (BBC, 1988–) presenter Miriam O'Reilly (both sacked 2009), were seen to be the subjects, and casualties, of both sexist and ageist logics. Summarily ejected from their posts due to their status as 'older' women while their 'veteran' male colleagues continued to thrive in a media that only considers ageing a problem for women, these particular cases were arguably lent a heightened currency by the fact that this discrimination was seen to be operative at the BBC, and thus at the heart of a public service institution. Whilst there was a significant groundswell of support for the women involved in these cases, the events also made visible the weight of historical prejudice against the older woman in these TV roles. In April 2014, remarks made by former newsreader Michael Buerk in the *Radio Times* demonstrated that the battle fought by O'Reilly et al., was still very much simmering away, when he was condemned for commenting that, 'If you got the job in the first place mainly because you look nice, I can't see why you should keep it when you don't' (cited in Collier, 2014). Although the emphasis on the visual here foregrounds the corporeality of the ageing woman as the key 'problem' faced by the older female wanting to maintain a career in the television industry, the cases also highlighted how the relationship between age and authority, and even affability, are *gendered*.

Thirdly, the burgeoning body of work on ageing women and femininities speaks to a context where the notion of 'generation(s)' (and ensuing generationalism) has become an increasingly potent and evident cultural touchstone. The discourses of postfeminism have been widely criticised for a preoccupation with young women as their subject. Though the second-wave was also held to account eventually for similarly privileging the interests of women's earlier life stages, under postfeminism this exists alongside an even more virulent drive to present the relationships between generations of women (or 'waves' of feminism) as inherently divisive. Recent feminist scholarship has sought to call out this focus on hostility and competition – a counter-product in some respects of the 'individualism' of postfeminism (Gill, 2007) – and this is a position which has arguably lent itself to a greater interest in the (once so widely neglected) ageing female subject. But this notion of 'generation(s)' is also useful in providing a context for the growth of scholarship in the field in thinking about a generation of women academics as ageing subjects themselves. Though one should not overgeneralise here in terms of the differences among individual career trajectories, and should be mindful of how the issue of privilege must be flagged up here in ways that did not occur sufficiently in the original discourses of second-wave feminism, the 'second-wave' of Feminist Media Studies scholars are now into and entering their 40s and 50s. They are thus perhaps inevitably more reflective about age and ageing and looking around them to find or create spaces where this issue can enter more decisively into academic and public discourse (and generally privileged in ways that enable them to pursue this). Clearly, when Feminist Media Studies was first emerging in tandem with the second-wave, pioneering scholars were embedded in the labour of establishing a new field, at a time when the wider cultural agenda did not give such an explicit currency to ageing. When the focus on 'woman' as a homogenous subject was challenged from the 1980s onwards, race, class and sexuality were primarily at the fore as the most significant forms of difference; a context which, as we have outlined here, is now shifting across numerous cultural, media and disciplinary contexts.

Celebrity studies, ageing and the academy

Following a long history of virtual neglect, then, Feminist Media Studies and Film Studies have begun to focus more attention on representations of female ageing. There is now a growing body of scholarship in this field, dealing with film (Markson, 2003; Wearing, 2007; Tally,

2008; Whelehan, 2009; Chivers, 2011; Jermyn, 2014; Do Rozario and Waterhouse-Watson, 2014), 'makeover TV' (Weber, 2009), television drama (Tincknell, 2012; Wilson, 2012; Wearing, 2012), TV comedy (White, 2014; Rawitsch, 2014), reality TV (Holmes and Jermyn, 2014; O'Brien Hill, 2014), popular music (Hibberd, 2014) and cross-media forms (Negra, 2009). We can equally point to conferences and research networks, such as 'Women, Ageing and the Media' (WAM) funded by the Arts & Humanities Research Council (AHRC) Research Networks and Workshops Project (2008–); the 'Age Spots and Spotlights: Celebrity, Ageing and Performance' symposium at Birkbeck, University of London in 2011; and the 'Acting Their Age: Women, Ageing and the Movies' conference held at Newcastle University in 2012.

By comparison, Gerontology, and later Feminist Gerontology, obviously has a much longer history of thinking about the social, cultural and political significance of age and the ways in which this impacts upon the life course, whether physically, economically or socially. Furthermore, the relationship between *media* and ageing has increasingly moved from the margins to the centre of the field (Harrington and Brothers, 2010: 28) (e.g., Martin and Warren, 2009, Yoon and Powell, 2012, La Ware and Moutsatos, 2013), although there are still calls to 'expand the range of ... textual forms that we consider when we examine how people make sense of their life course progression' (Harrington and Brothers, 2010: 28), suggesting that a great deal of media territory remains unchartered in this regard. Indeed, it is interesting that whilst studies of the media are increasingly present in Gerontology and Feminist Gerontology, as well as wider social sciences work on ageing, celebrity appears to be all but *absent* as a pivotal 'text' which might yield crucial insights into how our culture makes sense of the ageing woman; how 'she' should be imagined, and how she is culturally policed and (within subjectively narrow parameters) celebrated. This neglect may well point to discourses of cultural value: despite becoming a buoyant and established field which draws on work across disciplines, Celebrity Studies still has to defend its project against academic and popular value judgements about the apparent 'triviality' of its subject matter. Thus, this omission of celebrity from fields such as Feminist Gerontology may well speak to its enduring low cultural status in some quarters.

This neglect may also be related to the ways in which celebrity culture, in popular discourse at least, is often now assumed to speak to the interests of a younger audience. Even if this presumption were to be unambiguously proven to be the case, there is something of a disjuncture at work here, since Gerontology concerns itself with *age and ageing*, rather than simply with 'old' age. In fact, there is no real evidence to suggest that older people (in itself a problematically subjective term) are indeed somehow entirely removed from the realm of celebrity culture. Note, for example, how celebrities regularly pervade the pages of magazines targeting those in 'middle-youth' and above, from *Woman* to *Saga* (in the UK) to *AARP* (in the USA), while popular celebrity-focused programmes such as *Strictly Come Dancing* (BBC, 2004–) and *Dancing with the Stars* (ABC, 2005–) are widely seen to have significant cross-generational appeal. Furthermore, across all age ranges, from Lindsay Lohan and Gwyneth Paltrow on the one hand, to Cher and Judi Dench on the other, celebrity culture is quite frequently concerned with pointing out those (overwhelmingly female) celebrities who are or are not ageing 'well' throughout the ageing spectrum, underlining the sense in which the 'problem' of ageing is not one which is seen to only concern the apparently 'old'.

The work within Feminist Media Studies outlined above has sometimes incorporated celebrity case studies as one site in which discourses on ageing femininity come into circulation, such as Abigail Gardner's (2012) essay on Dolly Parton, Josephine Dolan's (2012) work on Helen Mirren, and Diane Railton and Paul Watson's (2012) and Kristyn Gorton and Joanne Garde-Hansen's (2013) analyses of Madonna. It is, however, within Star and Celebrity Studies (which does, of course, often intersect with Feminist Media Studies) that we might expect such work to be most visibly and concertedly undertaken. While we pointed above to the problematic absence of celebrity in Gerontology, it would be remiss indeed not to acknowledge that 'ageing' has more often than not been absent in Star and Celebrity Studies: it is only very recently that the discipline has begun to more evidently interrogate how ageing is imbricated in celebrity culture. One notable strand of work has been concerned with analyses of how ageing is figured in particular star and celebrity images (Gates, 2010; Holmlund, 2010; Wearing, 2012; Jermyn, 2012; Smith, 2012; Brown, 2012; Allen and McCabe, 2012; Jermyn, 2014); another has looked to examine how ageing represents a structural inequality both at the level of representation and career opportunity/longevity (Carman, 2012; Fairclough, 2012; Jermyn, 2013). It is fair to say that, across both approaches, the majority of this work has been written by women, about women – and indeed (as both Weidhase and Wearing note in their essays in this collection), about *white* women, so that questions of race and ethnicity thus constitute another problematic area of 'absence' in this field.[1]

In this regard, the fact that Star and Celebrity Studies has only more recently begun to pay attention to ageing is notable given that these fields have a long-standing relationship with feminism. But whilst there is an established history of reading star images with regard to gendered ideologies (e.g., Dyer, 1986; Stacey, 1994), it is only more recently that celebrity culture itself has been recognised as deeply and structurally gendered (across the spheres of 'talent', work and the body, for example), drawing attention to how celebrity culture has qualitatively different approaches to representing men and women (Williamson, 2010; Holmes and Negra, 2011; Tyler and Bennett, 2011). As Holmes and Negra (2011) argue, male and female celebrities are circulated through, and subject to, qualitatively different representational practices which demand analysis in their own right. Given that such work has only recently begun to emerge, it is perhaps not surprising that studies of how ageing enters this matrix are only now beginning to develop.

Pedagogies of ageing: approaching celebrity culture

Star and Celebrity Studies scholars have long since argued that celebrity culture exerts a pervasive, if complex, influence on social consciousness, and emphasis has been placed on the role that stars and celebrities play in shaping social identity. As already acknowledged, they can be viewed as fulfilling a pedagogic function, or as Chris Rojek puts it, as 'informal life coaches' who provide us with tips, images and models which span fashion, diet, morals, politics and taste – influencing the construction of a 'personal lifestyle architecture' (Rojek, 2012). The 'architecture' that Rojek references principally addresses women – especially in terms of the gendered emphasis on the body, and the fact that female celebrities are primarily circulated as corporeal signifiers. Furthermore, rather than celebrities simply representing aspirational figures of idolisation, emphasis has increasingly been placed upon discourses of judgement and condemnation within female celebrity culture, with such images and debates playing a key role in shoring up the boundaries of 'appropriate'/'inappropriate' models of class and gender (Tyler and Bennett, 2010; Holmes and Negra, 2011), as well as *age*. Looking at the contemporary celebrity context – and despite considerable shifts in masculinity – Sontag's pronouncement that 'Men are "allowed" to age, without penalty, in several ways that women are not' (1972: 73) still remains entirely pertinent, over 30 years after it was first made.

This neglect has existed despite the considerable and apparently accelerating visibility of age to the postfeminist context of celebrity culture, a context which evinces an 'abject dread of ageing' (Fairclough, 2012: 92). Whilst there remain marked inequalities across male and female celebrity when it comes to career opportunities, pay and longevity (issues which have been debated to some extent in the popular media in recent years), celebrity culture for the most part concerns itself with the realm of the corporeal and physical, meting out (often contradictory) judgements regarding women's ageing physicality and sexuality. In fact, if celebrity culture can be conceived of as a form of 'disciplinary regime' where responses to discourses of gender and class are concerned (Tyler and Bennett, 2010), it seems crucial that we factor ageing, and specifically female ageing, into this context.

The concept of female celebrity culture playing a pedagogic function in relation to age is arguably most clearly articulated in gossip magazines, on gossip blogs and on Internet sites. No longer simply contained as part of the coverage in *heat* magazine or in the caustic asides of perezhilton. com, the revelations of '20 celebs that aged terribly' (ForeverCeleb, 2014) or 'Young celebrities who are aging badly' (Williams, 2014) are sites – and thus spectacles – in *their own right*, entirely separate from any kind of 'story' or editorial copy. Men do appear on these sites, but not in the same vast numbers as women, and the latter often receive far more virulent treatment. Indeed, the pictures of female celebrities in particular often compare images taken some 15–20 years apart, thus meaning that it is often simply *age itself* which is being imaged and spectacularised here. As Fairclough has observed, celebrity bodies 'are still revered and aspired to, but they are also exposed, examined and scrutinised in order to reveal their outward corporeal construction' (2012: 91). Nowhere are these contradictions more evident than in the discursive circulation of celebrity plastic surgery. First, there is the suggestion that women should perpetually 'fight' and 'battle' the natural vicissitudes of the ageing process (whether in terms of surgical interventions, diet, lifestyle or consumer products), and the insistence that celebrities are socially and financially *well* placed to take on this 'fight' is widely recognised in media coverage. As Amy Lamare ponders here:

Aging is something we are all going to do, some of us better than others. When it comes to celebrities, it's a bit shocking when they don't age well. After all, they have money at their disposal. From anti-aging products, to taking care of your hair, to plastic surgery – these stars can afford to maintain their best face for many years. Sometimes though, even all the money in the world and every preventative measure you take can't stop the march of time. And sometimes too much plastic surgery trying to maintain a youthful visage can backfire. Let's take a look at 14 Celebrities Who Haven't Aged Well. (Lamare, 2014)

As this suggests, the management of the ageing self is often articulated in terms of a neo-liberal rhetoric of personal responsibility (Fairclough, 2012: 92) (although there is simultaneously the suggestion that even such self-vigilance and labour cannot compete with 'nature'). At the same time, such discourses coexist with the overt 'shaming' of celebrities who make the postfeminist labour of the youthful (or 'ageless') self *too* apparent – a form of abjection that occurs when the female body fails 'to conform to acceptable aesthetic or cultural norms' (Dolan and Tincknell, 2012: xi). These discourses then, in turn, coexist with apparent appreciations of 'graceful agers' (ibid.) – those who are revered for appearing to mature 'naturally'. As concepts such as 'graceful' suggest, these discourses are also intimately bound up with *class* judgements about femininity as a bodily property (see Skeggs, 2003). In this respect, and much like the policing of the female body more widely in celebrity culture, this leaves an incredibly narrow and precarious tightrope for the female celebrity to walk: the aesthetic and discursive space in which one can age 'well' is severely delimited, as well as contradictory, capricious and subject to change.

But a consideration of the relationship between female, celebrity and ageing does not simply encompass the overt ways in which celebrity culture disseminates pedagogic lessons in appropriate ageing; it also includes the ways in which – even in the context of the 'new' visibility of ageing – the careers of 'older' public women are curtailed in ways that men's careers are not. Indeed, whilst the relationship between age and femininity is subject to an intense media gaze (Fairclough, 2012) in celebrity culture – with the female body pored over for signs of 'abject' ageing as well as evidence of cosmetic surgery – the older woman can conversely still be subject to a damning invisibility. The study of the relationship between female, celebrity and ageing also includes media scandals around the relationship between ageism and sexism (Jermyn, 2013), and it includes how audiences respond to these discourses, and how they negotiate them in relation to their own ageing life course. Yet as discussed in the next section, questions of audience reception have so far been conspicuous by their absence in this regard, despite their centrality in understanding how ageing female celebrities come to 'mean'.

Where next: the absent audience and beyond

Much of what we have discussed in this essay has been in one way or another about absence. By way of conclusion, we want to sound a note of caution about how a 'new' absence risks being instituted within the noted emergent work underway. We have already pointed above to the need for more work that looks beyond white women celebrities. What is also evidently lacking across all the spheres we have pointed to – Celebrity Studies, Feminist Media Studies and Feminist Gerontology – is attention to how women *respond* to discourses of female ageing in the media. Even despite the long history of empirical audience research in Feminist Media Studies, this is another arena in which the matter of ageing has gone largely neglected. There is an established tradition of participant research in Feminist Gerontology, where older women's voices have been brought to the centre, and Star and Celebrity Studies has much to learn from it in this respect. Although there *are* empirical studies of audience responses to stars and celebrities, it is very evident this approach has garnered far less attention than the discursive celebrity 'text'. As Graeme Turner has observed, Star and Celebrity Studies have predominantly invested in modes of analysis that are 'primarily textual and discursive' (2010: 13).

This imbalance has also structured the presently emergent attention to the relationship between ageing, gender and celebrity: research so far has predominantly focused on the ways in which *particular images and tropes of representation* play out a limited range of permissible corporealities, identities and behaviours. Little work with audiences to date, then, has focused on how people actually respond to discourses of ageing female celebrity, or how they consume such material as ageing subjects. Furthermore, whilst Feminist Gerontology may have a longer history of participant research, here, too, studies of how women respond to *representations* of female ageing, or may consume the media as older subjects themselves, have been scarce. With regard to celebrity, this might be seen as particularly pressing given that there seems to be a popular media consensus that the disparate treatment of male and female celebrities, whereby women are subject to more punitive media coverage and judgement about their actions and appearance, emanates from the desire of *women* to see *other women* fail (Negra and Holmes, 2008) – a double ideological manoeuvre in which women are blamed for their own subjugation. Women, especially older women, are very rarely given a space to *respond to* such claims. In this regard, we propose that empirical investigation of reception here has an important yet largely untapped political importance.

As has long been established within Media and Cultural Studies, textual construction does not determine audience response, and power cannot be 'read off' from media images alone. Such debates in studies of audiences have also long since foregrounded the importance of plurality in this regard, with due attention paid to the complexity of identities as they cross such axes as gender, class, sexuality and ethnicity. Furthermore, whilst gender has gradually become more central to Gerontology and sociological studies of ageing, there has been a call for a greater acknowledgement of cultural *difference* in this regard – especially, for example, with regard to ethnicity (Maynard et al., 2008: 31), although we would also foreground the significance of sexuality here, and the ways in which the ageing identities of lesbian women constitute a further invisibility in both popular media and academic spheres. This clearly has its own resonance for the study of the intersection between female celebrity and ageing, both in terms of representation and audience reception. After all, and as noted above, the media surveillance of the ageing female celebrity is largely played out on the body of the privileged *white heterosexual* woman, and this has been borne out in existing scholarship, with studies of, for example, Helen Mirren and Diane Keaton receiving the scrutiny of scholarly spotlight. How factors such as ethnicity and sexuality (as well as socio-economic circumstance) play a role in *how* we age, and how ageing identities are valued and judged, is clearly an urgent subject for debate.

In mapping some of the critical and disciplinary terrain through which the concern with ageing has been marginalised, explored and then come to greater visibility, we have concentrated primarily on Feminist Media Studies and Celebrity Studies. Although feminism has long since questioned (although not always entirely successfully) the emphasis on a homogenous conception of woman, and intersectionality has become a recurrent feature of feminist approaches to media forms, the extent to which age and ageing is figured within this matrix is only just beginning to emerge. We hope that this essay, and this book as a whole, can be part of the next installment.

Note

1. As noted in the Introduction, this collection seeks in part to address the overwhelming whiteness of existing work on ageing female celebrity, with essays by Weidhase and Wearing here bringing new attention to bear on black women subjects, though this is evidently a small step.

References

Allen, M. and McCabe, J. (2012) 'Imitations of Lives: Ageing Men, Vocal Mimicry and Performing Celebrity in *The Trip*', *Celebrity Studies*, 3(3), pp.150–163.

Brown, W. (2012) 'Channel Hopping: Charlotte Rampling in French Cinema of the Early 2000s', *Celebrity Studies*, 3(1), pp. 52–63.

Carman, E. (2012) '"Women Rule Hollywood": Ageing and Freelance Stardom in the Studio System', *Celebrity Studies*, 3(1), pp. 13–24.

Chivers, S. (2011) *The Silvering Screen: Old Age and Disability in Cinema* (Toronto: University of Toronto Press).

Collier, H. (2014) 'Michael Buerk Criticises Female Presenters Who "Cry Ageism"', *The Guardian*, 8 April, available at: http://www.theguardian.com/media/2014/apr/08/michael-buerk-female-presenters-ageism-looks [accessed 26 February 2015].

Currie, E. (2009) 'Equality Is Fine, but This Absurd Bill Will Be a Disaster for Women and Britain', 29 April, *Daily Mail* online, available at: http://www.dailymail.co.uk/debate/article-1174171/EDWINA-CURRIE-Equality-fine-absurd-disaster-women-Britain.html [accessed 10 December 2014].

de Beauvoir, S. (1971) *The Coming of Age* (London: Norton) (reprint 1996).

Dolan J. (2012) '*The Queen*, Aging Femininity, and the Recuperation of the Monarchy', in A. Swinnen and J. A. Stotesbury (eds), *Aging, Performance and Stardom: Doing Age on the Stage of Consumerist Culture* (Zurich and Berlin, LIT Verlag), pp. 39–53.

Dolan, J. and Tincknell, E. (2012) (eds) *Aging Femininities: Troubling Representations* (Cambridge: Cambridge Scholars Press).

Do Rozario, R. and Waterhouse-Watson, D. (2014) 'Beyond Wicked Witches and Fairy Godparents: Ageing and Gender in Children's Fantasy on Screen', in I. Whelehan and J. Gwynne (eds), *Ageing, Popular Culture and Contemporary Feminism: Harleys and Hormones* (Basingstoke: Palgrave Macmillan), pp. 233–247.

Dyer, R. (1986) *Heavenly Bodies: Film Stars and Society* (London: Routledge).

ESRC (2014) Festival of Social Sciences exhibition, 'How to get to 100 – and enjoy it', OXO Tower, London, October – November.

Fairclough, K. (2012) 'Nothing Less Than Perfect: Female Celebrity, Ageing and Hyper-Scrutiny in the Gossip Industry', *Celebrity Studies*, 3(1), pp. 90–103.

ForeverCeleb (2014) '20 Celebrities That Aged Terribly', http://foreverceleb.com/20-celebrities-that-aged-terribly/, 25 May [accessed 17 February 2015].

Gardner, A. (2012) 'Grit, Glitter and Glamour: Tracing Authenticity in the Aging Artifice of Dolly Parton', in J. Dolan and E. Tincknell (eds), *Aging Femininities: Troubling Representations* (Cambridge: Cambridge Scholars Press), pp. 183–194.

Gates, P. (2010) 'Acting His Age? The Resurrection of the 80s Action Heroes and Their Aging Stars', *Quarterly Review of Film and Video*, 27, pp. 276–289.

Gill, R. (2007) 'Postfeminist Media Culture: Elements of a Sensibility', *European Journal of Cultural Studies*, 10(2), pp. 147–166.

Gorton, K. and Garde-Hansen, J. (2013) 'From Old Media Whore to New Media Troll: The Online Negotiation of Madonna's Ageing Body', *Feminist Media Studies*, 13(2), pp. 288–302.

Greer, G. (1991) *The Change: Women, Ageing and the Menopause* (London: Hamish Hamilton).

Gullette, M. M. (1997) *Declining to Decline: Cultural Combat and the Politics of the Midlife* (Virginia: University of Virginia Press).

Gullette, M. M. (2004) *Aged by Culture* (Chicago: University of Chicago Press).

Harrington, C. L. and Brothers, D. (2010) 'A Life Course Built for Two: Acting, Aging and Soap Operas', *Journal of Aging Studies*, 24, pp. 20–29.

Hibberd, L. (2014) 'Grown Up Girls: Newspaper Reviews of Ageing Women in Pop', in I. Whelehan and J. Gwynne (eds), *Ageing, Popular Culture and Contemporary Feminism: Harleys and Hormones* (Basingstoke: Palgrave Macmillan), pp.124–139.

Holmes, S. and Jermyn, D. (2014) 'The "Pig", the "Older Woman" and the "Catfight": Gender, Celebrity and Controversy in a Decade of British Reality TV', in B. Weber (ed.), *Reality Gendervision: Sex and Gender on Transatlantic Reality TV* (Durham and London: Duke University Press), pp. 37–53.

Holmes, S. and Negra, D. (eds) (2011) *In the Limelight and Under the Microscope: Forms and Functions of Female Celebrity* (London: Continuum).

Holmlund, C. (2010) 'Celebrity, Ageing and Jackie Chan: Middle-Aged Asian in Transnational Action', *Celebrity Studies*, 1(1), pp. 96–112.

I'm a Celebrity.. Get Me Out of Here! (2014), television programme, ITV1, December 6.

Jermyn, D. (2012) '"Glorious, Glamorous and That Old Standby, Amorous": The Late Blossoming of Diane Keaton's Romantic Comedy Career', *Celebrity Studies*, 3(1), pp. 37–51.

Jermyn, D. (2013) 'Past Their Prime-Time: Women, Ageing and Absence on British Factual Television', *Critical Studies in Television*, 8(1), pp. 73–90.

Jermyn, D. (2014) 'The (un-Botoxed) Face of a Hollywood Revolution: Meryl Streep and the "Greying" of Mainstream Cinema', in I. Whelehan and J. Gwynne (eds), *Ageing, Popular Culture and Contemporary Feminism: Harleys and Hormones* (Basingstoke: Palgrave Macmillan), pp. 108–123.

Lamare, A. (2014) '14 Celebrities Who Haven't Aged Well', *YourDailyScoop!*, http://www.yourdailyscoop.com/14-celebs-who-havent-aged-well/#ixzz3RcGCgwcz, 12 February [accessed 13 February 2015].

La Ware, M. and Moutsatos, C. (2013) '"For Skin That's Us, *Authentically Us*": Celebrity, Empowerment, and the Allure of Anti-aging Advertisements', *Women's Studies in Communication*, (36), pp. 189–208.

Markson, E. W. (2003) 'The Female Aging Body through Film' in C. A. Clarkson (ed.), *Aging Bodies: Images & Everyday Experiences* (California: AltaMira Press), pp. 77–102.

Martin, R. and Warren, L. (2009) 'Look at Me! Images of Women and Ageing', http://www.representing-ageing.com/about.php [accessed 16 December 2014].

Maynard, M., Afshar, H., Franks, M. and Wray, S. (2008) *Women in Later Life: Exploring Race and Ethnicity* (Berkshire: McGraw Hill).

Negra, D. (2009) *What a Girl Wants: Fantasizing the Reclamation of Self in Postfeminism* (Oxford: Routledge).

Negra, D. and Holmes, S. (2008) 'Introduction' to special issue, 'Going Cheap?: Female Celebrity in the Tabloid, Reality and Scandal Genres', *Genders*, 48, http://www.genders.org/g48/g48_negraholmes.html.

O'Brien Hill, G. (2014) 'The Older Mother in *One Born Every Minute*', in I. Whelehan and J. Gwynne (eds), *Ageing, Popular Culture and Contemporary Feminism: Harleys and Hormones* (Basingstoke: Palgrave Macmillan), pp. 187–202.

Railton, D. and Watson, P. (2012) '"She's So Vein: Madonna and the Drag of Aging', in J. Dolan and E. Tincknell (eds), *Aging Femininities: Troubling Representations* (Cambridge: Cambridge Scholars Press), pp. 195–206.

Rawitsch, E. (2014) 'Silence Isn't Golden, Girls: The Cross-Generational Comedy of "America's Grandma" Betty White', in I. Whelehan and J. Gwynne (eds), *Ageing, Popular Culture and Contemporary Feminism: Harleys and Hormones* (Basingtoke: Palgrave Macmillan), pp. 172–186.

Rojek, C. (2012) *Fame Attack: The Inflation of Celebrity and its Consequences* (London: Bloomsbury).

Skeggs, B. (2003) *Class, Self, Culture*. London: Routledge.

Smith, S. (2012) '"Get Off Your Asses for These Old Broads!"': Elizabeth Taylor, Ageing and the Television Comeback Movie', *Celebrity Studies*, 3(1), pp. 25–36.

Sontag, S. (1972) 'The Double Standard of Ageing', *Saturday Review of Literature*, 39, pp. 29–38.

Stacey, J. (1994) *Stargazing: Hollywood Cinema and Female Spectatorship* (London: Routledge).

Tally, M. (2008) 'Something's Gotta Give: Hollywood, Female Sexuality and the "Older Bird" Chick Flick' in S. Ferriss and M. Young (eds), *Chick Flicks: Contemporary Women and the Movies* (New York and London: Routledge), pp. 119–131.

Tincknell, E. (2012) 'Dowagers, Debs, Nuns and Babies: The Politics of Nostalgia and the Older Woman in the Sunday Night Television Serial', in J. Dolan and E. Tincknell (eds), *Aging Femininities: Troubling Representations* (Cambridge: Cambridge Scholars Press), pp. 53–68.

Turner, G. (2004) *Understanding Celebrity* (London: Sage).

Turner, G. (2010) 'Approaching Celebrity Studies', *Celebrity Studies*, 1(1): 11–20.

Tyler, I. and Bennett, B. (2010) '"Celebrity Chav": Fame, Femininity and Social Class', *European Journal of Cultural Studies*, 13(3), pp. 375–393.

Wearing, S. (2007) 'Subjects of Rejuvenation: Aging in Postfeminist Culture' in Y. Tasker and D. Negra (eds), *Interrogating Postfeminism: Gender and the Politics of Popular Culture* (Durham: Duke University Press), pp. 277–310.

Wearing, S. (2012) 'Exemplary or Exceptional Embodiment?: Discourses of Aging in the Case of Helen Mirren and *Calender Girls*', in J. Dolan and E. Tincknell (eds), *Aging Femininities: Troubling Representations* (Cambridge: Cambridge Scholars Press), pp. 145–160.

Weber, B. (2009) *Makeover TV: Selfhood, Citizenship, and Celebrity* (Durham and London: Duke University Press).

Whelehan, I. (2009) 'Not to Be Looked At: Older Women in Contemporary British Film', in M. Williams and M. Bell (eds), *British Women's Cinema* (London: Routledge), pp. 170–183.

White, R. (2014) 'Funny Old Girls: Representing Older Women in British Television Comedy', in Whelehan, I. and Gwynne, J. (eds), *Ageing, Popular Culture and Contemporary Feminism: Harleys and Hormones* (Basingstoke: Palgrave Macmillan), pp. 155–172.

Williams, M. (2014) 'Young Celebrities Who Are Already Ageing Badly, *Madamenoire*, http://madamenoire.com/326342/celebrities-who-are-aging-bad-lyyoung-celebrities-already-aging-badly/ [accessed 17 February 2015].

Williamson, M. (2010) 'Female Celebrities and the Media: the Gendered Denigration of the "Ordinary" Celebrity', *Celebrity Studies*, 1 (1): 118–120.

Wilson, S. (2012) 'Beyond Patriarchy: *Six Feet Under* and the Older Woman', J. Dolan and E. Tincknell (eds) *Aging Femininities: Troubling Representations* (Cambridge: Cambridge Scholars Press), pp. 123–132.

Woodward, K. (1999) *Figuring Age: Women, Bodies and Generations* (Indiana: Indiana UP).

Yoon, H. and Powell, H. (2012) 'Older Consumers and Celebrity Advertising', *Ageing and Society*, (32), pp. 1319–1336.

2
Reconfiguring Elinor Glyn: Ageing Female Experience and the Origins of the 'It Girl'

Karen Randell and Alexis Weedon

Elinor Glyn (1864–1943) was a fêted English author and celebrity figure of the 1920s who – while in her 50s and 60s – was constantly in the Hollywood press. She wrote articles for *Cosmopolitan* magazine on how to attract and keep men and 'racy' stories about love and romance, many of which were turned into films – most famously *Three Weeks* (Crosland, 1924)[1] and *It* (Badger, 1927). Decades on, the idea of the 'It Girl' continues to be pertinent in the postfeminist discourses of the twenty-first century and has been applied by the world's glamour press to up-and-coming young actresses and models from Marilyn Monroe and Edie Sedgwick to Alexa Chung and Kate Upton. However, many other contemporary stars, including both older women and men, such as Helen Mirren, Judi Dench, Diane Keaton, Meryl Streep, George Clooney and Matthew McConaughey, have also been credited with having 'It' on screen and off. This evokes Glyn's original definition of 'It' where the sexual attraction and charisma was not linked to gender nor age, but to a person's manner and sense of allure. Her formulation of the term was developed at the beginning of the century and became central to popular culture of the 1920s. Yet despite being a hugely influential and instrumental figure in her day, until very recently Glyn has been a peripheral figure in histories of this period, an older woman marginalised in accounts of the youth-centred 'flapper era'.

This chapter thus focuses on Glyn at the age of 56 and her American period in the 1920s when she rose to celebrity status. She was invited by Hollywood producers to advise on film adaptations of her books, coming to their attention because she was already a well-known romantic novelist in England. We frame her self-determined public status through the lens of Celebrity Studies by using her publications and films, as well as archival material such as letters and articles, to reconfigure an understanding of Glyn in terms of celebrity and ageing. In particular, we argue that Glyn's construction of herself as a mature and sexually experienced woman, able to advise young women in Britain and America on relationships through her magazine articles, films and fiction writing, remains relevant to contemporary debates about ageing female celebrity. Confident in her voice and opinions, Glyn sought out the opportunities provided by radio, magazine and the proliferation of women's associations to speak on etiquette and romance, marriage, and beauty, thus crafting her own public image. For these audiences, she was the interpreter of Paris fashions and a traveller who had seen the courts of Russia, Spain, Britain, and Egypt, and had circulated in high society in France and the USA. This exoticism as a world traveller coupled with her intimate knowledge of the décor and haute couture of the courts of Europe, helped to generate the celebrity persona which she cultivated and publicly projected. Audiences for her talks on the advocacy of sexual freedoms, discussions of marriage and divorce and the roles of women were heightened by perceptions of her character and the rumoured indiscretions of her own sexual mysteries. In fact, her affairs, and particularly her affair with Lord Curzon were discretely unspoken.

Glyn's early attempts at purposefully constructing her own public identity may appear naive in today's age-conscious celebrity. And we must remain mindful of the extent to which the advice and insight she shared could ever hope to address the interests or experience 'of women', as if they were a homogenous group. However, studying Glyn provides us useful insights into the construction of celebrity in the context of the relationship between novel publication and the growing internationalisation of the magazine industry. Glyn saw, and manipulated to her own advantage, the formative role of Hearst's magazine empire in the development of Hollywood's discourses of stardom, and her status as an older woman did not distract her from a self-conscious construction of celebrity within that world. In fact she used it, as we will discuss, to her advantage.

Placing age at the centre of the narrative

The longevity of Glyn's oeuvre, which spanned the first three decades of the twentieth century, marks her as a star who carries what Deborah Jermyn has described elsewhere (in relation to Diane Keaton) as a 'heightened (and gratifying) sense of history' (2012: 37). Glyn's overt acknowledgement of the changing social roles and freedoms of women is clearly marked in the crafting of dialogue in magazines and novels – particularly across generational boundaries, such as when grandmothers write to their coming-of-age granddaughters, and daughters correspond with their mothers. In her persona as the older woman, 'Madam Glyn', she gives advice to young lovers through magazine articles. Similarly, Glyn's authorial celebrity was intentionally enmeshed with her own life, as she publicly endorsed her own novel by playing her most scandalous fictional character on stage (as discussed below). She appeared to enjoy being the subject of press interest and actively sought to 'keep herself before the public' (Barnett and Weedon, 2014: 46). While she experienced the validation of commercial and popular success from a wide international audience consisting largely of women, she also experienced the dismissal of her romantic fiction as 'valueless' by the male judiciary. Much like 'outspoken', modern-day, older female celebrities such as journalist and broadcaster Janet Street Porter or former MP Edwina Currie, Glyn also experienced the censorship of mature female sexuality by the establishment (Moody, 2003).

Glyn entered Hollywood as the industry was stabilising its studio system. Richard deCordova reminds us that the studio system relied on constructed stars who, as well as exuding such qualities as 'charisma, beauty, exceptional talent, and luck', are also determined by the 'star system' which sought to deliver products that were 'highly individuated' (1990: 9). Such commodification through studio-controlled publicity and fan bases often disallows a sense of autonomy for the star over their mythological image. This problematic commodification was understood by Glyn: she was part of the 'Hollywood machine' and wrote prolifically for Hearst's International Magazine Company, publicising new films and stars. Such insights into the construction of the star may have enabled Glyn to understand how to market her own celebrity image in order to enhance her value for the film contracts that she secured through her own author-named company. Thus, although Glyn was one of a number of 'Eminent Authors' invited to Hollywood by Famous Players-Lasky Corporation in 1920 to lend credibility to their productions, she also used this platform to launch her own image. Through her involvement in emerging media practices across radio, cinema and the press she developed a notion of author-celebrity that we might recognise in cross-media authorship today.[2] Moreover Glyn understood the power of the interrelated, inter-textual text – in which she interwove her own social capital as an older woman whose age spoke of wisdom rather than obsolescence, her association with British and European aristocracy, and her currency as an internationally renowned novelist – to aid her visibility and raise the stakes for her contracts. As we will discuss further, she was not only a person who Daniel Boorstin might describe as a 'celebrity...who is well-known for their well-knowness' (1961: 58 in Turner, 2004: 5), but a woman who understood the 'cultural and economic processes' of her own celebrity potential (ibid.: 5).

Emily Carman has argued that the contractual and economic independence given by freelancing enabled A-list female stars in the 1930s and 1940s to extend their careers 'beyond what is generally imagined of female actors', citing the examples of Irene Dunne and Barbara Stanwyck who worked as stars into their 40s (Carman, 2012: 14). In parallel to this, Barnett and Weedon (2014) argue that Glyn's significance today as an author is as a pioneer of early cross-media business practices. Like Carman's stars, she gained an independent agency, though this was through the establishment of a family-owned company to market her intellectual property rights (founded in 1924). She contracted the rights to her books and stories to Elinor Glyn Ltd, who then leased film options and sold subsidiary rights, syndicating her articles and stories to the major newspaper and magazine companies in the USA and Britain. Glyn was also a friend of William Randolph Hearst and a companion of Marion Davies and understood the value of networking in Hollywood. As a result, she worked with directors Cecil B. DeMille, Sam Wood, Alan Crosland, and film stars Gloria Swanson, Rudolph Valentino, Elisa Landi, and Mary and Douglas Fairbanks. She became intimate with the film studios, gaining contracts with Paramount and MGM and working with Irving Thalberg, and she featured in many celebrity biographies.

Glyn ensured that her stories, characters, opinions and insights were publicised throughout different media outlets. During the 1920s she appeared and spoke on radio and in her films to promote her ideas on love, fashion and romance through magazine articles, short stories and novels, becoming a prominent and highly visible ageing woman and public figure speaking on issues of the heart. Having control over her contracts gave her agency in her career. It also enabled her to specify how her name and image were used and – as Carman suggests of the A-list female film stars – Glyn led on her work 'creatively as well as financially' since she wielded power over set design, costume and direction (2012: 15). In her authorial and stage persona, she constructed herself as the experienced woman – a mother, teacher, guide and movie-making Circe – harnessing the storytelling power of the film to enchant her audience and reveal unspoken truths (Barnett and Weedon, 2014). One of her significant tropes was to frame the older woman on a dais or in a picture frame. For example, in her magazine dialogues, later published in the book *Flirt and the Flapper* (Glyn, 1930), she employs the artifice of a framed portrait coming to life, while in her film *Knowing Men* (Glyn, 1930), she places herself on a dais behind a writing desk, ready with a wave of her quill to cut to a series of vignettes to show the viewer how men 'really' are. In both instances she breaks the verisimilitude and places an accent on the role of the older woman by focusing attention on the poise and attractiveness of the full body portrait. The older woman is the centre of attention, not the men of the film title or the young flapper in the story. The older woman still has 'It'.

Defining 'It': more than youth appeal

So what was and is 'It'? In the original novella, 'It' could be attributed to both men and women and was a 'strange magnetism which attracts both sexes' (Barnett and Weedon, 2014: 129). The novella (a story of an experienced man, John Gaunt, who exudes 'It') was reproduced in *Cosmopolitan* in the same year as Clarence G. Badger's 1927 film. Glyn adapted the story (screenplay by Hope Loring) after meeting Clara Bow in 1926 who, she said, exuded 'immense attraction', and held a 'scintillating fascination' for the viewer (Glyn, n.d.: 2). In her article 'In defence of Clara Bow', Glyn describes her magnetism in more detail:

> Her large lovely eyes flashed with life, her tiny figure seemed all alive with desire to go! Just as race-horses strain before starting their race! She expressed vitality. She talked in the toughest vocabulary I had ever heard in the film colony! But it was apt and very funny. (Glyn, n.d: 2, author emphasis)

In the original novella, Glyn created 'It' as ageless and ungendered: men 'wanted to be buddies with "It men" just as women wanted to date them' (1927: 145). She described the dynamics of 'It' thus:

> To have 'it'... He or she must be entirely unself-conscious and full of self-confidence. Indifference to the effect he or she is producing, and uninfluenced by others. There must be physical attraction but beauty is unnecessary. Conceit or self-consciousness destroys 'It' immediately. (1927: 129)

Even before 1926 when the Bow film was first mooted, Glyn had long been developing her conceptualisation of 'It'. In her fiction and non-fiction writings on love, passion and marriage she often created characters with 'It'. In the novel she wrote for the American market, *The Man and the Moment* (1915), she describes how having 'It' takes the person beyond conventional social mores: 'Some people can err and sin in every way, and yet there is something about them which causes them to be forgiven ... call it having 'it' – some people have it, and some people have not' (Glyn, 1915: 82). Such stories focus on romantic love leading to sexual passion and legitimise the exploration of romantic and sexual pleasure for her readership of all ages.

In her famous series of 'Truth' articles, Glyn, acting as an older and experienced sage, advises the young woman seeking to cultivate 'It':

> when all the outward things are as perfect as she can make them ... she must begin acquiring the magnetism of mind necessary to demon- strate 'it'. She must become complete master of her emotions and of her thoughts ... Complete self confidence is necessary to 'It' and the slightest touch of self-consciousness when with others, destroys all 'It'. (Glyn, 1927–1930, No 2 and No 3)

Glyn it seems was not 'terrorised ... [by] the process of ageing', as Margaret Morse suggests befalls so many women (Morse, 1988: 21), but rather she embraced her age and sexual experience to remind young women that inner confidence is the way to cultivate 'It', and to exude the necessary sexual allure to be successful with men. There is never any sense in any of Glyn's writings that she embraces the notion of the 'neuterization of feminine identity' which Morse suggests is often seen within the context of the ageing female image (ibid.). In fact, Glyn often places herself at the forefront of artistic visibility within her work.

In her short story 'Such Men Are Dangerous' (1933), the main char- acter undergoes body-changing surgery in order to make himself more attractive, and the disabled protagonist of *Man and Maid* (1922) has a transformation which is noticed by the heroine: 'You are changed since last time ... you always have ... Some kind of attraction that has no name' (Glyn, 1922: 125–126). Glyn then self-references to demonstrate her ability to place her own celebrity at the core of the narrative, 'Oh! you know what Elinor Glyn writes of in her books – that's 'it' – Some kind of attraction that has no name – but I am sure has a lot to do with love' (Ibid.). This inter-textual reference undermines the male transformation narrative of the story situating the female authorial voice and the notion of 'It' as the central focus for the reader.

Such referentiality continues in the 1927 film *It*, where Glyn, now aged 63, appears in the film as herself to tell the main male character and the viewing audience exactly what 'It' is.[3] The film which centres on a shop girl, Betty Lou (Clara Bow) and her intense love for her department store boss, Cyrus Waltham Jr (Antonio Moreno), contains an early scene at the Ritz where Cyrus is dining with friends. Glyn is introduced into the narrative because the group are discussing reading her novella, and one of the guests says to Cyrus, 'of course you're reading Elinor Glyn's latest story 'It' ... what is "it"?' At this point, Glyn arrives at the restaurant. As she does so, there is a moment of pause. The restaurant guests all turn toward the entrance. Glyn enters at the top of the stairs, as if entering stage right in the theatre, the heavy draped curtains behind her, the stairs in front of her and the ornate candelabra at each side creating a proscenium arch as she takes her place centre-stage. She stands still (as if to acknowledge her audience – both within the diegesis and in the cinema) before a waiter takes her gloves. As she very slowly descends the stairs the maître d'hôtel bends into an extraordinary low bow at the foot of the staircase, not lifting his eyes from the floor until Glyn is in front of him. Glyn is heavily made up, her glossy (red) hair, is swept into a smooth braided bun and her long, loose, dark silk gown gives her a regal air as she glides across the restaurant to greet the diners.

Figure 2.1　Elinor Glyn in *It* (Clarence G. Badger, 1927)
Source: *It*. Copyright: Public domain.

Cyrus stands to greet her and she smiles at him as his guests ask her what 'It' is. She says:

Self confidence and indifference as to whether you are pleasing or not – and something in you that gives the impression that you are not all cold. That's IT!

Pointing a finger at Cyrus' chest she says:

If you have 'IT', you will win the girl you love.

All eyes are on Glyn as she speaks, giving an insight into her celebrity status and how her glamour and well-preserved physicality give her an air of authority as someone who can still advise the young. After speaking to Cyrus and his guests, Glyn sweeps across the room with a regal wave. Her presence is felt for several moments more as Cyrus is asked whether he believes in 'It'. Her entrance to the Ritz gives us a contemporaneous perception of how Glyn was received during this period. This cameo appearance, the excitement of the restaurant guests and the overzealous politeness of the maître d'hôtel, all alert us to her celebrity appeal. Watching this scene now, it is tempting to imagine her entering the many Hollywood parties that she attended in a similar manner, and this scene unquestionably captures the air of glamour Glyn cultivated and her undoubted celebrity status. Hollywood memoirs of her time featuring Glyn suggest that she was always an alluring presence in any room. Samuel Goldwyn, for example, stated that:

As a matter of fact, Mrs. Glyn is one of the greatest social assets I ever knew. Not only may she be relied upon always to wear the most exquisite of gowns, but her narratives and her comments usually keep a whole roomful of people in an uproar of mirth. (1923: 239)

Having Glyn appear in the film that celebrates her philosophy of attraction alerts us to the high profile that she enjoyed during the 1920s, while it also demonstrates her ability to be what Goldwyn above describes as a 'social asset': the room comes alive and the narrative is arrested while she appears. Glyn is, to use Tom Gunning's term, a moment of 'attraction' herself (1990: 56–62). Age is signified here as not only exuding glamour, but also wisdom. It is understood that in some way Elinor Glyn 'knows' about the allure of 'It', that she has herself been in thrall of 'It' and that through this entrance she herself still exudes 'It'. The ageing female here is celebrated in ways that do not conform to the 'girling' (see Jermyn, 2012: 1) of older women seen in contemporary discourse. As Jermyn suggests, postfeminist culture requires women to efface the signs of ageing (ibid.), whereas Glyn responds to her age by revelling in the attention given to her sexual wisdom, something that she can only have attained through time.

Consumerism and 'It'

Several months before the movie was released, the more specific answer to the burning 'What is "It"?' question was well known: Clara Bow was 'It' and thereafter the notion of 'It' and the 'It Girl' was synonymous with young female stars of the screen and flappers in the commercial world: young women with confidence and sexual presence. At this point, to a certain extent, Glyn lost authorial and commercial control over the concept of 'It.' It takes on a life of its own, losing its ambiguous gender and age orientation and instead becoming the epitome of young female sexual allure. Thinking about Glyn and her ageing celebrity seems especially pertinent at a time when, as Jermyn has suggested, the older woman has become an important 'new' (that is, rediscovered) audience for the Hollywood film industry, while the '"greying" of mainstream cinema has gathered momentum' (Jermyn, 2014: 146). The ideas that Glyn ignited at the beginning of the twentieth century, about sexual allure and physical and emotional confidence, were set against a back-drop of growing commercial interest in beauty and ageing. Glyn never identified 'It' solely with youth, in contradiction to the Hollywood machine and studio system that celebrated young stars such as Gloria Swanson, Clara Bow and Mary Pickford. Her stories gave a different account, including ones about older women with 'It' loving younger men; of young men and older men with 'It'; and of self-improvement for both men and women of any age. However, when in February 1927 her story 'It' first appeared in *Cosmopolitan,* numerous adverts sat along-side the story aimed at women to improve skin, nails, weight loss, fashion and hair, undermining Glyn's notion that 'It' was ageless and genderless.

One such advert for hair colouring, for example, runs with the head-line: 'Is Your Husband Beginning to Look Around?' and goes on to state that, 'Smart women never let themselves look old! Gray hair, however handsome, denotes advancing age. We all know the advantages of a youthful appearance'. This advert has a lithograph of a presumably

Figure 2.2 Page from *Cosmopolitan* (1927) showing adverts alongside Glyn's story, 'It'

Source: Copyright: University of Reading, special collections.

married couple walking arm in arm. It is hard to discern the age of the woman as she walks away, but the man's head is turned and we can see that he is middle-aged and wearing a homburg (Figure 2.2). We might assume his wife to be of a similar age. He has turned to stare at a single young woman with black glossy hair. Shockingly (or rather perhaps depressingly) the advert cautions women that if they do not take care of their ageing looks they are likely to be replaced by a younger model illustrating how enduring such cultural discourses have remained in the almost 90 years that have passed. Even a fleeting look through a current copy of *Cosmopolitan* will highlight that ageing is similarly and enduringly figured in remarkably similar ways as a 'problem' which women must both combat and conceal still today.

Glyn and a developing narrative of celebrity

Instead of seeing her ageing as a problem to be solved Glyn embraced her impending middle age by expanding her horizons and developing her multimedia celebrity status as early as 1908 when, at the age of 44 she travelled to the US following the success of her novel *Three Weeks* (1907). This book focused on the sexual passion of an older woman and gained attention through its controversial narrative which centred on the predatory love affair of the middle-aged Queen of Sardalia, with a much younger man, Paul Verdayne. In her memoirs, Glyn conveys her excitement at this new start in her life. 'It seemed a very big adventure to be thus travelling about by myself, in the role of "Elinor Glyn the famous authoress" instead of in the company of my husband ...' (Glyn, 1936: 138). She had become the source of press interest:

> It appeared that the most fantastic stories had been printed while we were yet at sea. I myself was the heroine of *Three Weeks*, it was said, and one paper even published a number of names (derived from the 'Peerage', I imagine) of probable 'Pauls'. This avalanche so confused me that I fear I had no sensible answers ready ... They were all so kind and so eager ... Whether it was on account of this good first impression that I have always been shown such kindness by the American press. (Glyn, 1936: 138–139)

Glyn wrote later that, 'Whether you were "for" or "against" *Three Weeks* was quite an important matter in the United States in the Spring of 1908' (Glyn, 1936: 163) – not least because it promoted promiscuous sexual behaviour which was led by an older woman (Glyn, 1936: 163). In Britain, the press were very hostile, and the criticism was severe enough for Glyn herself to take to the stage on her return to the UK. To 'prove there was nothing "improper" in the story' (Glyn, 1936: 137), she performed 'the Lady' opposite the 27-year-old Charles Bryant in a private showing of the play, inviting most of British high society. The play was considered a success, and Glyn signed a contract. However, when it was submitted to the Lord Chamberlain (Glyn, 1936: 209), he forbade public performance, giving no reason for his decision. A later adaptation of the story had to be altered so that the leading actors were closer in age and the child resulting from the affair was removed (Kuhn, 2008). In defending the 'truth' of her story, Glyn became an actress in her 40s, publicly affirming her own sexuality and making love on stage to a man

17 years her junior – aided, one assumes, by the eroticism of the tiger skin upon which she lay with a rose between her teeth.

Later, when she returned to the US in the 1920s, America provided her with a bigger arena than Britain, via the press, through which to construct her celebrity. She was so well known that her opinions ran as headlines; the press noted where she went, what she wore, and what she said. For example, in 1925, the *Los Angeles Examiner* reported, 'Age-Long Social System Very Hard on Women, Declares Elinor Glyn'. This editorial in 'the paper for those who think' was accompanied by a portrait of Glyn who by now was 61 years old and was quoted as saying that society requires that 'women must suppress all their natural instincts and conform to certain rigid principles' (Anon, 1925). This ageing celebrity advocates the sexual rights of women and highlights the inequalities in 1920s society, 'For Mary will be just as tempted as Harry – and the odds are all against her' (Anon, 1925: 3). In her writing, Glyn often uses the first person, validating her celebrity status through her personal contact with screen icons and the mentoring role she had with them, or connecting with a younger female readership through her characters or advice columns. She told her readers about the 'moving picture people' through articles such as 'Douglas and Mary as I knew them'; 'Rudolph Valentino as I knew him'; 'The Elissa Landi I know'; 'Gloria Swanson as I knew her'; 'Gloria as a mother'; and 'The screen's most attractive woman [and man] – and why'. Elsewhere she asked her readers. 'Should you marry a screen star'? and advised them who represented 'The best prospects for a husband among the film stars' (RUA MS4059 Box 13).[4]

Glyn's construction of her celebrity and attitude – both positive and negative reactions – to ageing is evident through her writings. The literary form which Glyn often used, the magazine dialogue, was akin to a play script. It allowed Glyn to explore the contradictions of age through an exchange between the older and younger generation. In *The Flirt and the Flapper,* the shifting language of sexual expression and politics are problematised. Glyn contrasts the US in the 1920s with that of the time of her youth in the 1860s. In the dialogue, the older Flirt asks the 19-year-old thrill-seeker somewhat incredulously 'What will you do when you are fifty?', contrasting her mature perspective and her status as a former beauty (the character is a painted portrait come to life). In this dialogue, as through Glyn's writing career, she shows an awareness of how words and meanings, and even grammar, have changed. By seeking to understand the flapper's terms (e.g., dope, dough, hooch, boy-friend, heavy, wise) she explores the new sexual politics which have been changed irrevocably by figures such as Sigmund Freud and

Havelock Ellis. Even the concepts of old and young are being redefined to refer – somewhat cynically – to knowing how to 'play' your men. 'What is "to think old"?', the older woman asks. 'To know what your boy-friend's likely to put over from you, and to be up to his game and get something on him first', replies the flapper (Glyn, 1930: 108–109). Glyn implies here that 'thinking old' for the young is not to do with age, and she equates this concept with being both worldly wise and materialist. For Glyn these terms were not necessarily pejorative – as her novel plots and the descriptions of her fashionable interiors demonstrate.

Glyn carefully framed and controlled her public image by commissioning postcard portraits which she sent to newspapers to accompany her articles or to feature in journalists' interviews. These rarely reveal her age and the photographic and low-resolution printing technology was flattering. Some are signed with her characteristic signature – a signature famously used in her film *It*. She also used her image to promote Lux soap (an endorsement also undertaken by many female film stars in the period). For a while, her image was everywhere – in the papers and on screen – and she was even selected as one of a series of famous British authors on Wills cigarette cards. On one of her own later postcards, Glyn is shown as a small figure in her large living room sitting on her sofa, surrounded by her tiger skins and cats. It is a carefully staged interior, portraying Glyn as a glamour icon and fashion-setter.[5] This picture was probably from the period when she moved to a flat in Connaught Place, Bayswater, which she filled with 'her fine collection of French furniture and pictures, her beautiful silks and brocades, her tiger skins' (Glyn, 1936: 320).

While the wealth of her experience was a feature of her public image, her age was often omitted from the narratives about her as the memoir below illustrates. In the 1920s, Glyn was part of the social circle of Hollywood, where celebrities and stars mixed. Samuel Goldwyn remembers meeting her at a party at the home of Douglas Fairbanks Jr in 1922, and his description of her exemplifies how it was her performance that held her audiences in thrall. Significantly, her apparent allure is seen as ageless:

> She has the trick, so I found, of convincing you that her voice is some far-away, mysterious visitant of which she herself supplies only a humble and temporary instrument of escape.
>
> For example, when she remarked, 'Isn't this pool beautiful?' it sounded like some lonely Buddha's prayer echoing down through the ages from the far heights of Tibet. (Goldwyn, 1923: 238)

In a scrapbook of the newspaper serialisation of *Love's Blindness* (1926), Glyn cut and pasted portraits of herself, adding captions which underscored the meaning of her facial expressions. Photographs of her smiling innocently had added handwritten ironic captions such as, 'Good as gold!!' and 'In the best of temper! (got on better with the Charleston!)'. Straight provocative looks into the camera lens have captions such as, 'Just try it on!', 'What price glory!' or more sharply 'Touch not The Cat without Glove'. These public photographs (for release to the press) become flirtatious photographs when re-captioned for her personal use, illustrating her keen understanding of the performance of her public and private image. The scrapbook reveals her character through an engaging moment between her and her agent (lover) John Wynn, for whom she wrote flirtatiously in the book plate 'Property of *JOHN WYNN from Elinor Glyn* School, *Top* grade, *First* Class'. In this private document for the two of them, it is evident that Glyn understood the effect of her presence and image and actively embraced the freedom to perform her sexuality through her photographs. The witty and flirtatious epitaph also suggests that – at the age of 62 – she was thoroughly enjoying the experience.

Glyn's legacy

While we opened this chapter noting how Glyn had been largely excised from many histories of this period, it is interesting to note that her influence on the articulation of female sexual pleasure has very recently been noted in a high-profile instance of contemporary British culture, the widely celebrated and exported ITV drama *Downton Abbey* (2010–). In series 5 episode 3 (aired in the UK, 5 October 2014), Lady Mary Crawley is having a coded discussion with her brother-in-law about her sexual attraction (or otherwise) to a new suitor:

> Mary: The point is I wasn't seeing him clearly, but now I do. He's a nice man, a very nice man, but not... I mean of course we talked about things, but I think my judgement rather was clouded by...
> Tom: By what Miss Elinor Glyn likes to write about in her novels...
> Mary: Maybe, but I seem to have got over that now.

This recent reference in a period drama, which firmly locates Glyn as a celebrity in 1924, shows that, however unjust the neglect she has been subject to historically, she has not entirely faded from our cultural consciousness. Indeed, in 1996, she was selected by Marian Fowler as one of five women of style in *The Way She Looks Tonight* (1996) and featured alongside Jacqueline Kennedy Onassis, Empress Eugenie of France, Marlene Dietrich, the Duchess of Windsor, and Eugenie Bonaparte. A decade earlier, biographers Meredith Etherington Smith and Jeremy Pilcher called Glyn and her sister the 'It' Girls (Smith and Pilcher, 1986). In their vivid portrait, the sisters certainly have dramatic flair. The facts bear this out: Glyn exhibited a talent for the theatrical when she participated or orchestrated the *tableaux vivants* held in some of the country houses she visited early in her marriage, and later in Hollywood. 'Lucille' Lady Duff Gordon, Glyn's older sister, dressed royalty and stars, and popularised sexy lingerie. Together they created the *mise-en-scène* of Glyn's films. What is most certain is that Elinor Glyn, confident in herself, apparently undiminished by age, and aware of her own sexual magnetism, constructed a persona where she evidenced that she herself had 'It'.

Her legacy lies in the notion of the 'It Girl' which, though changed, has retained a currency in our understanding of female celebrity, and it says much about the gendered nature of contemporary fame. Nowadays, it is more associated with female bright-young-things, rising Hollywood stars. Historicising celebrity through a reconsideration of Glyn provides insights into early practices in constructing a media persona. She was a highly visible media presence and her celebrity narrative portrayed her as an authentic, independent, successful, wise and experienced older woman. As 'Madam Glyn' she claimed to offer empowerment, engaging with and rewriting normative expectations of beauty and attractiveness. She did this through control of her own career and, like freelance A-list actresses of the 1930s, was able to directly affect the *mise-en-scène* of her films and her own star appearances through her contractual negotiations extending her career into her 50s and 60s. Strikingly, Glyn was adept at driving the multilinearity of interrelated written and visual texts enabling her to promote her work across media platforms. To be sure, we cannot consider this address to women to have been articulated (nor certainly received) in universal terms – as predicated on a homogenous conception of 'woman' as a subject. Glyn spoke from the position of a white, upper-class woman – privileges that enabled her to become a voice to be heard.

Nevertheless, Glyn is a complex historical figure. She can be read as an 'Eminent' romantic novelist who was brought in to bolster the reputation of Hollywood or as the British author who was banned by the censors for portraying an older woman's sexuality on stage and in film. She certainly upheld the overall status quo of patriarchal dominance by recommending marriage (albeit for love) but was also a pioneer in creating a popular forum for the expression of female sexuality at any age through her literature, the wide circulation of her magazine articles and the writing and directing of her films. The challenge for future researchers working within Celebrity Studies, as the discipline continues to forge new methodological approaches and areas of conceptual enquiry, is to recognise the importance of the historical example to highlight both the changes and continuities that exist across female celebrity in different periods. Glyn constitutes a major historical instance of an ageing woman star who contested dominant cultural discourses that rendered older women marginal – and as such her story offers up a significant precursor to the debates around the gendered inequities of fame that we see taking place with increasing vehemence and regularity today.

Acknowledgements

Our thanks to the University of Reading, Special Collections and Mrs Elspeth Chowdharay-Best for her permission to quote from the Elinor Glyn collection, which is referenced throughout as RUA, Ms 4059. Thanks also to the Margaret Herrick Library of the Academy of Motion Picture Arts and Sciences, Los Angeles, for permission to quote from Samuel Goldwyn (1923) *Behind the Screen* held in the reference collection. The research in this chapter arises in part from Weedon (PI) AHRC-funded project on cross-media cooperation in Britain in the 1920s and 1930s (AR112216). Last but not least, a huge thank you to Danielle Roberts and Charmaine Cummings for finding us the time to write this.

Notes

1. This novel and subsequent film includes the famous tiger skin 'moment' in which a loose-clad Aileen Pringle lounges on a tiger skin waiting for her young lover Paul (Conrad Nagel) with a rose between her teeth.
2. Samuel Goldwyn organised Eminent Authors in 1919 as a division of his film company and other studios followed suit (Rogers, 2005).
3. Clara Bow plays Betty Lou Spence, a lingerie salesgirl who falls for her department store owner boss, Cyrus Waltham Jr (Antonio Moreno). She contrives to meet him at the Ritz – where Cyrus and his dinner guests are introduced to Elinor Glyn – by persuading Cyrus's best friend to take her on a date there. Later, Clara is invited on a date with Cyrus (in spite of the fact that he is engaged) to Coney Island and they fall in love. A misunderstanding about her roommate's baby leads Cyrus to think that she is an unmarried mother and he calls off the affair. Heartbroken Betty Lou follows Cyrus to his yacht where he

is holding a party and she accidently falls overboard. Cyrus jumps in to save her, the couple reunite and a romantic happy ending is assured.
4. These are titles of Glyn's magazine articles in typescript as listed in RUA MS4059 Box 13
5. Christmas card postcard portrait to Betty Ross (1935–1938). Available at http://www.manuscripts.co.uk/images/pic8138.jpg [accessed 12 November 2014]. Archived description of an item.

References

Anon (1925) 'Age-Long Social System Very Hard on Women, Declares Elinor Glyn', *Los Angeles Examiner*, 25 August, RUA 4059. Box 19. n.p.

Barnett, V. L. and Weedon, A. (2014) *Elinor Glyn as Novelist, Moviemaker, Glamour Icon and Businesswoman* (Farnham and Burlington, VT: Ashgate).

Boorstin, D. (1961) *The Image: A Guide to Pseudo-Events in America* (New York. Atheneum).

Carman, E. (2012) 'Women Rule Hollywood: Ageing and Freelance Stardom in the Studio System', *Celebrity Studies*, 3(1), pp. 13–24.

DeCordova, R. (1990) *Picture Personalities: The Emergence of the Star System in America* (Illinois: University of Illinois Press).

Fowler, M. (1996) *The Way She Looks Tonight: Five Women of Style* (New York: St Martins Press).

Glyn, E. (n.d.) 'Gloria Swanson as I Knew Her', RUA 4059. Box 11. TS.

Glyn, E. (n.d.) 'In Defence of Clara Bow', RUA 4059. Box 11. 'It'.

Glyn, E. (1915) *The Man and the Moment* (London: Duckworth).

Glyn, E. (1920a) 'Three Dialogues', RUA 4059. Box 11. Cutting of published version, p. 578.

Glyn, E. (1920b) 'Are Women Changing?', RUA 4059. Box 11. TS, p. 4.

Glyn, E. (1922) *Man and Maid* (London: Duckworth).

Glyn, E. (1927) *The Wrinkle Book or, How to Keep Looking Young* (London: Duckworth).

Glyn, E. (1927–1930) 'The Truth IT' No 2 – No 3. RUA 4059. Box 11. TS.

Glyn, E. (1930) *The Flirt and the Flapper: Dialogues* (London: Duckworth).

Glyn, E. (1933) 'Such Men Are Dangerous', in E. Glyn, *Saint or Satyr? And Other Stories* (London: Duckworth).

Glyn, E. (1936) *A Romantic Adventure* (London: Nicholson).

Glyn, E. (1939a) 'To Women', RUA 4059. Box 11. TS. 4 April.

Glyn, E. (1939b) 'The Message of Elinor Glyn to the Older Women of Britain', RUA 4059. Box 11. TS.

Goldwyn, S. (1923) *Behind the Screen* (New York: George H. Doran Co.).

Gunning, T. (1990) 'The Cinema of Attractions: Early Cinema, Its Spectator, and the Avant-Garde', in T. Elasaesser (ed.) *Early Cinema: Space Frame Narrative* (London: British Film Institute), pp. 56–62.

Jermyn, D. (2012) '"Glorious, Glamorous and That Old Standby, Amorous": The Late Blossoming of Diane Keaton's Romantic Comedy Career', *Celebrity Studies*, 3(1), pp. 37–51.

Jermyn, D. (2014) 'The (un-Botoxed) Face of a Hollywood Revolution', in I. Whelehan and J. Gwynne (eds) *Ageing, Popular Culture and Contemporary Feminism: Harleys and Hormones* (Basingstoke: Palgrave Macmillan), pp. 108–123.

Kuhn, A. (2008) 'The Trouble with Elinor Glyn: Hollywood, *Three Weeks* and the British Board of Film Censors', *Historical Journal of Film, Radio and Television*, 28(1), pp. 23–35.

Moody, N. (2003) 'Elinor Glyn and the Invention of "It"', *Critical Survey*, 15(3), pp. 92–104.

Morse, M. (1988) 'Artemis Aging: Exercise and the Female Body on Video', *Discourse*, 10(1), pp. 20–53.

Rogers, W. (2005) *The Papers of Will Rogers: From the Broadway Stage to the National Stage, September 1915–July 1928* (Norman: University of Oklahoma Press).

Smith, M. E. and Pilcher, J. (1986) *The 'It' Girls: Elinor Glyn and 'Lucile'* (London: Hamish Hamilton Ltd).

Turner, G. (2004) *Understanding Celebrity* (London: SAGE).

Filmed

Downton Abbey. ITV, UK, 2010–.

It. Directed by Clarence G. Badger. US, 1927.

Knowing Men. Directed by Elinor Glyn. UK, 1930.

Three Weeks (aka *A Romance of a Queen*). Directed by Alan Crosland. US, 1924.

Three Weeks. Directed by Perry N. Vekroff. US, 1914.

3

Bette Davis: Acting and Not Acting Her Age

Martin Shingler

Towards the end of 1988, an 80-year-old Bette Davis, after seeing the first week's rushes of her scenes for Larry Cohen's *Wicked Stepmother*, was so shocked by her frail appearance that she withdrew from the project.[1] Emaciated and ravaged by time and illness (including breast cancer, a stroke and a broken hip), Davis quit, fearing that – as she later reported to Nina Easton of the *Los Angeles Times* – 'it could seriously be the end of anybody ever hiring me again' (Easton, 1988: 6). As it turned out this was the end, but it was actually a wonder that she was hired for this film in the first place. As Easton noted in her article, 'Bette Davis Smoking Over Stepmother', most studios were reluctant to hire actors with health problems due to the high cost of obtaining insurance to cover losses if s/he died or fell ill during production. In this instance, Larco Productions had acquired (no doubt, costly) insurance for Davis and the insurance company duly paid out to the tune of a million dollars when the aged star withdrew, enabling 44-year-old Barbara Carrera to be hired as a replacement.[2] Consequently, the film was completed and released (on video rather than in cinemas) in 1989. This, Bette Davis' final film, makes for painful viewing as she limps and stumbles through her scenes. Although struggling to move and deliver her lines, she does manage occasionally to glare malevolently with those celebrated eyes of hers, while puffing incessantly on a cigarette. Nevertheless, this was a sad end to a long and illustrious film career.

Bette Davis made 89 movies from 1931 to 1988. Despite her small stature, strikingly large eyes and a face that photographed well when sympathetically lit, she was rarely considered a beauty. Her appeal lay in her fiercely independent spirit, her unconventionality and rebelliousness (Shingler, 2008: 271). Through a combination of hard work, determination and courage, Davis became an acclaimed screen performer who favoured challenging roles, particularly feisty heroines, tragic victims and unscrupulous bitches in romantic dramas known as 'weepies'. Success at the box office from 1935 to 1945, combined with the support of the New York film critics and the jury of the Motion Picture Academy, made her a powerful person in studio era Hollywood. Indeed, by 1939 Davis was an intimidating figure, a challenging colleague and a defiant employee (Shingler, 1996: 127–128). Davis frequently defied convention, including shocking her public and critics with unusual portrayals and performances, with extreme characterisations, including larger-than-life and unsympathetic characters, realised through excessive costume and make-up combined with a performance style judged to be mannered, even 'hammy' (Shingler, 1999: 56). Notable examples include *The Private Lives of Elizabeth and Essex* (Curtiz, 1939), *The Little Foxes* (Wyler, 1941), *Mr. Skeffington* (Sherman, 1944), *All About Eve* (Mankiewicz, 1950), *The Star* (Heisler, 1952) and *What Ever Happened to Baby Jane?* (Aldrich, 1962). Having proven herself adept at realism and restraint with subdued roles in *The Petrified Forest* (Archie Mayo, 1936), *The Letter* (Wyler, 1940) and *Watch on the Rhine* (Shumlin, 1943), Davis relished opportunities to embrace excess and even the grotesque, courting controversy and dividing critical and popular opinion (Shingler, 2013: 31–32). One of the ways in which she did so was with her portrayals of old age. Hollywood, of course, is widely recognised as an industry relentlessly unforgiving of ageing among its women stars. In such a professional context, Davis' willingness to play older women rather than shy away from the fact of ageing, and her determination not to be ousted but to keep working as she aged, spoke to a career marked, as noted, by 'unusual performances' and bolstered a persona that embodied resilience and boldness even in her younger years.

Davis often aged beyond her years, for instance as the 60-year-old Queen Elizabeth I in *The Private Lives of Elizabeth and Essex* when the actress was just 31. For the next 50 years, ageing and old age played a major role in her career. Playing older women in her 30s enabled the star to enhance her credentials as an actor, proving that she was adept at portraying women very different from herself. In her 40s, Davis strove to convince film executives of the viability of films centred upon women of her own age when most studios were producing movies for adolescent and young adult audiences. In her 50s and 60s, Davis produced some astonishing versions of mature femininity, creating a gallery of female grotesques (see Brooks, 1999, and Morey, 2011). Meanwhile, in her 70s and 80s, Davis fought against infirmity and ill health to go on acting in films, occasionally producing some remarkably poignant depictions of old age.

This article explores some of the more remarkable aspects of Bette Davis' approach to old age, revealing that ageing played a key role in her longevity as a screen performer. It reveals how Davis' propensity to perform age in exaggerated and grotesque ways earned her the respect of gay audiences as a cult star at the point when mainstream audiences and major studios had little use for her. Bette Davis was not only one of Hollywood's most accomplished creators of ageing femininity but also one of the most radical. Indeed, as this essay suggests, her presentations of age were as provocative and challenging as her portrayals of gender, a topic that I have previously examined elsewhere (Shingler, 2008). Indeed, the two were inescapably interwoven, since the very persistence of her image and performances over many decades, not just as an 'old star' but as an enduringly and atypically visible ageing *woman* star, in itself unsettled one of the gendered inequities at the heart of Hollywood. By investigating this here, I hope to show how a critical awareness of ageing and old age, and the imbrication of this with her gender, provides a fuller understanding of Davis' controversial star image.

Too old?

From the moment she came to prominence in 1935 with an Oscar-winning leading role in *Dangerous* (Green), Bette Davis was considered too old to be a major star. At 27, she had exceeded the average age of female film stars in Hollywood, which before 1940 was 20–25, as Edgar Morin has noted (1957/2005: 36). When Davis became the top female star at Warners (Warner Bros.), after winning her second Oscar for *Jezebel* (Wyler, 1938), she was 30 – much too old. Nevertheless, over the next seven years, Davis defied expectation by becoming one of Hollywood's most commercially successful and critically acclaimed film stars. Part of her success lay in her proven ability to convincingly play women younger than herself. After winning an Oscar for her role as the 20-year-old Julie Marsden in *Jezebel*, a 31-year-old Davis won rave reviews for her appearance as the spirited 20-year-old Charlotte Lovell in *The Old Maid* (Goulding, 1939). Three years later, she appeared in a short flashback scene as naïve 20-year-old Charlotte Vale in *Now, Voyager* (Rapper, 1942) and over the next two years played more 20-year-olds in *Old Acquaintance* (Sherman, 1943) and *Mr. Skeffington* (Sherman, 1944). However, as I noted in my essay 'Masquerade or Drag?', Davis felt too old at 35 to convincingly play her character in *Mr. Skeffington* at the age of 25 and so compensated with an excess of feminine frills and poses, along with a falsetto voice, rendering her performance of young femininity a masquerade to the point where this evokes a palpable sense of female impersonation or drag (Shingler, 1995: 182).

The concept of femininity as masquerade, as articulated by psychoanalyst Joan Riviere in her essay 'Womanliness as a Masquerade' (1929), suggests some interesting reasons for Davis' extraordinary feminine display in *Mr. Skeffington* (Riviere, 1929/1986). In particular, it suggests that Davis, at the peak of her power in Hollywood in 1944, adopted an excessively feminine characterisation as a means of concealing the power she wielded at Warners at this time (Shingler, 1995: 185). For Riviere, one of the main reasons for powerful women's adoption of excessive femininity in the early part of the twentieth century was to conceal their power from men due to an unconscious fear of retribution. However, Kathleen Woodward's re-articulation of masquerade in terms of youthfulness sheds a different light on a performance such as Davis' in *Mr. Skeffington*. In her essay 'Youthfulness as a Masquerade,' Woodward notes that 'masquerade with respect to the ageing body is first and foremost a denial of age, an effort to erase or efface age (or to put on youth)' (Woodward, 1988–1999: 121). This can involve the addition of desired body parts (e.g., falsies or wigs) or the removal or concealment of those that indicate advanced age, along with face lifts and the remodelling of the body's shape in order to erase the effects of gravity. During the early sequences of *Mr. Skeffington*, in which Davis plays the 25-year-old Fanny Trellis Skeffington, the actress dons heavy make-up and a wig, along with an excess of lace, silks and chiffon, in order to disguise her own bodily signs of middle age, while simultaneously adopting a noticeably animated set of gestures, movements and facial expressions in order to signify both a youthful energy and self-consciousness. All of these operate to mask the fact of Davis' age in a bid to create a character ten years younger.

Kathleen Woodward's conceptualisation of youthfulness as masquerade considers such acts to be less defensive than in Riviere's original articulation, regarding masquerade as a strategy of defiance rather than defence. This lends it a much more aggressive dimension and, consequently, it seems more relevant for a consideration of Bette Davis' performances of age, leading to the possible conclusion that Davis' excessive display of youthful femininity in this film was intended to signal that, since she felt uncomfortable performing 25-year-old characters at 35, she was not prepared to perform this in more natural or credible ways. Another interesting aspect of Woodward's conception of youthfulness as masquerade is that it incorporates aspects of the grotesque, which again seems to be particularly relevant for understanding Davis' performances of characters younger than herself after 1944. As I discuss in my essay 'The Naked Ugliness of *Beyond the Forest* (1949),' her portrayal of the destructive small-town siren of King Vidor's 1949 film offers a version of femininity as masquerade that is more deeply rooted in the grotesque. Here, not only does the 41-year-old Davis appear as Rosa Moline in an incongruous long black wig and tight-fitting costumes but her face also appears to melt during her death scene, becoming strangely distorted.

While *Mr. Skeffington* was a commercial success, garnering positive reviews and earning Davis an Oscar nomination, *Beyond the Forest* did badly at the box office, with Davis being heavily criticised for her performance and characterisation (see Shingler, 2013: 32). Here, Davis' frustration at having to play a young beauty was evident to audiences and critics alike, signaling that Davis could no longer go on playing such young characters in her 40s. Nevertheless, she did play a character in her 20s during some of the early flashback scenes of *Payment on Demand* (Bernhardt, 1951). This film, which also did badly at the box office, proved to be the last time Davis was required to play such a young character on screen.

Acting her own age

It was during the making of *Payment on Demand* that Davis announced it was time for her to start playing middle-aged characters. In an undated and unsourced article entitled 'Star Wishes More Mature Parts Were Written' and held at the Bette Davis Collection at the Howard Gottlieb Archival Center at Boston University, a 41-year-old Davis is reported to be 'back at work playing a fortyish mother, and, she said yesterday, she thinks other almost middleaged stars ought to act their ages too'.[3] Here, Davis bemoans the lack of opportunities in Hollywood for women of her age. Interviewer Aline Mosby, quotes Davis as stating that, 'It's too bad that Hollywood has made a complete fetish of the 18-year-old heroine,' that 'Anyone at that age is the dullest person' and that 'Screen plays should be written more and more with mature roles' because 'Beyond 30 is when a person gets interesting' (Mosby, 1950). Davis is also reported to have declared that, 'When an actor reaches a certain age, he must have the courage to give up the young roles and go out to find the parts he can play at that age', adding that, 'It's too bad that there are very few written'. By this time, then, Davis not only had the courage to play middle-aged characters but also to publicly berate Hollywood studios for their failure to supply established actresses of her generation with interesting leading roles. Having previously fought for equal pay for male and female stars, for better working conditions and more control over her roles, Davis now had a new cause to fight for.[4]

The fighting spirit that was the keynote of Davis' star image at Warners in the 1930s was still evident in *Payment on Demand*, which she made at RKO in 1950.[5] Here Davis portrayed a wife whose husband suddenly announces that he wants a divorce after 20 years of marriage. Davis' character fights to secure her home and wealth, along with custody of her two teenage daughters, but she also learns of the danger of ageing and loneliness for women. At one point she is told by an older divorcée (played by ageing Broadway star Jane Cowl), who has succumbed to alcoholism and the questionable charms of a young and parasitical lover, that time can become an avalanche and loneliness a disaster for older women. The film features many flashback scenes, charting the entire history of Joyce Ramsay's marriage. However, Davis spends much of the film in a grey wig, suggesting that her character is older than the actress herself. Consequently, this film did not present Davis with much of an opportunity to play a character her own age. However, a few months later she was given that opportunity. As Margo Channing in Twentieth Century Fox's production of Joseph L. Mankiewicz's *All About Eve*, Davis played a 40-year-old Broadway diva forced to make way for a younger actress, Eve Harrington (Anne Baxter). Frustrated by having to play 20-year-olds on stage in the absence of mature roles, and outmanoeuvred by Eve (her fan turned personal assistant, understudy and rival), Margo eventually forsakes the theatre in favour of marriage to her lover Bill Sampson (Gary Merrill), a man eight years her junior. The age gap between Margo and Bill is continuously highlighted in the dialogue, as is the fact that even at her 'advanced' age, Margo remains the most childlike of all the characters in the film; hence her tantrums, sulks, play acting offstage and self-evident need for attention, approval and affection.

All About Eve features Davis' most heartfelt and nuanced performance in a role that she completely inhabited. Once this film had proven its worth at the box office and with the judges of the Academy of Motion Picture Arts and Sciences (garnering eight nominations and two awards), her career appeared to be back on track, particularly after her stellar performance as an ageing unemployed, bankrupt and alcoholic movie star trying to make a comeback in *The Star* in 1952, which earned Davis another Oscar nomination.[6] However, the 1950s proved to be a disappointing decade for Davis, with only a handful of starring roles. She endured years of unemployment and was largely reduced to playing character parts and supporting roles until, in 1962, she made her own remarkable comeback opposite Hollywood stalwart Joan Crawford in *What Ever Happened to Baby Jane?* This modestly budgeted film was directed by Robert Aldrich, produced independently by Seven Arts Associates and distributed by Warner Bros. after numerous Hollywood studios had rejected it on the grounds that its 50-something stars were no longer 'bankable' (Davis, 1987: 136). After the film took an impressive $1,600,000 in rental on its opening weekend in October 1962 and grossed almost four million dollars during its initial run in the US, Davis and Crawford temporarily regained a significant degree of star power (Sikov, 2007: 345).

Davis received her first Oscar nomination in ten years for her role as Jane Hudson, the middle-aged has-been child star, who cruelly persecutes her paralysed ex-movie star sister Blanche (Crawford). Occupying a netherworld between childhood and middle age, fantasy and reality, a delusional Jane plans her comeback in show business despite her worn out voice and body. The curious combination of a mature body and a childish personality recalls Margo Channing of *All About Eve*, only transformed here into something darker and more disturbing, even psychotic and gruesome, particularly when Jane starves, terrorises and brutalises her disabled sister.

Bleak and bold, *What Ever Happened to Baby Jane?* enabled Bette Davis to produce an extraordinary performance of ageing femininity, one that Jodi Brooks has interpreted as a refusal to be discarded as an ageing star, arguing that plot and the extra-textual significance of Jane's crisis for Davis herself blur here. (Brooks, 1999: 234). Raging against the film industry's tendency to discard mature actresses, Davis reclaimed the limelight by situating her ageing body at the centre of a compelling gaze, providing a grotesquely humorous and horrific spectacle, perfectly crafted but excessive, tasteless and unconventional. In this movie, Davis proved with her Oscar-nominated performance that she was still a great actress as well as a bankable star. She also proved, with a strenuous physical performance, that she could still withstand the rigors of filmmaking at 54. Meanwhile, by making a generic shift from romantic drama to horror/thriller/exploitation, she also demonstrated an ability to reinvent her star image and win new fans, including teenagers and males, to augment and substitute for her waning fan base of older women (i.e., her loyal fans from the 1930s and 1940s).

By the early 1960s, Davis had aged noticeably. Years of heavy smoking and drinking, combined with a lack of exercise, dieting, beauty treatments and cosmetic surgery resulted in the loss of her slim physique and the development of noticeable bags under her eyes, as well as jowls and wrinkles. Compared to her *Baby Jane* co-star Joan Crawford, who was older by five years, Davis looked considerably aged and out of shape. Unlike Crawford, Davis made little attempt to disguise her age on or off the screen. In fact, while Crawford's stardom relied upon her being considered beautiful, glamorous and stylish, Davis built her reputation by being considered plain, bad and unsympathetic.

Playing old when young

Bette Davis had played unsympathetic and old characters ever since she was 31. This began in 1939 with her role as an embittered spinster in *The Old Maid*, her character ageing 20 years, from 20 at the start of the film to 40 at the end. After portraying a 60-year-old Elizabeth Tudor, Davis played the ambitious 40-year-old Regina Giddens in Lillian Hellman's *The Little Foxes* in 1941. In 1944, her character aged more than 20 years in *Mr. Skeffington*, from an attractive woman in her mid-20s to a prematurely aged 49-year-old whose youth and beauty have been destroyed by diphtheria, leaving her grotesquely haggard.

Philip and Julius Epstein's adaptation of Elizabeth von Arnim's novel *Mr Skeffington* (1940) departed significantly from the original text by featuring scenes of the main protagonist in her 20s and 30s, as well as giving her a child. The novel was a tragicomedy about the double standard of ageing for men and women, highlighting how age can be both psychologically traumatic and socially debilitating for attractive childless women. In fact, the novel almost exactly illustrates Susan Sontag's thesis on the sexual inequalities of age as set out in her essay, 'The Double Standard of Ageing', published in 1972.[7] Von Arnim's novel presented Fanny Skeffington on the eve of her 50th birthday as a once admired and beautiful woman reduced to an aged crone, one who elicits horrified reactions from former admirers. The author details her character's haggard features repeatedly throughout the novel, including the hollows in her cheeks and heavy pouches beneath her eyes, her false yellow curls that substitute for her once bountiful and radiant hair and the heavily scented body and painted face that makes this aristocratic woman easily mistaken for a prostitute.

Davis chose to wear a rubber mask to create Fanny Skeffington's grotesquely aged appearance and did so against the wishes of her director Vincent Sherman and her scriptwriter-producers, the Epstein brothers. By doing so, she remained faithful to Elizabeth von Arnim's original conception. By presenting Fanny's aged appearance as a mask or masquerade, Davis was in effect affirming her own youthfulness. In other words, by seemingly having to adopt an excessive and obvious set of accoutrements to achieve the appearance of old age, the actress demonstrated that even at 35 she could only achieve this via artificial means. Despite feeling too old to play her character at 25, it was imperative at this point in her career that Davis prove that in her mid-30s she was still sufficiently youthful to be a bankable star in Hollywood. She did so by adopting agedness as a masquerade.

Resembling Mrs Skeffington

By 1988, Bette Davis had become the very image of her character at the end of *Mr. Skeffington*. Thomas Quinn Curtis of the *International Herald Tribune* was struck by this resemblance when he met the 80-year-old star in Paris, where she was publicising her book *This 'N That*. In his article 'Bette Davis: "Never Say Die"', he describes her as,

> a frail little woman with hollow cheeks. She stands on her spindly legs as erect as a grenadier at attention, her eyes alert. She resembles her portrayal on the screen of the haughty Mrs. Skeffington taking the advancing years in her proud stride. (Quinn Curtis, 1988)

While diphtheria robbed the fictional Fanny Skeffington of her youth and beauty, cancer and a stroke very nearly robbed Bette Davis of her life and career in June 1983. Having discovered a lump in her left breast, the star had a mastectomy and then suffered a major stroke nine days later. Her doctors declared that she was unlikely to ever work again. However, they were proven wrong (despite a fall that broke Davis' hip later in the year) when Davis returned to work in 1984, appearing in a Warner Bros. television production of Agatha Christie's *Murder with Mirrors* (Lowry, 1984), which aired in the US on CBS television in February 1985.[8] This introduced audiences to Bette Davis' emaciated body, contorted mouth and thin, stilted voice. The left side of her face was visibly impaired by the facial drag caused by the stroke, while her movements and gestures betrayed the fact that her left arm and leg were severely weakened; and it remains striking, and uncommon, to see such evidence of how the physical challenges of 'advanced old age' are made visible on screen. These remained evident two years later when Davis finally returned to the big screen after a seven-year absence to reclaim her status as a film legend alongside Lillian Gish in *The Whales of August* (Anderson, 1987). Cast as two elderly widowed sisters spending time together at their summerhouse on the New England coast, Davis played the older bad sister Libby

Strong opposite Gish's good and long-suffering Sarah Webber. The film, adapted by David Barry from his off-Broadway play and produced by the independent production company (appropriately called) Alive Films again provided a rare look at advanced old age. This quiet, gentle and nostalgic film contains some heart-rending close-ups of Davis' withered hands and face, her skeletal body with its loose covering of tissue-paper-thin skin. There is a palpable sense here of witnessing someone with one foot in the grave; someone, though, who remains tenacious, fiery, determined and indomitable. Throughout the film, shots of framed photographs of a youthful Bette Davis reveal the full extent to which time had ravaged her.

Despite her various physical impairments, Davis created an eloquent and moving performance as the bitter 90-year-old Libby, blind and fragile, domineering and rude, lonely and lost. This was a haunting portrayal of a woman who has become a shadow of her former self, almost a ghost, hovering between life and death. It would have made a fitting final film for Davis. It certainly earned her good reviews in *Variety* and the *New York Times*. A *Variety* review on 13 May described her as looking 'gaunt, grim and disturbed' but insisted that she had nonetheless produced a performance that was 'restrained in such a way that may even increase its power' (Anon, 1987). Three days later, Vincent Canby of the *New York Times* reported that in *The Whales of August* Davis' 'famous features had suddenly been ennobled by time, the familiar mannerisms subdued and enriched' (Canby, 1987). Nevertheless, despite her restrained performance, Davis' characterisation of Libby Strong retained aspects redolent of her earlier grotesque roles, such as her long white wig (obviously not the actress' own hair) and mannered speech patterns, recalling the likes of Fanny Skeffington, Rosa Moline and Baby Jane Hudson.

It was Fanny Skeffington that Davis most resembled in her public appearances during the mid-to-late 1980s, being similarly adorned in elaborate wigs, heavy make-up, gloves, hats and veils. However, if the 35-year-old Davis had used a grotesquely aged mask to highlight her own youthfulness in 1944, over 40 years later Davis' extraordinary appearance seemed to accentuate her age. As an old and physically impaired woman, Davis donned her excessively feminine accoutrements for her public engagements, fusing the trappings of youth and age. In so doing, she continued to shock and disturb, just as she had done throughout her career, challenging conventions of decorum and good taste, defying the social codes of age-appropriate behaviour. In this, Davis also resembled the character Elizabeth Hunter in Patrick White's novel *The Eye of the Storm* (1973) who, in her 80s, performs a masquerade of youthfulness that involves taking pleasure in the artificial and the inappropriate (e.g., by wearing a long wig, deep red lipstick and garish clothes) in order to defy her old age and powerlessness (Woodward, 1998–1999: 126). Davis' final incarnation presented her less in terms of youth than femininity, as though she was staging one last bid at womanliness despite the efforts of age and cancer (as well as the medics who performed her mastectomy) to rob her of her outward signifiers of femininity. After her cancer treatment and stroke, Davis refused to give up smoking. She also refused to give up work and womanliness. Cigarettes and bright red lipstick substituted for what she had lost: her power and health. Though physically diminished, Davis retained her intelligence, wit and willpower. She also made every effort to display them. By recreating her appearance at the end of *Mr. Skeffington*, she evoked the time when she was at her most powerful as a star, recalling the moment when she was the controlling force behind her films, one that no one (that is, no man) could prevent from having her own way. What had once been a masquerade that had, in part, concealed such power now signified something very different. At the point where Davis was losing power, control and independence, she donned the same mask in order to transform powerlessness into self-determination. By this time, although fêted as a Hollywood legend, Davis was no longer an A-list movie star whose appearance in a film could guarantee huge global sales at the box office. Indeed, Davis had been operating mainly at the fringes of the film industry since the 1960s, occasionally making small independent films but more often starring in made-for-television movies, while maintaining her public profile as a celebrity with personal appearances on TV chat shows, at film festivals and book signings. Nevertheless, despite being marginalised, Davis had never retired in defeat but rather had gone on defying expectation just as she had throughout her career with a determination to work in an industry that continued to privilege youth and beauty for its female stars. Even at 80, Davis showed no signs of retiring gracefully from the spotlight.

In November 1988, Thomas Quinn Curtis reported to readers of the *International Herald Tribune* that Davis wanted the leading role in the film version of Alfred Uhry's play *Driving Miss Daisy*.[9] He also claimed that Davis had told him that she wanted another opportunity to play Queen Elizabeth I.[10] It was a month later that Nina Easton informed readers of the *Los Angeles Times* that Davis had withdrawn from the set of *Wicked Stepmother* so that her appearance would not jeopardise any further acting prospects. Even here, then, was an indication that Davis intended to continue working in the film industry. It was only Davis' death on 6 October 1989 that confirmed the fact that the star's long film career was finally over.

Conclusion

> If a female star could last for a decade, she really paid off. If she could last for two decades, she was a phenomenal success. If she lasted longer than that, she was a miracle, and today we can call her a legend. (Basinger, 2007: 320)

As Jeanine Basinger has noted, Bette Davis was one of a minority of female stars of the 1930s and 1940s who survived for more than three decades, earning the title of 'legend' (ibid.). Davis endured so long partly because she was never considered to be one of Hollywood's great beauties, the glamorous persona she developed during her heyday relying less on her good looks and attractive figure than her power, independence and panache. Although her power diminished during the late 1940s, Davis found herself a more permanent niche as a film celebrity, a cult star and an icon: most notably, as a gay icon (see Sikov, 2010). However, as revealed in this essay, the longevity of Bette Davis' film career was in part determined by her ability to perform age as well as to reinvent herself as she aged.

What this essay also reveals is that Davis' most remarkable, celebrated and memorable performances of ageing and old age were darkly comic, such as in *Mr. Skeffington, All About Eve, What Ever Happened to Baby Jane?* and *The Whales of August*. In all these instances, ageing and old age were something to laugh about, but they were also disturbing, presenting uncomfortable truths humorously (that is, with black humour), presenting the reality of ageing and old age through a high level of artifice (i.e., masquerade) and gross exaggeration (i.e., the grotesque). It is perhaps fitting, then, that in her end-of-life autobiography *This 'N That*, Bette Davis provided a troubling and darkly humorous joke about old age.

At the start of the book's fourth chapter, Davis described an embroidered pillow among her personal possessions bearing the inscription 'Old Age Ain't No Place for Sissies' (Davis, 1987: 49). This curious item of soft furnishing works as a gag on several levels. Firstly, the brutal reality of the statement (that old age is tough) is transformed into an item designed to (literally) cushion the blow of this realisation. Secondly, it implies that Sissies (i.e., effeminate gay men) do not do old age, not necessarily because they die young (say, of AIDS-related illnesses, although this appeared to be the case in 1987) but because they frequently deny the signs and effects of old age, erasing them by whatever means they can. Davis, of course, was neither a Sissy nor a gay man (although by the 1980s it was widely accepted that many of her fans were) and in that sense, old age was a place that she was prepared to go, somewhere, in fact, she would take her fans, gay and straight. Finally, the statement works as a gag by means of the double negative 'Ain't No Place' that transforms it into an assertion of the opposite of what it appears to be at first sight. In other words, old age *is* a place for Sissies, just as it is for everyone else. Davis was a perfectionist and an intelligent and articulate woman who, despite a refined persona, revelled in bad taste and ribaldry. The use of this statement's non-standard but idiomatic double negative no doubt appalled and delighted her in equal measure. Despite its ambiguities, this phrase clearly proclaimed that she was going into old age as a fighter not a wimp.

What Davis insisted upon at the start of a chapter entitled 'Well On Our Way' is that old age is something everyone must face if they go on living. Male or female, gay or straight, film fan or movie star, life inevitably gets harder and everything ultimately becomes hard work. Time eventually destroys, diminishes and degrades. Ultimately it brings long-time survivors (like Davis) down. And so, for Davis, this unpalatable truth becomes a cruel joke. For an actress whose ability to move and speak fluently had been severely diminished by time, age was surely no joking matter. However, in her advanced old age, Bette Davis found a neat way of using humour, suitably black humour, to acknowledge the one fight she knew she could never win. It was one of many harsh lessons she had learned throughout her life, as well as being one of the recurrent themes of her films. In the end, no one knew this better than Bette and no one proved this better than Davis.

Notes

1. Larry Cohen, a specialist in low-budget horror movies, was *Wicked Stepmother*'s writer-director and executive producer.
2. Barbara Carrera, former Bond girl with Sean Connery in *Never Say Never Again* (Kershner, 1983), was best known for her role in the television series *Dallas* from 1985–1986.
3. If Davis was, as this article states, almost 42 at the time, this piece was published shortly before 5 April 1950.
4. For details of Davis' fights for equal pay, autonomy and better working conditions, see Paul McDonald's *The Star System* (2000: 52–57 and 62–65).

5. Davis was released from her long-term contract with Warner Bros. in 1949 and subsequently operated as a freelance artist seeking work on the open market. In theory, this expanded her opportunities as she could apply for suitable roles at many different studios; but actually it reduced them, since the common practice was that each studio prioritised actors under contract when casting parts. As Emily Carman has observed, while freelancing proved advantageous for some female stars (e.g., Irene Dunne and Barbara Stanwyck), enabling them to maintain their Hollywood careers well into their 40s, for others (e.g., Ruth Chatterton and Miriam Hopkins), it accelerated their decline (Carman, 2012: 14–18). Although Davis was able to gain roles at several studios in the early 1950s, mostly at Twentieth Century Fox, after 1952 this became much harder.

6. Anne Morey's essay 'Grotesquerie as Marker of Success in Aging Female Stars' (2011) rescues films such as *All About Eve* and *The Star* from charges of misogyny, conceiving of them as empowering for Bette Davis, their grotesque aspects operating as acknowledgements of acting prowess. Using the term 'elegiac grotesque' to denote 'a role in which actresses play female stars at the end of their powers', Morey observes that such films not only reveal the acting skills of older actresses but also the negative effects of female stardom and the toll they take on the personal psychology and private life of the star, particularly as they age and become increasingly redundant (Morey, 2011: 105).

7. Sontag's essay was first published in *Saturday Review* on 23 September 1972 (pp. 29–38). It is included in Vida Carver and Penny Liddiard's *An Ageing Population* (1978), pp. 72–80.

8. As with many female stars of the studio era, Bette Davis found more consistent employment in television during the 1970s and early 1980s (see Smith, 2012). While she made no films between 1981 and 1986, Davis regularly appeared on television and in made-for-TV movies, such as *Right of Way* (Schaeffer, 1983) in which she co-starred with Hollywood legend James Stewart. This comedy-drama about the (lack of) rights of old people in society, involved a married couple, Mini (Davis) and Teddy Dwyer (Stewart), both aged 78, who decide to commit suicide after discovering that Mini has a terminal illness. Barbara Leaming has noted that such television productions provided 'substantially more income and prestige than the shoddy films to which, by and large, she had devoted herself in recent years' (Leaming, 1992: 267).

9. *Driving Miss Daisy* (Beresford, 1989) was produced by the Zanuck Company in 1989, featuring Jessica Tandy in the title role. It won four Oscars, including one for Best Actress for Tandy, who also won a Golden Globe and a BAFTA award.

10. Quentin Crisp played the elderly Queen Elizabeth I in Sally Potter's *Orlando* (1992). Bette Davis could have been magnificent in this role.

References

Anon (1987) Review of *The Whales of August*, *Variety*, 13 May, np.

Basinger, J. (2007) *The Star Machine* (New York: Alfred A. Knopf).

Brooks, J. (1999) 'Performing Aging/Performance Crisis (for Norma Desmond, Baby Jane, Margo Channing, Sister George – and Myrtle)', in K. Woodward (ed.) *Figuring Age: Women, Bodies, Generations* (Bloomington and Indianapolis: Indiana University Press), pp. 232–247.

Canby, V. (1987) 'In Cannes Limelight: Gish and Davis', *New York Times*, 16 May, np.

Carman, E. (2012) '"Women rule Hollywood": Ageing and Freelance Stardom in the Studio System,' in *Celebrity Studies*, 3 (1) pp. 13–24.

Carver, V. and Liddiard, P. (1978/1985) *An Ageing Population* (London: Hodder and Stoughton in association with The Open University Press).

Davis, B. with Herskowitz, M. (1987) *This 'N That* (New York: G.P. Putnam's Sons).

Easton, N. J. (1988) 'Bette Davis Smoking Over Stepmother,' *Los Angeles Times*, December, pp. 1, 6.

Leaming, B. (1992) *Bette Davis: A Biography* (London: Weidenfeld & Nicolson).

McDonald, P. (2000) *The Star System* (London: Wallflower Press).

Morey, A. (2011) 'Grotesquerie as Marker of Success in Aging Female Stars', in S. Holmes and D. Negri (eds) *In the Limelight and Under the Microscope: Forms and Functions of Female Celebrity* (New York and London: Continuum), pp. 103–124.

Morin, E. (1957/2005) *Les Stars*, translated by R. Howard (Minneapolis and London: University of Minnesota Press).

Mosby, A. (1950) 'Star Wishes More Mature Parts Were Written,' date and journal unidentified, available in 'Scrapbook 50: 1948–1951' at the Bette Davis Collection at the Howard Gottlieb Archival Center, Boston University, USA.

Quinn Curtis, T. (1988) 'Bette Davis: "Never Say Die"', *International Herald Tribune*, 5–6 November, np.

Riviere, J. (1929/1986) 'Womanliness as a Masquerade', in V. Burgin, J. Donald and C. Kaplan (eds) *Formations of Fantasy* (London and New York: Methuen), pp. 35–44.

Shingler, M. (1995) 'Masquerade or Drag?: Bette Davis and the Ambiguities of Gender', *Screen*, 36(3), pp. 179–192.

Shingler, M. (1996) 'The Fourth Warner Brother and Her Role in the War', *Journal of American Studies*, 30, I, April, pp. 127–131. Reprinted in Walter L. Hixson (2002) (ed.) *The American Experience in World War II: The American People at War: Minorities and Women* (New York: Cambridge University Press).

Shingler, M. (1999) 'Bette Davis: Malevolence in Motion', in A. Lovell and P. Kramer (eds) *Screen Acting* (London: Routledge), pp. 46–58.

Shingler, M. (2008) 'Bette Davis Made Over in Wartime', *Film History: An International Journal*, 20(3), pp. 269–280.

Shingler, M (2013) 'The Naked Ugliness of *Beyond the Forest* (1949)', in C. Nally and A. Smith (eds) *Naked Exhibitionism: Women, Gendered Performance and Public Exposure* (I. B. Tauris), pp. 19–40.

Sikov, E. (2007) *Dark Victory: The Life of Bette Davis* (New York: Henry Holt and Company).

Sikov, E. (2008) '"Don't Let's Ask for the Moon – We Have a Star!" Bette Davis as Gay Icon', *Screen*, 49(1), pp. 86–94.

Smith, S. (2012) '"Get Off Your Asses for These Old Broads!": Elizabeth Taylor, Ageing and the Television Comeback Movie,' *Celebrity Studies*, 3(1), pp. 25–36.

Von Arnim, E. (1940) *Mr Skeffington* (London: William Heineman), reprinted by Virago Press (1993).

Woodward, K. (1988–1989) 'Youthfulness as a Masquerade', *Discourse*, 11(1), pp. 119–142.

FILMOGRAPHY

All About Eve. Directed by Joseph L. Mankiewicz. US, 1950.
Beyond the Forest. Directed by King Vidor. US, 1949.
Dangerous. Directed by Alfred E. Green. US, 1935.
Driving Miss Daisy. Directed by Bruce Beresford. US, 1989.
Jezebel. Directed by William Wyler. US, 1938.
The Letter. Directed by William Wyler. US, 1940.
The Little Foxes. Directed by William Wyler. US, 1941.
Murder with Mirrors. Directed by Dick Lowry. US, 1985.
Mr. Skeffington. Directed by Vincent Sherman. US, 1944.
The Old Maid. Directed by Edmund Goulding. US, 1939.
Orlando. Directed by Sally Potter. UK, 1992.
Never Say Never Again. Directed by Irvin Kershner. US, 1983.
Now, Voyager. Directed by Irving Rapper. US, 1942.
Old Acquaintance. Directed by Vincent Sherman. US, 1943.
Payment on Demand. Directed by Curtis Bernhardt. US, 1951.
The Petrified Forest. Directed by Archie Mayo. US, 1936.
The Private Lives of Elizabeth and Essex. Directed by Michael Curtiz. US, 1939.
Right of Way. Directed by George Schaefer. US, 1983.
The Star. Directed by Stuart Heisler. US, 1953.
Watch on the Rhine. Directed by Herman Shumlin. US, 1943.
The Whales of August. Directed by Lyndsay Anderson. US, 1987.
What Ever Happened to Baby Jane? Directed by Robert Aldrich. US, 1962.
Wicked Stepmother. Directed by Larry Cohen. US, 1987.

4
Moms Mabley and Whoopi Goldberg: Age, Comedy and Celebrity

Sadie Wearing

Introduction

In keeping with the representational imbalances of popular culture, interest in ageing and celebrity has to date been preoccupied with white female performers and the ways in which their ageing is pathologised, celebrated or erased.[1] Against this background, and reflecting this volume's concern to extend critical work on celebrity and ageing, this chapter explores the role age and ageing plays in the celebrity and performances of two black female comics, Jackie 'Moms' Mabley and Whoopi Goldberg. My argument here is that Mabley and Goldberg can be linked. Firstly, this is with regard to their roles in the history of African American comic celebrity, and secondly, it relates to the ways that the content of their comedy repeatedly poses questions about the cultural construction of (and meanings attached to) age. This can be understood through the ways in which their embodied comic performances both foreground and render ambiguous the ageing female body in celebrity representation. Both performers can be read as revealing some of the ways in which the history of racialised representation shapes available forms of bodily presentation with regards to ageing, but both refuse to conform to the conventional meanings attached to these and use their comedy as a means to redefine and comment upon cultural expectations of age and femininity. Both figures exceed the limitations and meanings assigned to them, and they thus have 'something to tell us'[2] about the cultural tropes of ageing, sexuality, ethnicity and the temporality of celebrity.

This chapter does not represent the first bid to link the stand-up comedian Jackie 'Moms' Mabley with the actress and comedian Whoopi Goldberg. Critics interested in the dynamics of gender and comedy in general, and black American comedy in particular, have frequently connected the two performers (Haggins, 2007; Watkins, 1994; Brevard, 2013; Dresner, 1991). Earlier in her career, Goldberg, in fact, wrote and performed in a play based on Mabley and has fostered the perception of this close association, recently directing her first film, a documentary account of Mabley's life and work, *Whoopi Goldberg Presents Moms Mabley* (Goldberg, 2013). The film's construction of, and tribute to, Mabley is the starting point for this chapter's exploration of the meanings of celebrity that circulate around these two figures, and my analysis of the film centres on three interrelated areas. Firstly, attention is paid to the ways in which the film reveals a certain amount of ambiguity in Mabley's celebrity status, which is complicated by the imagery that narrates her 'personal' life. Secondly, I elaborate on the broader significance of Goldberg's homage and tribute to Mabley in relation to both the history of black comic performance and the creation of a celebrity archive. Finally, I use the film as a conduit to the content and presentation of Mabley's comedy and its unique delineation of the ageing, gendered body, arguing that the long gestation of her comic performance of an older black woman troubles constructions of both race and age. The chapter then goes on to look briefly at the evolution of Goldberg's own comedy act and maturing celebrity voice, with particular reference to her one-woman Broadway show originally performed in 1985 and revived in 2005. Goldberg's routine (like Mabley's) explicitly confronts tropes associated with age, and her (re)iteration of these performances over time similarly works to complicate the celebrity performance of ageing.

Celebrity, comedy and racialised contexts

Some of the key works in Celebrity Studies have recognised the centrality of processes of racialisation to the understanding of the social significance of stars. Indeed, Richard Dyer's virtual inauguration of the field in *Heavenly Bodies* (2004) uses case studies of Paul Robeson and Lena Horne to illustrate the dilemmas facing the performers in a production and cultural context dominated by whites with limited representational strategies open to them and facing what has been termed elsewhere the 'burden of representation'. Studies of African American comedy have shown how, in racialised and unequal societies, humour is a potent force which offers possibilities for subversion as well as redeployments of the status quo (Watkins, 1994; Williams 1991, 1995; Krefting, 2014; Haggins 2007). Critics interested in gender and comedy have produced important insights into the potential subversion of commonplace assumptions about, for example, the cultural worth of the ageing female body (Finney, 1994; Arthurs, 1999; Mellencamp, 1992). My interest here is in examining the intersection of comedy, celebrity and ageing in relation to the images of Mabley and Goldberg. In a visual field which is marked by race and racism, the twin spectres of hyper visibility (in confined, often demeaning roles and stereotypes) and invisibility (in relation to limited opportunities and access) faced by black performers are ongoing key concerns for cultural critics. For Nicole Fleetwood, the affective resonances of what she theorises as 'iconicity' continue to be important to the project of Black Cultural Studies, even as it distances itself from what she describes as the 'scene of punishment' (2011:13); that is, the focus on representations *of* rather than *by* black performers and visual artists. This describes the heavy burden placed on the imagery of black cultural producers. In her analysis she points to the 'exhaustion' for black cultural performers and producers whose work is routinely 'measured within arts traditions as demonstrative of black experience' (2011:14). She suggests that, although not endorsing the term 'post black', it should be acknowledged that: 'This exhaustion is with the privilege of iconicity in black representational practices and dominant visual culture. The concept of "post black" registers a profound frustration with normative ways of understanding black representational practices and dominant visual culture' (ibid.) Although made in relation to a different set of cultural practices than my concern here with celebrity, comedy and ageing, this caution is important. I am not claiming either Mabley or Goldberg as illustrative of black experience, but I am concerned with how the circulation of celebrity discourse around them does have recourse to a broader set of debates about representation.³ I am interested in the ways in which Goldberg's own celebrity is used to produce Mabley as a star, and the ways that she invokes her 'representativeness'. There are some interesting paradoxes at work here in that, on a banal level, Mabley's fame is the inaugurating object of Goldberg's film, and yet the film is equally invested in a project of 'recovery' which suggests that the subject herself is far from secure in the celebrity archive. This is also significant in terms of ageing as it foregrounds the temporal dynamics of celebrity as well as the ways that age is figured within histories of representation.

Whoopi Goldberg presents Moms Mabley

Goldberg's film opens with a blank screen and the sound of applause which dissolves to archival footage from *The Smothers Brothers' Comedy*

Hour, 1967. A head shot of the young, white, male comic presenter, Tom Smothers, fills the screen to introduce:

A lady who has been one of the most popular comediennes in the United States for over 40 years. Now some of you may not have heard of her yet, she's only recently started doing television. But she's often been called the funniest woman in the world. Meet Moms Mabley.

Mabley enters the studio, in the Moms' attire of an unglamorous flowery housecoat, oversize shoes, small hat and no teeth, declaring to the audience, 'You know Moms don't like old men, no, any time you see me with my arms around an old man I'm holding him for the police'. At this point Goldberg's voice-over starts and she explains:

I don't know whether it was the voice or the clothes or just her whole being. There was something about her that knocked me out.... Her impact on me was profound and I really wanted to know if she impacted on other people like that. So, there's not much more I can tell you about her so let me just introduce herself to you.

From the start of the film, we are faced with a paradox surrounding Mabley's fame. This paradox is that she is lauded for her longevity, her age and what this might signify in terms of her accrued value as a celebrity. At the same time, it is not expected that this particular audience will be familiar with her at all. This contradiction further is foregrounded in Goldberg's film by her own commentary, which mirrors the archive footage in its presentation of Mabley as a surprisingly unknown but long-standing 'star'. For both presenters, then, Mabley is a star, and moreover she has been a star for decades. But she is one who is recognised as only partially visible and as needing (to reverse the usual saying) 'every introduction'. This is particularly interesting in relation to age since it demarcates the 'mainstream' television audience – both in 1967 and in 2013 – as separated by generation and from Mabley's presumed existing audience. The reference to 'television' in the archive clip can be read as an explicit acknowledgement of the largely (racially) segregated audiences that Mabley had spent the first part of her career performing to, and thus functions as a reference to the television 'crossover' (mainstream, white) audience. The 'what can I tell you?' identification of Goldberg's 2013 invitation to 'meet' Mabley also perhaps signals that Mabley's fame was produced in primarily black audience contexts[4] (a point reiterated in the film through the use of a number of black comics recounting their first exposure to Mabley). No such reticence, however, is evident in the way that Goldberg herself is presented in this opening: she clearly requires no introduction and it is her autobiographical trajectory that the film (at this point) seems most interested in, as it explicitly raises the question of how Mabley figures in Goldberg's celebrity story. In this regard, celebrity works in the film in rather contradictory ways since although Mabley is the subject of the documentary because of her stardom, her stardom also registers as something that needs to be recovered through the retrieval of a 'lost' historical record (and via the subjectivity of someone who is better known). In addition, the documentary 'reveals' a dimension of Mabley's life, in relation to her gender presentation and sexuality that, whilst apparently not hidden during her lifetime was, nonetheless not an overt aspect of her public persona.

Goldberg's film simultaneously resists and reproduces the productive confusions between the figure of 'Moms' and the performer who took on an ex-boyfriend's name, Jackie 'Moms' Mabley. This oscillating impulse between maintaining Mabley's Moms persona as the object of the documentary and revealing the figure 'behind' the performance remains unresolved. The film thus sets up Mabley as an enigmatic figure, one whose fame is structured around longevity both in terms of her career, as well as her performance of an embodied reminder of time. This is the 'granny' persona around which her act was based, and which remained constant over the half century of her performance career.

Age, comic personae and the category of celebrity

Given the ways in which Mabley is presented in the documentary, it might seem at first counterintuitive to describe Jackie 'Moms' Mabley as a celebrity, if one of the conditions of celebrity is a reproduction of an oscillating dynamic of public and private 'self', of elements of performance and persona playing out across a range of spaces. Mabley's act was highly consistent and, as I shall return to, consistent in its reproduction and repudiation of aged embodiment. However, this consistency also marks the separation of comic persona ('Moms') from the more elusive 'private' figure behind the image. During her lifetime, there was little consistent press interest in her 'private' life, and she appears to have worked to maintain this. In Elsie Williams' scholarly account of her life and work, this reticence is understood as deliberate (Williams, 1995: 42). But it is also (a point similarly made in Goldberg's film) understood as both historical and cultural.

Goldberg points out in her film that very little is known about the 'life' of Mabley, although the same stories are retold in virtually all accounts of her work and life. Often repeated aspects of biography include that she was raped (twice) as a young woman, with both rapes resulting in pregnancies and adoptions, and she left home on her grandmother's encouragement and performed in vaudeville acts on the 'Chitlin' Circuit' in singing, dancing and eventually comedy routines. She performed as a 'blackface' comedienne in tent shows in the early 1900s prior to her success in musical comedies and as a stand–up comic (Watkins, 1994: 154). She was the first woman to appear solo at the Apollo Theater in New York and was associated with figures in the Harlem Renaissance including Langston Hughes and Zora Neale Hurston, with whom she wrote a play (see Monroe, 1994). Stories of her early hardships are central to both her biographical narration and her stand-up acts, which frequently include a cutting put-down to those who talk of the so-called 'good old days':

Whit good old days? When?

I was there. Where was You? (Mabley, 2004)

Goldberg's film situates Mabley within a historical context of racial segregation that dictated where black acts performed and for whom. The history of the move into a crossover space is alluded to in the film, both in its content and form. It tells the history of Mabley's journey from the black circuit to the Apollo Theater, to the emblematic Criterion Theatre, into television and finally a feature film (*Amazing Grace*, Lathan, 1974). The film features many contemporary iconic comics (black and white, male and female) delivering Mabley's lines and recounting how indebted they are to her. This production of genealogy both registers the hardships and inequality faced by black performers, whilst also historicising them. At the level of iconography then, the film produces an account of Mabley's fame which establishes it as belonging to a past whose hardships have, allegedly, largely been overcome.

In this regard, Mabley's early life and career are read as emblematic of the wider processes of exclusion, occlusion and omission. At one point in the film Goldberg says: 'When you look at Moms' history I guess it's the history of black folks in America because all of the information is not there so I realised I was not in a position to do a biography but here's some things'. This lack of detailed knowledge about Mabley's actual life is complicated by the ways Mabley used the persona of Moms as a conduit for telling stories which seem to reveal something of her own history, whilst at the same time remaining 'in character'. For example, the story Moms frequently relates in her act about being married off by her father as a very young girl to 'an old, old, man', to whom being married was like 'Pushing a car. Up a hill. With a rope'. The actual details of this are unknown, but Goldberg suggests the story had resonance for many. This stresses Mabley as both emblematic of collective pain and simultaneously as unique. After all, as Goldberg explains, Mabley 'was one of the few stars'. This oscillation between 'like us' and 'not like us' has become axiomatic in relation to thinking about celebrity, but the stress is placed here on politicising the collective aspect of the celebrity which is 'the story of black folks'.

The use of archival material, particularly photographs, also reinforces this collective and individual dynamic. The film uses photographs of Mabley in performance, in publicity shots and backstage, and also utilises 'establishing' film footage of Harlem in the early twentieth century. These photographs, too, reveal an interesting dimension to Mabley's celebrity status. In publicity shots and studio portraits she looks nothing like the 'Moms' comic persona, and these photographs are crucial to the revelations around her sexuality that Goldberg presents. Mabley is thus 'recovered' – both as epitome of homely 'ordinariness', *and* as star. Her stardom is, in part, revealed through the reproduction of a number of extremely arresting black and white images of Mabley both backstage and seemingly un-posed, and in studio and publicity portraits. These photographs are significant in that they draw attention to the discrepancy between Mabley's consistently aged feminine persona and her lived embodiment at this key stage in her stardom – as neither old nor emphatically feminine. Her star image is thus bifurcated between two extremes, furthermore the photographs, whilst on one level testifying to her star status are simultaneously used in the film as a form of revelation – the 'real' Mabley behind the Moms act.

One of the functions of the photographs is simply to demonstrate her unique status as 'the one woman amongst these men'. On the other hand, the stills are also used as a visual accompaniment to the reminiscences of those who worked with Mabley in ways that recover her as a sexual and gender nonconformist. The Apollo historian Billy Mitchell tells Goldberg that 'Moms Mabley was the first lady I saw wearing men's clothes'. Accompanying this remark is a 1936 still of Mabley and Fats Waller. Mabley is wearing a light-coloured suit and Waller has his arms around her. Behind, two men look on and a young woman (possibly on a bicycle) looks off down left. The photograph is not a studio portrait and has a quality of movement and vitality to it which contrasts with another still, a studio portrait, which accompanies dancer Norma Miller's reminiscence of Mabley with whom she shared a dressing room: 'She and I and her girlfriend. She was real. She was Moms on stage but when she walked off that stage she was "Mr Moms"'. Accompanying this testimony is what appears to be a publicity still (it is autographed and clearly posed), which shows Mabley in a suit and tie with one leg raised on a chair and the other hand in her suit pocket. Miller continues:

> On stage she was really Moms... but you never saw her with a young man, you saw her with a young girl and there was no question... we never called Moms a homosexual, that word never fit her. We never called her gay. We called her Mr Moms.

It is Goldberg who then takes up the theme, encouraging the audience to read this 'revelation' again in terms of a temporal distinction between then and now – both in terms of lived experience outside of heteronormative paradigms but also referencing the distinctive temporal differences in terms of celebrity culture. As Goldberg puts it:

> See in that time period it was nobody's business. Nobody's business and I will assume that when Moms came out of her costume and put on that silk shirt and that suit and those pants and that fedora and had those women on her arm I think everybody was like OK and so I think she was a woman among men and she was equal to those men and they treated her like a man and I think that was the secret to her longevity.

Something interesting is hinted at here in relation to the complex celebrity status of Jackie 'Moms' Mabley. On the one hand, we have Mabley functioning as a stand in for gaps in black history (about which 'we don't know much'), but she is simultaneously produced as an arresting visual presence with a public history which both 'fits' with the iconography of stardom. These are undoubtedly glamorous shots, yet they resist the restricted visual codes through which glamour (reified in terms of heterosexuality and gender conformity) is usually signalled. Furthermore, the photographs are used primarily as less a testimony to her stardom (which they clearly are) but rather as providing the viewer access to Mabley's 'real' self. What is not stated explicitly here (but which is alluded to in the photograph) is an explicit reference to the distinction in *age* between the offstage Mabley and the Moms persona, a discrepancy which alters, of course, as the performer herself ages. It is to this aspect of Mabley's celebrity that I now turn.

The Moms persona, unlike the 'Jackie Mabley' still images that Goldberg presents to us, is entangled with the history of black female representation in the US, representations which have a generational logic. As Williams points out, there are points in Mabley's act where she explicitly calls upon this representational history in order to ridicule it. Williams traces Mabley's expressive style and delivery as having its roots in the history of slavery, which 'emerges as the pivotal genre through which African Americans have dealt with their experience in America' (1995: 4). She cites amongst others Langston Hughes for whom 'black laughter becomes a strategy for bearing or masking pain, an unconscious therapy to protect oneself at the expense of another' (ibid.). One such oblique commentary on the problematic framing of all older black women in relation to the Mammy stereotype is made by Moms in performance when responding to 'some old Klan' who 'accidently' refers to her as 'Mammy'. The response is an unequivocal rejection of the assumptions underlying such a designation:

> No damn MAMMY. Moms
> I don't know nothin'
> 'bout no log cabin;
> I ain't never seen
> No log cabin ..
> Split level in the suburbs
> Baby! (Jackie Mabley, cited in Williams, 1995: 11)

The complexity of this rejection lies in the ways in which the character that Mabley adopts is caught up in the representational history of black women in the US which has historically largely relegated them to (at best) the supporting role. The comic irony here is of course that Mabley's success as 'Moms' – a character based, in part, on her own grandmother (Williams, 1995: 74) – produces a celebrity who then invades spaces of power (this excerpt comes from a routine about Moms visiting the White House as a guest of and advisor to the president), thus overturning in carnivalesque or trickster fashion established hierarchies and power dynamics. Another similar instance is the 'call' to the lighting crew in *Boarding House Blues* to 'Make me look like Lena Horne – not *Beulah*, LENA!'. As Williams argues, in these moments there seems to be 'a ghost, a stereotype stalking [M]oms and falling prey to the performer's humour' (Williams, 1995: 74; see also Haggins, 2007: 150). If we explore this persona in relation to the figuration of ageing, there is also something of a tension since Mabley both 'played' age and also grew into it – her comic persona 'Moms' is predicated on a mature femininity which loathes 'old men' (and loves young men). The old male body is the butt of many of Mabley's routines which link the old man to dirt, impotence, senility and weakness, and being 'so ugly it hurt my feelings'. Women's bodies, including Moms' own, are also ridiculed in her routines ('I got a mirror, I can see what's happening', as Mabley puts it with reference to her young man's attempts at duplicitous sweet talk). 'Old' in Mabley's routines is associated with both individual bodily ageing *and* the hardships and oppressive regimes (both public and private) of the past, but the extreme disidentification with 'old' as spoken through the voice of the revered grandmother figure offers a complex positioning. One element of this is summed up with such lines as, 'I don't want nothing old but some old money. Buy me some young ideas', which relates to both the active position Mabley takes up in civil rights politics, as well as the lasciviousness of her persona. Her feminist politics can also be traced in the speaking back or reversing the comic ritual of denigrating women, whilst performing in a role that twists the expectations and social significations of age, gender and sexuality, as Haggins and Williams both point out.

There is thus a paradoxical note to the Moms' persona in terms of embodiment. Feminist Critical Race Studies insights have established how 'black women have been historically imagined and represented through their bodies which bear the markers of their deviance from white norms of feminine propriety and attractiveness' (Young, 1999: 68). This aged embodiment over time constitutes another intriguing paradox since it can be read as an unstable iteration of ageing which undermines the conceit that aged embodiment is fully naturalised. I am not suggesting here that Mabley's body did not change or indeed that her presentation of that body does not shift at all in the years between, for example, two feature films that she appears in as 'Moms', *Boarding House Blues* (Binney) in 1948 and *Amazing Grace* (Lathan) in 1974. I am suggesting however, that the defining features of this comic performance of an older femininity do remain constant over this long period, drawing our attention to the performative dimension of both age and gender. The celebrity body thus 'introduced' by Tom Smothers in 1967 and the reiteration of that entrance in Goldberg's film of 2013 is an older black female body that is already complex – a celebrity body which in 'playing' age since the 1920s undermines the naturalisation of aged characteristics. As critics have noted, it is an embodiment which both relates to and comments on the female archetypes that Young argues offered the three main 'depictions' of black women – 'desexualized mammies, servants and wet-nurses... the "tragic mulatta"... finally... the black woman whose lasciviousness and hyper sexuality were inscribed on her body' (1999: 68). Mabley's act arguably reconfigures these elements into a whole that undermines their demeaning potential and cultural authority through her refusal to accede to the norms associated with the figuration. In her work, the 'safe' and unthreatening, desexualised 'mammy' is recouped as both desiring and nurturing, as Williams and Haggins both argue. Further, these elements are also rendered as political in both the sense of public, civil rights politics and cultural politics through Mabley's resistance to a nostalgic forgetfulness of the oppressiveness of the past. For Stallings, the sexual grandmother figure that Mabley cuts is radical because, in placing these elements together, she does nothing less than disrupt the entire racialised sex and gender order:

> The virtual desexualisation does not prohibit expressions of sexual desire. It merely un-names Mabley as woman. It allows for a bold show of sexuality through its deferring of gender. Whenever audiences might assume they are being provided with less taboo subjects, such as the family or sacredness of the grandmother, Mabley refers back to less comfortable discussion of sexuality and age. She never allows the audience to separate sexuality from gender, age or race. Her strategy makes it impossible for anyone to establish fixed boundaries or the 'norm'. (Stallings, 2007: 143)

In a related vein, but one which places Mabley against a civil rights and Cold War background, Bambi Haggins' reading of Mabley's comic persona suggests that, in the incorporation of civil rights and activism into her performance, she is treading a line 'within a stone's throw of the mammy' that positioned her: 'not simply within the black comic traditions of the past, in which the critique of mainstream America had to be coded and hidden, but also... within a new form of comic discourse in which the voices of marginalised people – including black women, would be heard' (Haggins, 2007: 150).

In Goldberg's documentary, too, the suggestion is made, by Joshua Gamson, that Mabley might be read as a 'bridge' between the vaudeville past and the confrontational politics of comedy that emerged later, and this is a bridge, in part at least, that is built by Goldberg. Goldberg acts in the film as 'author' of the documentary and as the intermediary to Moms Mabley. But she also makes an explicit identification with her in her own comedy routines which, like Mabley's, tell stories and also reflect a resistance to normative feminine embodiments (Haggins, 2007: 148).

Whoopi Goldberg's celebrity is by no means confined, as Mabley's was, to her 'stand-up' comic performances and singular personae (although the term 'stand-up' is not entirely accurate for either performer). Instead, her fame rests on decades of work across a range of genres, platforms and styles, including both serious and comic roles in film and television. Furthermore, her personal relationships have been subject to a level of scrutiny and debate that Mabley's have not.[5] As 'herself', she has most recently appeared as the host and moderator of the daytime talk show *The View* (1997–present). She is also well known as a serial presenter of the Academy Awards and has developed a profile as the producer of many of her own projects. The Mabley project, however, was her first film as director. The film is an HBO production and continues Goldberg's association with the company that also brought her Broadway performances to the small screen in *Whoopi Direct from Broadway* (1985) and *Whoopi Back to Broadway* (2005). These two performances – distributed as a twentieth anniversary DVD package in 2005 (Cullner) – present Goldberg at two very different points in her career, and these performances, especially read together, also provide a site for reflection on ageing, celebrity and comic performance. Goldberg's 'stand-up work' consists of character monologues. The stories offer a caustic commentary on cultural perceptions and attitudes to older women, embodiment and sexuality.

Ageing in Goldberg's *Back to Broadway*

To revive the same monologues after a 20-year absence begs a number of questions – questions similar to those already raised by Mabley in relation to the performativity of ageing. To recap, in Mabley's case, these revolve firstly around her construction of a persona who signifies 'age' but who, in remaining consistently 'old' over many decades, produces – in effect – an 'ageless' present, 'undoing' the cultural work of ageing (including assumptions around identity and ageing), in a context which has proscribed particular roles for older black women. Secondly, Mabley's iteration of celebrity is complex because of the ways that an alternate framing of her is evoked in the celebrity archive foregrounding quite different aspects of her identity and thereby unsettling the association of her purely with 'age'. In Goldberg's case, the staged 'return' to characters she originally played 20 years earlier also calls attention to the role of performance and performativity in the construction of ageing.[6] This is revealed through the juxtaposition of the two shows. When they are packaged together the viewer is encouraged to consider the processes of the ageing of the 'star' Whoopi Goldberg, whose 'return' to an earlier performance incarnation we witness. But the content of those performances, as we shall see, also unsettles any easy links between ageing, embodiment and identity.

Goldberg's routines famously have her shifting shape to encompass a bodily range of ages as well as genders, ethnicities, nationalities and abilities (see Dresner, 1991). Of the characters originally performed in 1985, this range is maintained with the inclusion of both the male 'junkie' Fontaine, the 'Crippled lady', and the introduction of a new character, the menopausal Lauralene. My discussion is going to focus on the two monologues which foreground ageing most clearly, namely the Jamaican maid in the 1985 production and Lauralene in the 2005 production. Between the 1985 and 2005 shows, Goldberg's body has clearly changed: she is heavier, and when asked by the interviewer about the background to the inclusion of the new character in the show, she says 'the size of my behind'. Whilst in both shows her clothing – like Mabley's – tends to downplay the significance of her gendered embodiment, the effect is somewhat different. For Mabley, the putting on of age in the Moms' attire speaks to a complex iteration of the production of age and gender as a space from which to undo some of the pernicious cultural work of the iconicity of the mammy and the disciplining of the sexuality of older women. In both shows, Goldberg's baggy shirt and jeans enables a performance which facilitates her crossing gender, age and ethnicity, thus drawing attention away from Goldberg's body to expose the ways in which these are always cultural productions and performances at some level.

This is not to suggest, however, that questions of age and material embodiment do not matter to Goldberg or Mabley. On the contrary, in their performances they both mine a rich comic vein in their account of the physical matter of the ageing body. Both male and female bodies are subject to comic dissection and are routinely laughed at for their unattractiveness and decrepitude. However, these elements of the grotesque can be read as also subversively drawing attention to the possibility of undermining these very norms. This is in keeping with the ways in which many feminist commentators have noted how comedy routinely exposes and undermines gender norms by presenting 'unruly' gendered bodies, both male and female (Mellencamp, 1995; Arthurs, 1999). In Goldberg's two Broadway shows, sexuality and age are, as with Mabley, drawn into comic proximity. The celebrity body, in both cases, is effaced through performance strategies which ameliorate its visibility while simultaneously addressing issues of gender, race, sexuality and power. One of the key characters in Goldberg's 1985 show is a Jamaican maid who, at the instigation of a rich old man, moves to live in the United States as his companion. She calls the old man 'old raisin' because he is 'incredibly wrinkled and very very tan'. Suspecting the old man of senility when he describes his vast house to her, she thinks he must have read *Gone with the Wind* and superimposed the book onto his own life. This is played for comedy effect when it turns out that the house is just as big and grand as he said. But it also introduces once again the spectre of the representational history of black women as servants given the iconic status of Hattie McDaniel's portrayal in the 1948 film. This may cue the audience into a reconsideration of this figure and in Goldberg's story the power dynamics of the relationship are revealed to be complex. The comic energy of the monologue is sustained by the descriptions of the old man's body as anything but desirable. Indeed, the description could be Mabley's when Goldberg describes his entry into her bedroom:

The man stepped in. Grinning. Not a tooth in his head, not a tooth. Naked.

Naked, naked. Naked as the day that he was born, child and the man was wrinkled beyond belief. Beyond belief. I took one look at him and all I wanted to do was iron him.

Nonetheless, Goldberg's character finds sexual satisfaction 'in praise of older men' and reverses any expectations the audience may have of a simple 'reading off 'of power dynamics from established economic and social hierarchies. There is also genuine pathos in the finale of this story where Goldberg's Jamaican maid becomes a 'millionairess' through the old raisin's will, but also finds she misses him, and pays a tribute to his generosity and sense of adventure. In this way, the audience is perhaps schooled into reconsidering both the comedy of disgust which relies on laughing at frail physical embodiment and also assumptions that power and emotion play out in predictable ways with clear victims and aggressors.

In the later show, whilst many of the original monologues are revived, the Jamaican story is not. In its place, however, there is another story where ageing is once again central. Lauralene is a lady of a certain age whose reflections on her present state of bodily discomfort – brought about by the menopause – instigates a series of reminiscences about her past and the ageing process in general. Pathos in this story again attaches to a very funny evocation of the humiliations of gendered ageing. But here the pathos is ratcheted up by the description of the suicidal impulses that are revealed as attendant on menopausal bodily changes for this character – a woman whose identity it emerges has always been bound up with her hormonal status and physical appearance. Once again a comparison with Mabley is instructive. Mabley has a routine in which she encourages an old friend to shoot herself because her physical deterioration disgusts Mabley, and the laugh comes when Mabley tells her to shoot herself two inches below her left breast, but she shoots herself in the knee. However, the laugh is complicated since the 'homely' embodiment of Moms is also implicated in the scene, with much of the humour coming from the juxtaposition between Moms' view of herself as desiring and desirable and this anti-glamorous presentation. In Goldberg's sketch, the figure of the depressive menopausal woman is eventually coaxed out of the bathroom where she is gathering up her pills, when the needs of her teenage child interfere. The dynamic of this might seem highly normative in comparison to Goldberg's earlier routines. But in fact the ending of this monologue is highly equivocal. It does not end on a straightforward celebration of recovery. Instead, the alienation from the body produced by the internalised cultural expectations of ageing is shown to be pervasive, toxic and potentially deadly, although it may be transcended (with support). As with Mabley, some very blunt dissections of the internalised disgust aroused by the ageing female body are produced and diffused through comedy.

Conclusion

The celebrity construction of Mabley is, as I have outlined, rather different from that of Goldberg. However, I have suggested here that when considered in relation to dynamics of ageing and celebrity, they can be very fruitfully linked. Both performers draw our attention to ageing in both the content and delivery of their comedy and in the ways that they show how aged figures, particularly women, are circumscribed and curtailed through cultural norms and expectations. Both, too, use comic embodiments to unsettle these presumptions. Further, Goldberg's film about Mabley also raises some intriguing questions about temporality and celebrity. In Mabley's case, her complex performance of age over time makes her celebrity status curiously ambivalent given her persona's liminal biographical references. The content of her comedy reflects, too, a paradoxical relationship to age, which it both relies upon and repudiates. The 'old man' routine links to a painful past, which is certainly cultural and was possibly also personal. Her evocation of the granny figure works to unsettle the racialised tropes of the desexualised figure of the mammy and thereby ameliorates some of its symbolic power. The Moms persona can also be read as a homage to Mabley's 'real' granny on whom she is reported to have based the character (Williams, 1995: 74), and this, too, is significant for thinking through the representational politics of the older black female figure. Goldberg's comedy incorporates reflections on the cultural politics of ageing in ways that are both similar to and distinct from Mabley's repertoire. Her identification with Mabley and her homage to her can be read as perhaps a related form of appropriation, a claiming of a genealogy in the face of a wider historical erasure. Finally, Goldberg's film 'recovers' a more multifaceted Mabley, beyond the mask of the aged granny figure, always on the hunt for young men, and thus produces both a complex star from the archive and a recalibration of her own celebrity authority.

Notes

1. As an example, some of my own work on ageing and celebrity (Wearing, 2007, 2011, 2012) has focused on the dynamics of representations of white women across a range of genres and platforms, from European arts cinema to makeover television. Whilst 'race' has been an element of these analyses, this exclusive focus can also be read as problematically reproducing assumptions over the absence of black representation. For a related discussion of this tendency and the importance of reading both absence and presence in popular culture, see Springer (2007).
2. The original title of Goldberg's film about Mabley, under which it appears to have been shown at film festivals, is *Moms Mabley: I Got Something to Tell You* (one of Mabley's catchphrases). HBO, however, have distributed, broadcast and released it as a DVD under the title used in this chapter.
3. In the double sense of representation meaning (minimally) both standing in for (representativeness) and referring to cultural production.
4. A point both made and also implicitly challenged in the documentary with the inclusion of Jerry Stiller whose identification with black acts is laughingly accounted for by his Jewishness. A less celebratory look at the period notes that white comics routinely appropriated or 'stole' material from black performers, see Nachman (2003) .
5. Scandals have included her then boyfriend Ted Danson's appropriation of 'blackface' at a 'roast' which elicited hugely unfavourable publicity for Goldberg (Brevard, 2013; Haggins, 2007).
6. For examination of the vexed relation between performance and performativity and the ways in which these need to be both kept apart and thought of in rela-

tion to one another, see Parker and Sedgewick (1995). For an elaboration of ageing in relation to performativity and performance, see Basting (1998: 1–23).

References

Arthurs, J. (1999) 'Revolting Women: Women in Comic Performance', in J. Arthurs and J. Grimshaw (eds) *Women's Bodies: Discipline and Transgression* (London and New York: Cassell), pp. 67–90.

Basting, A. (1998) *The Stages of Age Performing Age in Contemporary American Culture* (Ann Arbor: The University of Michigan Press).

Brevard, L. (2013) *Whoopi Goldberg on Stage and Screen* (Jefferson: McFarland and Company).

Dresner, Z. (1991) 'Whoopi Goldberg and Lily Tomlin: Black and White Women's Humor', in June Sochen (ed.) *Women's Comic Visions* (Detroit: Wayne State University Press), pp. 179–192.

Dyer, R. (2004) *Heavenly Bodies: Film Stars and Society, 2nd edition* (London: Routledge).

Finney, G. (1994) (ed.) *Look Who's Laughing: Gender and Comedy* (Abingdon: Taylor and Francis).

Fleetwood, N. (2011) *Troubling Vision Performance, Visuality and Blackness* (Chicago: University of Chicago Press).

Haggins, B. (2007) *Laughing Mad: The Black Comic Persona in Post Soul America* (New Brunswick: Rutgers University Press).

Krefting, R. (2014) *All Joking Aside American Humor and Its Discontents* (Baltimore: John Hopkins University Press).

Mellencamp, P. (1992) *High Anxiety: Catastrophe, Scandal Age and Comedy* (Bloomington: Indiana University Press).

Monroe, B. (1994) 'Courtship, Comedy and African-American Expressive Culture in Zora Neale Hurston's Fiction', in G. Finney (ed.) *Look Who's Laughing: Gender and Comedy* (Abingdon: Taylor and Francis), pp.173–188.

Nachman, G. (2003) *Seriously Funny, the Rebel Comedians of the 1950s and 1960s* (New York: Pantheon Books).

Parker, A. and Sedgwick. E (1998) (eds) *Performativity and Performance* (New York: Routledge).

Springer, K. (2007) 'Divas, Evil Black Bitches, and Bitter Black Women in Postfeminist and Post-Civil-Rights Popular Culture', in Y. Tasker and D. Negra (eds) *Interrogating Postfeminism* (Durham: Duke University Press), pp. 249–276.

Stallings L. H. (2007) *Mutha is half a word intersections of folklore, vernacular, myth and queerness in black female culture* (Columbus, Ohio University Press).

Watkins, M. (1994) *On the Real Side: A History of African American Comedy* (Chicago: Lawrence Hill Books).

Wearing, S. (2007) 'Subjects of Rejuvenation: Aging in Postfeminist Culture', in Y. Tasker and D. Negra (eds) *Interrogating Postfeminism* (Durham: Duke University Press), pp. 277–310.

Wearing, S. (2011) 'Notes on Some Scandals: The Politics of Shame in *Vers le Sud*', in R. Gill and C. Scharff (eds) *New Femininities: Postfeminism, Neoliberalism and Identity* (Palgrave Macmillan), pp. 173–187.

Wearing, S. (2012) 'Exemplary or Exceptional Embodiment? Discourses of Aging in the Case of Helen Mirren and *Calendar Girls*', in J. Dolan and E. Tincknell (eds) *Aging Femininities: Troubling Representations* (Newcastle: Cambridge Scholars Press), pp. 145–157.

Williams E. A. (1991) 'Moms Mabley and the Afro-American Comic Performance', in J. Sochen (ed.) *Women's Comic Visions* (Detroit: Wayne State University Press), pp. 158–178.

Williams, E. A. (1995) *The Humor of Jackie Moms Mabley: An African American Comedic Tradition* (New York: Garland Publishing).

Young, L. (1999) 'Racializing Femininity', in J. Arthurs and J. Grimshaw (eds) *Women's Bodies: Discipline and Transgression* (London and New York: Cassell) pp. 67–90.

Filmed

Boarding House Blues. Directed by Josh Binney, US, 1948.

Amazing Grace. Directed by Stan Lathan, US, 1974.

Whoopi Goldberg Presents Moms Mabley. Directed by Whoopi Goldberg, US, 2014.

Whoopi Direct from Broadway. Directed by Thomas Schlamme, US, 1985.

Whoopi Back to Broadway the 20th Anniversary. Directed by Marty Callner, US, 2005.

Moms Mabley, Comedy Ain't Pretty. Audio CD, remastered original recording, 2004.

Moms Mabley, M.I.L.F. Audio CD, Universal Music Distribution, 2010.

5

'Je joue le rôle d'une petite vieille, rondouillarde et bavarde, qui raconte sa vie…' ['I am playing the role of a little old lady, pleasantly plump and talkative, who is telling the story of her life…']: The Significance of Agnès Varda's Old Lady Onscreen

Rona Murray

It is with an appropriate sense of urgency that feminist scholarship has turned to the idea of considering 'the matrix of gender, ageing and celebrity' (Jermyn, 2014: 3). This work joins a history of interventions such as those made by sociologists Kathleen Woodward (1999) and Julia Twigg (2004) who both identified a failure in feminist thinking to take account of the specifically gendered nature of aspects of old age. These writers questioned how academic feminism had failed to adequately reflect on ageing and the later stages of women's lives as vital to understanding women's (shifting) experience over the life course.

And in many ways, the work of a filmmaker and artist such as Agnès Varda speaks to some of these concerns, since she has brought ageing very visibly into the cultural conversation through her appearances onscreen in her own films. In these works, Varda turns the camera on herself, critically and meditatively reflecting on her ageing/aged self. As I will demonstrate in this essay, these moments and images are important not only as they offer an alternative to the invisibility of the ageing body, but also in the way in which they capture a female author working into old age productively and successfully. In addition, the longevity of her career allows an interplay between Varda as the 'auteur' filmmaker of French cultural history – a celebrated photographer and director since the 1950s known as the 'mother of the French New Wave',[1] by virtue both of prefiguring its evolution in her early work and by being its only woman filmmaker – and the working artist she is still today.

However, it is the manner in which Varda's celebrity is such a vital, contributing component to her performance of authorship that makes her a relevant case study for this collection. She is one of the intellectual stars of the French New Wave while also a popular figure – publically understood, too, as a mother and grandmother – with whom many audiences have seemingly forged a direct, emotional bond. This ensures that Varda in old age has increased, rather than decreased, in visibility, since her work demonstrates a symbolic marriage of past and present. She has established a vibrant persona, both within her films themselves and as the celebrity filmmaker appearing on television, a medium which has always included the work of auteur filmmakers as part of its cultural remit in France. Varda, therefore, has been visible throughout her career in this mass medium and can now accede to a particularly French kind of celebrity in old age, in which her gender is an essential component.

Deborah Jermyn opened an earlier collection examining the relationship between women, celebrity and ageing by asking: 'When does a woman become an old woman?' She argued that the image of an ageing Jane Fonda shown excitedly preparing for a date in a L'Oreal advert at that time exemplified how 'such "girling" of older women is both symptomatic of postfeminist culture and indicative of a wider move to push back the boundaries of ageing' (Jermyn, 2014: 1). Where women are visible in older age, therefore, they are often seen expressing the same desires and aspirations of younger women, aspirations that can be fulfilled through the purchase and consumption of the 'right' commodities. Older women are pressured never to abandon their youthfulness, if not their 'girlishness'. In contrast, Varda's celebrity identity at this time is very deliberately built upon the promotion of herself as *an ageing woman* with all the experience that implies, as a mother, grandmother and widow now in the later life stages.

The following analysis thus seeks to illustrate how Varda's celebrity persona interacts with her own textual performances onscreen, and generates a powerful representation of an ageing woman who is a successful auteur filmmaker within the French film industry. The fact of her ongoing creative practice constitutes an important social statement in itself, one which resonates beyond French culture in the way in which it demonstrates a female author at work and sustaining her career into old age. However, since Varda has made ageing a subject of her work from the very beginning of her career, her appearances onscreen are also a crucial development of her subject matter. Varda as a young woman artist stared at the faces of the old women living in her district and captured them with her camera, reflecting on the horrors of old age in *L'Opéra-Mouffe* [*Diary of a Pregnant Woman*] (1958). Now, Varda the old woman artist looks at her own image with an understanding of what old age really means from the inside looking out. An added dimension is that Varda's life has been lived in public, through her work and through her marriage to a French icon in filmmaker Jacques Demy. Her popular image allows her to underline Varda-the-woman as part of Varda-the-artist, and in fact this is an essential part of her approach to her work. It is possible to trace her career-long commitment as a filmmaker to witnessing the ordinary lives of others, and this has made her incomparably well-placed to explore her own. Understanding the relationship between gender, celebrity and old age in Varda's persona and work is to look at how she herself understands these relationships, and harnesses their emotional resonance in her own appearances in the films of her third – and fourth – age.

Varda – *une petite vieille* – onscreen

In the opening to *Les plages d'Agnès* [*The Beaches of Agnès*] (2008), Varda appears walking backwards across a beach, to symbolise the journey she is about to take into her past during the course of the film. It is to be one that travels through events in her life, experiences and art, and in this moment she appears as both woman and artist. She is instantly recognisable with her trademark hairstyle – dyed wine-red but with a circle of white at its centre. Seemingly at ease with old age, in fact, drawing attention to it, she has left the roots substantially visible. As she walks, she comments on her action: *'Je joue le rôle d'une petite vieille, rondouillarde et bavarde, qui raconte sa vie....'* ['I am playing the role of a little old lady, rotund and talkative, who is telling the story of her life...']. Crucial here is the interplay between 'the little old lady' and the French icon or star.

Who is this apparently ordinary old lady and what extraordinary quality qualifies her to take the audience on such a tour? Born in 1928, Agnès Varda began her filmmaking career in the 1950s with the feature *La Pointe-Courte* (1955).[2] Set in the French fishing village of the title, the film has been credited as a forerunner of *la nouvelle vague* or

Figure 5.1   Screen shot of Varda in *Les plages d'Agnès* [*The Beaches of Agnès*] (2008)

French New Wave, the influential post-war movement which saw the transition of critics such as François Truffaut and Jean-Luc Godard into celebrated filmmakers. Characterised by a desire to challenge the established forms of cinema in France, which were seen as staid and lacking innovation, these male critics found inspiration in American cinema. In their view, Hollywood films had cultivated a cinematic language in which the creative centre was the director – a figure who they dubbed the 'auteur'. As a group of filmmakers, they came to be fêted as auteurs themselves with their innovation in subject matter and style. Varda, the only woman associated with this group, not only made films before and alongside her fellow *cinéastes* in this early period, but has continued to work consistently since then. She originally trained as a photographer and studied art history, and she has often blended still and moving images in her work. In her later years, she has increasingly moved into art installation, exhibiting at the Fondation Cartier in 2006 and experiencing in her own words the pleasure of 'the old filmmaker transformed into the young material artist' ['*la vieille cinéaste se transforme en jeune plasticienne*'] (de Julie, 2013). From her first film in 1955 right up to the present day, Varda has acted as her own producer through her company, Ciné-Tamaris, based near her home on Rue Daguerre in Paris. She has continued to work consistently since the early 1950s, making diverse films, from feature length dramas such as *Cléo de 5 à 7* [*Cleo from 5 to 7*] (1962) or *Sans toit ni loi* [*Vagabond*] (1985) to a number of documentary and short 'essay' style films, which allows her to explore a subject or argument utilising still and moving images in creative and sometimes challenging juxtapositions.

Notions of French stardom and celebrity

Su Holmes, in revitalising Richard Dyer's classic work on stardom within contemporary Celebrity Studies, wrote that his work on the 'common discursive structures through which stars were circulated' continues to be important (2005: 10). By highlighting the individuality of the director, the New Wave critics created a discursive context for them to be considered stars or even celebrities. Therefore, in thinking about the kind of public figure Varda constitutes, and how this has functioned in her old age, it is necessary to think about French discourses of stardom and celebrity, specifically the greater presence of 'elite' or 'high' culture in popular culture. Arguably, this generates a particular French category of celebrity, that of the intellectual. John Gaffney and Diane Holmes described how in the 1950s and 1960s there were:

> '...a range of intellectuals who were household names, including Barthes and Lévi-Strauss. With Jean-Paul Sartre and Simone de Beauvoir, indeed, the intellectual and the popular cross paths, for they were themselves part of trendy Paris café society, along with celebrities such as the singer Juliette Greco. (Gaffney and Holmes, 2007a: 2)

French intellectuals could cross over to popular culture, therefore, and for a country sensitive to American cultural domination, not least through the cinema, this was one important aspect by which French culture could regard itself as different, even superior.

If an auteur or intellectual can be a star, then Varda certainly seems to qualify. However, as suggested above, academic 'discursive structures' around French celebrity are different to those in the UK and US. Natalie Heinich has written about the underdevelopment of Celebrity Studies as part of traditional academic disciplines in France, which she attributes in part to the strong influence of '*les élites*' and an attitude that regards mass culture unworthy of study (2011). This could necessitate some 'borrowing' of concepts in order to describe Varda, although the widely influential work of French sociologist Edgar Morin in the 1950s and 1960s includes the term '*Olympiens*'[3] to describe figures in modern mass culture that are: 'superhuman in the role they embody, human in their private lives'[4] (1962: pp. 145–146).

Varda was certainly an icon or '*Olympien*' and a model of the French intellectual in French television's construction of her in the decades following the New Wave, as archival television sources preserved at *L'institut d'audiovisuel* (INA)[5] in Paris demonstrate. She is featured, in 1971, discussing the shooting of her first film *La Pointe-Courte* (1955), as a young filmmaker (*Agnès présente ses films*, 1971). An episode of *Apostrophes*, a long-running arts discussion programme (on *Antenne 2*), featured her female-centric, feminist film *L'une chante, l'autre pas* [*One Sings, the Other Doesn't*] (1977) in its 'ciné-club' segment (1979). In 1991, *Soir 3* covered the Cannes premiere of *Jacquot de Nantes* (*Journée à Cannes*, 1991), her drama based on Demy's autobiographical reminiscences about his childhood in Nantes during the war.

These examples show Varda as holding 'intellectual stardom' in these earlier decades, helped by television's cultural role.[6] The public and private self have always intermingled for Varda through her partnership with Demy. Married from 1962 until his death in 1990, they raised two children: Rosalie Varda (by actor-director Antoine Bourseiller) and Mathieu, her son with Demy. In a behind-the-scenes insight, *Jacques Demy et Agnès Varda à propos de leur couple, de leurs films* [*Jacques Demy and Agnès Varda on Being a Couple and Their Films*] (1964) the intellectuals are visited at their home and studio on Rue Daguerre. Each half of this famous couple is interviewed on questions relating to the nature of happiness – a question that is as much philosophical as it is prompted by the title of Varda's then current project, her complex, feminist family melodrama *Le Bonheur* (1965). Here, the married auteurs of the French New Wave seem to have evolved into an iconic representation of important French values in the decades subsequent to *la nouvelle vague*, which were evidently transferable overseas. In 1965, they were photographed by William Klein for American *Vogue* for a feature entitled 'People are talking about...' which enthused about Demy, Varda and Rosalie: 'This family is movie-struck...Working separately, easily, gaily, Varda-Demy form a brilliant unit' (Klein, 1965: 90). Moving to Los Angeles in the late 1960s, when Demy was courted by the American studios, Varda describes how their New Wave aura acted as a calling card. They were 'halo-ed with the reputation of *la nouvelle vague*. We spent time with Warhol, Jim Morrison, the young ones who were emerging such as Spielberg, Lucas, Scorsese, and Coppola, but we also met Hollywood legends like Gregory Peck and Mae West'[7] (Ferry, 2014). Alongside the international marketability of the glamour of performers such as Catherine Deneuve, it seems clear that French intellectual chic could also travel.

In later life, Rue Daguerre is Varda's home again and is a familiar setting through which she invites her film audiences into her private world. There is an increasing personalisation of her popular image as she ages. Her public persona has increasingly represented the 'human' over the 'superhuman', just as Richard Dyer describes the increasing 'ordinariness' of the star persona in his development of Morin (and others) into the ordinary/extraordinary dyad, increasingly relevant to Varda: 'in the early period, stars were gods and goddesses, heroes, models – embodiments of *ideal* ways of behaving. In the later period, however, stars are identification figures, people like you and me – embodiments of *typical* ways of behaving' (1998: 21–22) [original emphasis]. Varda's growing 'typicality' – what I will call her 'celebrity value' as opposed to her '*Olympien*' stardom – reflects her own dual sense of herself, as a woman ('Agnès') and an artist ('Varda'). The relationship between these entwined identities is arguably part of her particular power as an artist in old age.

Varda onscreen as a French celebrity

Varda makes an interesting parallel case to Godard. Both may have begun as a 'stars' of the French New Wave; however, whilst they both continue to work into their 80s, he remains generally inaccessible to the public. His New Wave stardom was built partially through this mystique. Even as he moved to the margins in his style of filmmaking from the 1970s onwards, Alison Smith described how his celebrity remained strongly cast as 'Monsieur Cinéma', and his image 'as the spokesperson of new currents of culture' in France post-May 1968 persisted in popular consciousness, even despite his relative disappearance from view (Smith, 2007: 147–148). Unlike Godard, Varda has remained a representative of the New Wave but has accrued a much more popular form of celebrity. The 'mother' or 'grandmother of the New Wave' is more accessible as a real mother and a grandmother. *Le Grand Journal*, a popular nightly news programme broadcasting from Cannes in 2013 featured her as the President of the Caméra d'Or jury for that year. The French artist-intellectual is comfortable beside *Jamel Debbouze*, an actor-producer from an alternative comedy background. Varda plays along good-humouredly with his teasing: 'Also, I need to tell you your hair colour is not finished yet…I'm just saying you have forgotten one or two things…' When a joke about going to bed with her firmly slides him over the line into being offensive, the intellectual New Wave auteur curbs him with a witty but definite put-down. Their exchanges are 'current' enough to

Figure 5.2   Jamel Debbouze and Agnès Varda trade remarks on *Le Grand Journal* (2013)

Source: Canal Plus/Closer.fr

make the programme's online 'zapping' account – the online digest of entertaining clips for that day (*Jamel Debbouze*, 2013).[8] Elsewhere, in a programme for television channel *France 2*, Mathieu Demy is asked what his mother would be as a series of objects. If Varda were a piece of clothing, what would she be? Mathieu answers it would be a 'spotted dress', recalling her typical style. If she were a sport? The marathon, states Mathieu, because she never stops. Varda is then interviewed for her responses and talks openly about her relationship, personal and professional, with her son (*Portrait D'Agnès Varda*, 2001). Varda enters French popular culture as a patrimonial figure (an '*Olympien*') but her manner is warm and accessible as '*Agnès*'. In no sense does this imply inauthenticity in Varda's behaviour or a constant, conscious construction of a role. In Varda's case, as she ages, her star image functions positively to keep her, Demy and her children firmly visible in the public eye and, as a female author, contributes to her ability to work into old age.

Varda and French femininity

The Varda visible on television and in her work is the same woman who has utilised her private self as a means of exploring her signature themes in her art throughout her career, mainly through her short films. However, old age has opened up new possibilities for her to bring this person into the public domain, and to represent a number of contradictions in her persona as a *French* female artist. This is because French femininity itself can be said to contain and sustain a number of contradictions borne out of its historical roots. At the beginning of the twentieth century, French female public figures took a form that incorporated both public and private features:

> Work and femininity seemed much more compatible than before. Although this was a culture that still preferred women to be wives, the ideals of self-fulfilment that female celebrities performed legitimately included careers. (Berlanstein, 2004: 83)

Despite this, repressive attitudes still prevailed in a religiously conventional country (with a strong Catholic church) symbolised by the government's pro-natalist policies.[9] Post–Second World War, these contradictions became 'profound' as described by Gaffney and Holmes in relation to *Elle* magazine, which:

> ...invited its readers to see themselves as a new generation of emancipated women, now (at last) full citizens of their country with the right to vote finally won in 1944, but also as specifically French women, elegant, domestically competent, culturally aware and willingly responsible for the quality of their (heterosexual) relationships. (Gaffney and Holmes, 2007b: 15)

They were women who could demonstrate a 'feminine quality that combined social equality with the maintenance of a very traditional role as (sooner or later) wife and mother' (Gaffney and Holmes, 2007b: 15). Even in the case of French women activists, Ginette Vincendeau has noted that feminists in the public eye such as Julia Kristeva and Hélène Cixous have achieved their position 'partly because they endorsed the accepted signs of "French femininity"' whilst Catherine Deneuve can balance a 'combination of feminist positions and glamour' making her a '"very French" feminist' (2000: 206). Strength, therefore, is acceptable if coupled with an outward maintenance of feminine beauty.

Varda has always been visible and vocal, alongside actresses such as Catherine Deneuve, in her support of women's rights and her avowed status as a feminist. Both Deneuve and Varda were signatories to the famous anti-abortion manifesto drafted by Simone de Beauvoir, *Manifeste des 343*, in 1971, protesting about the infringement of women's right to choose. And yet, Varda was contemporaneously a wife and mother to daughter Rosalie, and, shortly thereafter (in 1972), the mother of Mathieu Demy. In some quarters this might have been considered contradictory, but was entirely possible in the discursive structure these French public women inhabited. Rather than these competing demands seeming irreconcilable, the evidence is that French women could bear these contradictions without withdrawing into their private life or having to disown certain forms of more politically challenging behaviour.

This milieu does not make French feminine/female celebrity immune to ageism. In his analysis of *Paris Match* covers (from 1949–2005), Alain Chenu concluded that 'female beauty comes to the fore with adolescence and declines with maturity' (2010: 102). However, this was not a constraint on Varda who was never a 'glamorous' intellectual in Vincendeau's terms. She could, thus, transition more easily into 'Agnès' or the *'petite vieille'* in the public's perception and make use of its warmth and communicative power in her films, notably *Les glaneurs et la glaneuse* (2000).

Ordinary and extraordinary – the Varda of *Les glaneurs et la glaneuse* and *Les plages d'Agnès*

Varda's persona in old age is one which critics in France and elsewhere have found easy to write about, and audiences to engage and empathise with, as shown in the response to the first appearance of *'la petite vieille'* in *Les glaneurs et la glaneuse* [*The Gleaners and I*] in 2000. In her early 70s then, Varda travelled around France exploring the meaning of gleaning and recycling in modern France. She interviewed those who collect food to survive and those who glean for political and environmental reasons, and also examined art-history representations of gleaning. Its awards success and its popularity with a wider audience spawned a follow-up film, *Les glaneurs et la glaneuse – deux ans après* [*The Gleaners and I – two years on*] (2002), in which the filmmaker returned to a number of the people seen in the first film and included new subjects who had directly responded to the first feature.[10] Varda clearly made for an affecting onscreen presence. Direct and distinctly unsentimental in her approach, the ageing woman with two-tone hair sat down with people from all social backgrounds with consummate ease and great empathy.

By the time of *Les plages d'Agnès*, Varda's walk backwards is clearly an invitation from both the public and private woman – 'Agnès' and 'Varda' – to travel through a series of public and private reminiscences. As she begins her story, she is seen directing her crew on the beach, in Kelley Conway's words, as the 'experienced professional film-maker at work' (2010: 132). The film is thus able to 'assert Varda's status as an active, ever-evolving artist, and to memorialise her oeuvre in photography, film and installations' (Conway, 2010: 126) linked by Varda's commentary. The interplay of 'Agnès' and 'Varda' is also part of the filmmaker's onscreen reflection on her own celebrity and is as potent in establishing her as an auteur as her appearance directing on the beach. In one sequence, Varda browses a flea market (she is herself a practiced gleaner) and rifles through a set of study cards on French cinema, finding herself and Jacques Demy. In a direct reference to their dual status in French culture, she comments: 'Before we were cinema cards with cardboard heads, we were flesh and blood beings'.[11] Of course, she has to buy them. In another memory, she revisits the presentation of her feature, *Cléo de 5 à 7*, at Cannes in 1963. Joking, she notes the differences between herself and the film's beautiful lead actress, Corinne Marchand, who embodies the tall, blonde glamour of a French film star. The 'petite' filmmaker is dressed in an outfit made by a costumier from the national theatre (where she worked as a photographer) and she is announced as 'Varga'. Varda laughs at her incongruity in the world of celebrity, literally in costume and 'confused' in the announcer's mind with the Varga Girls of the Casino de Paris. These entertaining vignettes – blended seamlessly into the structure of the essay film (discussed below) – are 'Agnès' at her most ordinary, even while they demonstrate her long-standing participation in this other world.

However, this is not her attempt to downplay or neutralise her intellect or place in film history. The purpose behind this becomes most clear in her adaptation of René Magritte's photomontage '*Je ne vois pas la [femme] cachée dans la forêt*' ['I do not see the woman hidden in the forest'] (1929) in which the image of a naked female sits in the centre of photographs of French surrealists, all with eyes closed. In Varda's version, her photographic image is at the centre of a similar montage, surrounded by the *nouvelle vague* male auteurs (eyes open). She has placed her finger on her lips. Here I am, Varda seems to suggest playfully, at the centre of the New Wave, but how many people knew that I was always there? Chris Marker, her friend and New Wave compatriot, asks her about that history in voiceover: 'And what about you, La Varda?' The woman who could be credited as anticipating the experimentation of the French New Wave with *La Pointe-Courte* and who has subsequently sustained a continuous career, now recognises it is up to her to ensure that her oeuvre is seen as a body of work. 'Agnès' and her celebrity reminiscences is as much part of that 'memorialisation' as is her performance onscreen as the director. Her celebrity 'brand' is, after all, useful to her as a producer. The recent collection of her entire oeuvre, a DVD boxset entitled *Tout(e) Varda* (2012),[12] presents a witty cartoon version of the ageing Varda on the outside of the box. She is instantly recognisable. It is a friendly image of an old woman which, nonetheless, does not belie the substance and longevity of her achievements or her company's commercial power in producing it.

Varda – onscreen, playing the role of the old lady

Varda may ensure the preservation of hers, and Demy's, past work through her activities and to honour her position in French film history. She is, more than anything, still youthful in her continued verve to work, visible onscreen and, judging by recent news articles, strongly implanted in popular consciousness (e.g., Ferry, 2014; Duponcelle 2014). However, it is the way in which this persona allows Varda to extend an aspect of her previous work – a so-called *'cinéma d'auteur-témoin'* ('cinema of the author as witness') – that is the focus of this final section. Significantly, her opening invitation in *Les plages d'Agnès* continues thus: 'But it is others I'm interested in and who I like to film; others, who intrigue me, motivate me, make me ask questions, disconcert and fascinate me'.[13]

This is no idle claim. Back in 1975 on the making of her film *Daguerréotypes* (1976), Varda talked about the film and its focus on the *'quotidienne'* since it follows the shopkeepers of Rue Daguerre (Varda's 'Daguerreotypes'), her neighbours. She and her cinematographer Nurith Aviv hid behind the counters and inside the doorways to capture the rhythms of their day. She reflected on the experience:

> Perhaps I am constructing a cinema of the author as witness ... I think I am an 'auteur' but I recoil a little before that word, in the way that it can have a limited meaning. [*Peut-être fais-je un cinéma d'auteur-témoin ... je crois que je fais du cinéma d'auteur, mais je renacle un peu devant le mot 'auteur', si on lui donne un sens trop limité.*] (Amiel, 1975: 46)

Whilst Varda recoiled at the idea of being an 'auteur' in this quote, time and again she embraces her interest in people and in acting as a witness to their lives. This concept – of the *'cinéma d'auteur-témoin'* – is thus a useful one to frame Varda's own witnessing of her personal old age.

Important here is Varda's command of the essay form, a form of discursive documentary. Still after many years the essay film form continues to infuse her work with the spontaneity, wit and energy of a *'jeune plasticienne'*. In his historical review of this form, Corrigan cites Jacques Rivette's characterisation of this style as one in which 'the indefatigable eye of the camera invariably assumes the role of the pencil, a temporal sketch is perpetuated before our eyes'. (Rivette quoted in Corrigan, 2011: 68). According to Corrigan, the essay film can allow a more palimpsestic approach, more personal, even apparently 'amateur'. This apparent lack of sophistication entirely suits her intention to infuse the personal with the artistic, and she is seen by Corrigan as a key twentieth-century proponent of the form.[14] *Les glaneurs et la glaneuse* plays with ideas of old age throughout, leading to affective revelation. For example, images of the heart-shaped potatoes she has gleaned in the field are filmed in her studio as they decay and sprout roots. Through the artist's eye they are beautiful, one of many images of 'old age' that pepper the film and suggest the outline or palimpsest of an argument as they are juxtaposed with the quotidian of her *own* existence as an old woman. As Martine Beugnet states their originality points to a 'whole economy of consumption and refuse (throwing away and replacing with the new) where images of ageing are systematically excluded from the screen' (2006: 27).

This is best exemplified by a sequence from the film that has become critically famous. Turning her 'cinema of author as witness' upon herself, Varda (the artist) films herself in extreme close-up to examine her ageing skin. She has returned from travelling abroad, having attended

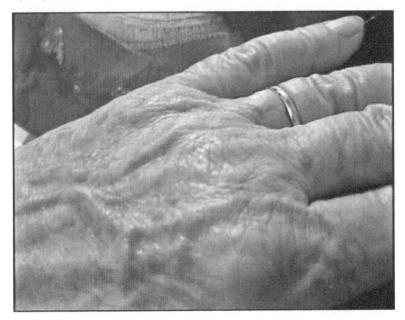

Figure 5.3 Varda observes her ageing skin

Source: Les glaneurs et la glaneuse (2000), Ciné-Tamaris

a presentation of her work in Japan, and empties out her suitcase. She holds a postcard of a Rembrandt self-portrait, painted in old age, and appears spontaneously to move the camera upwards from this to film her own hand and arm. The texture and surface of her skin, in the flat digital image, is juxtaposed with the image of the stain she has noticed on her ceiling. Whereas she has enjoyed the imperfection of the plasterwork (superimposing still pictures of artworks it reminds her of) her skin evinces more a sense of its difference for Varda as the cinematographer – its separateness from herself. She comments: *'J'ai l'impression que je suis une bête. C'est pire. Je suis une bête que je ne connais pas.'* ['I appear to myself as an animal. Worse than that. An animal that I don't recognise.']15

Since play and wit run through Varda's films, this seems a sudden moment of private fear, a confession to the camera, one which her interviewee Alain later told her was self-indulgent. Yet, a much younger Varda, reflecting on her early film *L'Opéra-Mouffe* (1958), acknowledged a similar fascination tinged with horror at ageing:

> '*L'Opéra-Mouffe* tells of how one can be at the same time pregnant, full of joy, happy, and at the same time to be aware that life is misery and old age, which is everywhere present around Rue Mouffetard. That contradiction interested me more since it was highlighted to me.' ['L'Opéra-Mouffe, *qui raconte comment on peut à la fois être enceinte, bêate de joie, heureuse, et en même temps savoir que la vie c'est la misère et la vieillesse, qui sont plus que partout ailleurs omni-présentes rue Mouffetard. La contradiction m'intéressait d'autant plus qu'elle était éclatante.'*] (Amiel, 1975: 45)

The woman may be afraid, but as the young artist she is inspired, driven, even forced, to try to explore these images publicly. In old age, as Mireille Rosello contends, Varda 'deliberately chooses not to equate old age and beauty...She is much more interested in her search for new visual and narrative grammars of old age' (2001: 34). Varda-the-artist is ever-present with Agnès-the-woman, each informing the other.

Rosello and Beugnet both rightly argue for the feminist potential of Varda's work in these films. Varda says herself that she made it her business to witness this part of life: 'I always liked bringing in old people, even very old people, senior citizens and beyond, in my films'.16 With typical humour, though, she sees imagining oneself as old as *'une sale blague'* ('a dirty joke'). If, as Julia Twigg (2004) has argued, the body can be regarded as a 'social text' and therefore the ageing body is 'not prediscursive, but fashioned within and by culture' (2004: 60), then Varda's representations onscreen are crucial. Twigg also points out that older women were excluded from feminism's early analysis of the female body, reflecting even there the 'gerontophobia of the wider culture' (Twigg, 2004: 60). Varda's diegetic persona is important in conjunction with her own commentary – in all these films – created as part of a personal, artistic expression, but as a body of work containing great political significance in this way for speaking what has gone largely unspoken.

However, ignoring her dimension as a public celebrity negates an important dimension of this persona. The conditions of French culture apparently allow Varda to hold and present the contradiction of being both intellectually engaged and a vulnerable woman in her work.[17] This filmmaker appears to be genuinely liked by her audiences, arguably because she seems familiar and ordinary. And her appearance as 'Agnès' on television allows her to point to a body of work that, amongst other themes and concerns, bears witness to old age, intellectually and emotionally.

Artist, woman, old age

Nowhere, however, does the conjunction of her artistic and celebrity personas and her act of witnessing come together more powerfully than in relation to Jacques Demy. Varda is, on one level, the public widow of the French icon who directed *Les parapluies de Cherbourg* (1964) and *Peau d'âne* (1970). In this role, she never shrinks from performing – onscreen and in interviews – an ordinary and extraordinary grief. Valérie Duponchelle's recent interview typically captures the interplay of this particular aspect of past and present in Varda, as the grieving widow for over 20 years following Demy's early death:

> After so many years at the heart of French cinema, she is tired of talking about herself, about TNP, about Jean Vilar; not so, regarding Jacques Demy; at his name her strong, firm voice falters immediately. [*Après tant d'années au coeur du cinéma français, elle se lasse de parler d'elle, du TNP [Théâtre national populaire],*[18] *de Jean Vilar; pas de Jacques Demy, dont l'évocation adoucit aussitôt sa voix nette et ferme.*] (Duponchelle, 2014)

Her work displays similar feeling and the essay form, in its 'sketching out' of many ideas, can hold without resolution the memory of great love and the presence of great grief. I would argue that her challenge to the 'narrative grammars of old age' is strongest here. As in *Les glaneurs et la glaneuse*, Varda peppers *Les plages d'Agnès* with images of her grief – performed by her using various material symbols of his absence, including her own dress – just as that earlier film contained more playful references to ageing. More so than her ageing skin, this testifies to a different kind of price that comes with old age and are arguably images which are just as 'systematically excluded from the screen'.

However, beyond the personal, Demy's widow uses her artistic experience to produce a community of stories as the author as witness. This is clearest in her art installation *Les veuves de Noirmoutier* [*The Widows of Noirmoutier*] (2004). Set in a place that Varda made a home with Demy, it contains a number of filmed interviews with widows and stories of different experiences of death, grief and memories of love. Chairs are placed for visitors with headphones to listen, intimately, to the revelations. Varda is filmed, but remains silent in her projected space. Marie-Claire Barnet comments on the exhibition:

> Varda mastered the subtle art of stirring a tide and flow of emotions, illuminating the ambiguity of all that is said or seen, not so much to avoid, but to bring us straight back to, the heart of messy feelings (the widows', her own, even ours). (Barnet, 2011: 105)

Liberating these unheard stories is a significant part of Varda's power as an auteur, made visible now that 'Agnès' has captured the public imagination. 'La Varda' was always there working with this purpose; old age has made her more visible and stimulated a further critical re-evaluation of her importance. It is a body of work, not just in its existence as a boxset or even in its thematic consistencies but also in one woman's constant renewal of a commitment to an idea of cinema to be as much communal as it is personal. Ordinary and extraordinary, Varda has found a way to sustain a truly powerful – feminine and feminist – cinema to bear witness for herself and others for over 60 years.

Notes

1. The chapter title refers to a passage spoken by Agnès Varda in her film *Les plages d'Agnès* (2008).How this sobriquet arose is unclear, but it has been taken up critically (e.g., Levitin, 1974).
2. Georges Sadoul (1965) described this film as 'genuinely the first film of the French *Nouvelle Vague*' (1965: 196).

3. Violette Morin expanded this term in her 1963 article to suggest, slightly differently to Morin, that these people were 'different *in kind* from other people.' (Dyer, 1998: 43)[original emphasis]
4. "...surhumains dans le rôle qu'ils incarnent, humains dans l'existence privée qu'ils vivent'.
5. INA is an organisation set up in 1975 with the express purpose of conserving French broadcast material for posterity.
6. To support and maintain national identity through a national culture, television companies had and have a statutory obligation both to arts programming and to funding film production for the cinema. Even as the relationship between French television and an idea of maintaining 'Frenchness' has become, in Lucy Mazdon's words, 'increasingly fraught', there has remained a role 'in disseminating a national popular culture and of the need (and indeed desire) to protect that role and that identity' (Mazdon, 2013: 190).
7. '*nous étions auréolés de la réputation de la Nouvelle Vague. Nous avons fréquenté Warhol, Jim Morrison, des petits jeunes qui débutaient comme Spielberg, Lucas, Scorcese* [sic] *et Coppola, mais on a aussi rencontré des légendes d'Hollywood, Gregory Peck et même Mae West*' (Ferry, 2014).
8. This is not to claim Varda's appeal reaches out into online youth culture; *Le Grand Journal* is marketed at a relatively middle-brow audience.
9. Historian James McMillan highlights these prevailing conservative attitudes pre–Second World War: 'As far as the legislators were concerned the role of women as wives and mothers was more than ever considered to be their paramount contribution to society' (McMillan, 1981: 189).
10. Varda shows a number of examples, and visits *correspondants*, in *Les glaneurs et la glaneuse – deux ans après* (2002).
11. '*Je pense qu'avant d'être des fiches de cinéma, avec des têtes de carton, on a été des êtres de chair et sang.*'
12. This appropriately and playfully can be translated as either 'Everything by Varda' or 'All of Varda'.
13. '*Et pourtant, ce sont les autres que j'aime filmer. Les autres qui m'intriguent, me motivent, m'interpellent, me déconcertent, me passionnent.*'
14. Corrigan, in examining essay films from 'Montaigne to Marker' includes Varda as an author who has helped to 'revitalise' the form by using its 'exploratory energy' that 'liberates it as a kind of testing of both expression and address' (2011: 70).
15. This recalls something of Simone de Beauvoir's own fear of ageing which she confronted in her work, especially *La Viellesse* (1970).
16. '*J'ai toujours aimé faire rentrer des vieux, der vrais grands vieux, le troisième le quatrième âge.*' This is represented in Varda's films by, for example, *Elsa la rose* (1966), *Daguerréotypes* (1976) and *7 P., cuis., s. de b...(à saisir)* (1984).
17. Her recent television series for ARTE encapsulates this dual persona in its French title *Agnès de ci, de là Varda* (2011) [*Agnès Varda: From Here to There*].
18. This was the 'People's National Theatre' established in 1920. Varda acted as the company's photographer in its time under the stewardship of Jean Vilar.

References

Amiel, M. (1975) 'Merci Agnès. Autour et alentour de *Daguerréotypes*', *Camera*, December, pp. 38–53.

Barnet, M.-C. (2011) 'Elles-Ils Islands': Cartography of Lives and Deaths by Agnès Varda', *L'Esprit Créateur*, 51(1), pp. 97–111.

Beauvoir, S. de (1970) *La Viellesse [Old Age]* (Paris: Éditions Gallimard).

Berlanstein, L. R. (2004) 'Historicizing and Gendering Celebrity Culture: Famous Women in Nineteenth-Century France', *Journal of Women's History*, 16(4), pp. 65–91.

Beugnet, M. (2006) 'Close-up Vision: Re-mapping the Body in the Work of Contemporary French Women Filmmakers', *Nottingham French Studies*, 45(3), pp. 24–38.

Chenu, A. (2010) 'From Paths of Glory to Celebrity Boulevards: Sociology of *Paris Match* Covers, 1949–2005', *Association Revue Française de Sociologie*, 51(1), pp. 69–116.

Conway, K. (2010) 'Varda at work: *Les Plages d'Agnès*', *Studies in French Cinema*, 10(2), pp. 125–139.

Corrigan, T. (2011) *The Essay Film: From Montaigne, after Marker.* (New York: Oxford University Press).

De Julie, M. (2013) 'Ageing and Memory in Agnès Varda's *Les plages d'Agnès*', *Senses of Cinema*, No. 67, July.

Duponchelle, V. (2014) '*Ça c'est... Paris! Agnès de 5 à 7;Tête-à-tête en salle de montage avec la cinéaste et artiste de l'image*', (Paris: Le Figaro).

Dyer, R. (1998) *Stars* (London: British Film Institute).

Ferry, J. (2014) 'J'ai rencontré Jacques Demy à Tours', *La Nouvelle République*, 3 August. Available at http://www.lanouvellerepublique.fr [accessed 5 October 2014].

Gaffney, J. and Holmes, D. (2007a) 'Introduction', in J. Gaffney and D. Holmes (eds) *Stardom in Postwar France* (New York and Oxford: Berghahn Books), pp. 1–6.

Gaffney, J. and Holmes, D. (2007b) 'Stardom in Theory and Context', in J. Gaffney and D. Holmes (eds) *Stardom in Postwar France* (New York and Oxford: Berghahn Books), pp. 7–25.

Heinich, N. (2011) 'La culture de la célébrité en France et dans les pays anglophones' ['Celebrity Culture in France and in Anglophone Countries'], *Revue française de sociologie*, 52(2), pp. 353–372. Available at www.cairns.info [accessed 10 December 2014].

Holmes, S. (2005) 'Starring...Dyer? Re-visiting Star Studies and Contemporary Celebrity Culture', *Westminster Papers in Communication and Culture*, 2(2), pp. 6–21.

Jermyn, D. (2014) '"Get a Life, Ladies. Your Old One Is Not Coming Back": Ageing, Ageism and the Lifespan of Female Celebrity', in D. Jermyn (ed.), *Female Celebrity and Ageing: Back in the Spotlight* (London and New York: Routledge), pp. 1–14.

Klein, W. (1965) 'People Are Talking about...', *Vogue*, 146(3), pp. 90–91. Available at www.vogue.com/archive [accessed 5 January 2015].

Levitin, J. (1974) 'Mother of the New Wave: Interview with Agnès Varda', *Women and Film*, 1(5–6), pp. 62–67.

Mazdon, L. (2013) 'French Television: Negotiating the National Popular', in D. Holmes and D. Looseley (eds), *Imagining the Popular in Contemporary*

French Culture (Manchester and New York: Manchester University Press), pp. 162–193.

McMillan, J. F. (1981) *Housewife or Harlot: The Place of Women in French Society 1870–1940* (Brighton, Sussex: The Harvester Press).

Morin, E. (1962) *L'esprit du temps: essai sur la culture du masse* (Paris: Grasset).

Morin, V. (1963) 'Les Olympiens', *Communications*, 2(2), pp. 105–121.

Rosello, M. (2001) 'Agnès Varda's *Les Glaneurs et la glaneuse*. Portrait of the Artist as an Old Lady', *Studies in French Cinema*, 1(1), pp. 29–36.

Sadoul, G. (1965) *Dictionnaire Des Cinéastes* (Paris: Paris Éditions du Seuil).

Smith, A. (2007) 'The Auteur as Star: Jean-Luc Godard', in J. Gaffney and D. Holmes (eds) *Stardom in Postwar France* (New York and Oxford: Berghahn Books), pp. 126–151.

Twigg, J. (2004) 'The Body, Gender, and Age: Feminist Insights in Social Gerontology', *Journal of Aging Studies*, 18(1), pp. 59–73.

Vincendeau, G. (2000) *Stars and Stardom in French Cinema*. (London and New York: Continuum).

Woodward, K. (1999) *Figuring Age: Women, Bodies, Generations*. (Bloomington, Indiana: Indiana University Press).

Filmed

7 P., cuis., s. de b ... (à saisir). Directed by Agnès Varda. France: Ciné-Tamaris, 1984.

Agnès de ci, de là Varda. Directed by Agnès Varda. France: Ciné-Tamaris/ARTE France, 2011.

Cléo de 5 à 7. Directed by Agnès Varda. France: Ciné-Tamaris/Rome Paris Film, 1962.

Daguerréotypes. Directed by Agnès Varda. France: Ciné-Tamaris/INA/ZDF, 1976.

Elsa la rose. Directed by Agnès Varda. France: Pathé Consortium Cinéma, 1966.

Jacquot de Nantes. Directed by Agnès Varda. France: Ciné-Tamaris/Canal Plus/ CNC, 1991.

Le Bonheur. Directed by Agnès Varda. France: Parc Film, 1965.

Les glaneurs et la glaneuse. Directed by Agnès Varda. France: Ciné-Tamaris, 2000.

Les glaneurs et la glaneuse – deux ans après. Directed by Agnès Varda. France: Ciné-Tamaris/C.N.C.P./Canal Plus/CNC, 2002.

Les parapluies de Cherbourg. Directed by Jacques Demy. France: Parc Film/Madeleine Films/Beta Film, 1964.

Les plages d'Agnès. Directed by Agnès Varda. France: Ciné-Tamaris/ARTE France, 2008.

La Pointe-Courte. Directed by Agnès Varda. France: Ciné-Tamaris, 1955.

L'Opéra-Mouffe. Directed by Agnès Varda. France: Ciné-Tamaris, 1958.

L'une chante, l'autre pas. Directed by Agnès Varda. France: Ciné-Tamaris, 1977.

Peau d'âne. Directed by Jacques Demy. France: Marianne Productions/Parc Film, 1970.

Les Veuves de Noirmoutier. [Art Installation]. Directed by Agnès Varda. France: Ciné-Tamaris, 2004.

Sans toi ni loi. Directed by Agnès Varda. France: Ciné-Tamaris, 1985.

Tout(e) Varda [DVD Boxset]. Directed by Agnès Varda. France: Ciné-Tamaris/ARTE Editions, 2012.

Television broadcasts

Agnès Varda présente ses films, 25 August 1971. Office national de radiodiffusion télévision française Montpellier. Available through: www.ina.fr [accessed 12 September 2014].

Apostrophes: Guy de Maupassant, 27 July 1979. Antenne 2. Available through: www.ina.fr [accessed 13 September 2014].

Interview d'Agnès Varda et Ludivine Sagnier, extrait de l'émission Le Grand Journal à l'occasion du 66ème Festival de Cannes 2013. Canal Plus. Available through: www.canalplus.fr [accessed 20 September 2014].

Jacques Demy et Agnès Varda à propos de leur couple, de leurs films: Démons et merveilles du cinéma, 19 December 1964. Office national de radiodiffusion télévision française. Available through: www.ina.fr [accessed 12 September 2014].

Jamel Debbouze taquine Agnès Varda sur sa coiffure, 23 May 2013. Extract from: *Le Grand Journal*. Available through: *Le Zapping de Closer* at http://www.dailymotion.com/video/x1055mq_ [accessed 20 September 2014].

Journée à Cannes, 12 May 1991. *France Régions 3*. Available through: www.ina.fr [accessed 13 September 2014].

Portrait D'Agnès Varda Par Son Fils Mathieu Demy, 22 April 2001. *France 2*. Available through: www.ina.fr [accessed 5 August 2014].

6
Ageing Grace/Fully: Grace Jones and the Queering of the Diva Myth
Nathalie Weidhase

Grace Jones, the celebrated black singer and disco diva, released her comeback album *Hurricane* in 2008 after a 19-year musical hiatus that saw her making professional DJ appearances but ceasing to release any new recorded material. *Hurricane*, and the promotional live performances that followed, were met with critical acclaim and extensive media coverage largely focusing on Grace Jones' supposedly 'ageless' body (Gardner, 2012), while neglecting the actual musical output that constituted her comeback. Throughout her career, Grace Jones has arguably queered a myriad of identity categories in her performances, including race, gender, sexuality and national identity (Guzman, 2010). Invoking the term 'queer' in both her status as a disco icon and as an identificatory figure for marginalised audiences, Jones has a long and pronounced history of unsettling and disrupting identity configurations such as gender, sexuality and race (Kershaw, 1997; Royster, 2012). Equally undisputed is her status as a (disco) diva (Lobato, 2007). But this chapter is concerned with the fusion between these two concepts, exploring how a particular queer diva ages in the spotlight. The diva has been identified as a potentially successful performance strategy for ageing, female, popular music performers (Jennings, 2012), and this chapter will explore the ways in which Grace Jones queers the concept of the diva during her comeback at the age of 60 through a queering of gender, race and sexuality. Through close analysis of the lyrical content of *Hurricane* (2008), the music video for the single 'Williams Blood' (2009) and a photo shoot with Chris Cunningham for *Dazed & Confused* magazine (2008), this chapter will explore the ways in which Jones' comeback continues to present queer 'lapses and excesses of meaning when the constituent elements of anyone's gender, of anyone's sexuality aren't made ... to signify monolithically' (Sedgwick, 1994: 8). I examine how these performances reconfigure the diva myth through the ways in which Jones performs both ageing and agelessness. Moreover, Jones' performance of the ageing diva embodies a vision of 'queer time' (Halberstam, 2005) where age becomes the dominant queering factor which not only subverts normative notions of ageing, but also reconstructs the diva myth itself as a performance strategy which facilitates those subversions.

Grace Jones: queer icon and disco diva

Grace Jones was born in 1948 in Spanish Town, Jamaica, and was raised by her grandparents after her parents moved away to work in the United States. Her father was a politician and clergyman who subjected Jones to a strict upbringing under the influence of the Jamaican Pentecostal church. As a shy child, she reportedly had only one friend and was often teased in school for her tall, slim appearance (Royster, 2012). At the age of 13, she followed her parents and moved to Syracuse, New York. Initially starting a major in Spanish at Syracuse University, she was approached by a model scout and moved to New York at age 18 to begin her modelling career. Moving to Paris in 1970, she modelled for (amongst others) Yves St. Laurent and appeared on the covers of *Vogue* and *Elle* (Royster, 2012). Her first album was released in 1977, shortly after which she met illustrator Jean-Paul Goude, who, in true Svengali-style, became influential in crafting her image as a disco diva and performance artist (Kershaw, 1997). She gave birth to son Paulo in 1979 and in the following years released a string of singles, albums and tours that confirmed her status as a queer disco icon (Lobato, 2007). Subsequently, she became the subject of academic inquiry with regard to her apparent subversion and distortion of racist and gender stereotypes (Kershaw, 1997).

At the same time, Jones' subversive performances of racist stereotypes are so complex and conflictual that their discursive connotations are not always clear. As Francesca Royster argues:

> She is so fantastic at becoming an object – animal, machine, space invader, multiplying robot, hurricane – that we might not hear her also explaining what it's like to be an object. Grace is so good at creating desire that we miss her read on where that hunger comes from, and what it costs. But it's there, in the force of her voice, in her lyrics, in the flash of her eyes. And in the highly theatrical staging of scenes of desire that occupy her work: from cage to studio to disco floor to stage. Her work is often overlooked as a project of

black critique because of the contradictions she raises and refuses to resolve. (Royster, 2012: 150)

Jones' image both embodies and arguably distorts racist and sexist stereotypes in such a way as to pose 'challenges of readability' (Royster, 2012: 147). Arguably, however, it is this very confusion that potentially forms a large part of her appeal to minority and marginalised audiences, who may perceive themselves to eschew strict normative identity categories in similar ways. And while it seems that the musical performance art of Grace Jones is beyond straightforward comprehension, it is useful to examine her performances of ageing through the lens of the diva. This is not only because it is a title she has worn with pride for the majority of her career, but also because the diva trope has been identified as a potentially successful performance strategy for the ageing female pop star, in which a skilled execution of this trope can capture the nostalgia of an earlier career and simultaneously accommodate and incorporate the signs of ageing in spectacular and performative ways (Jennings, 2012).

The diva myth: forms and functions

While the contemporary diva is often perceived as a 'powerful and entertaining, if pushy and bitchy, woman' (Springer, 2007: 255) – the latter description being particularly exaggerated in the cultural and mediated reception of black performers which builds on the stereotype of the 'angry black woman' (Springer, 2007) – the term has not always been burdened with overtly negative connotations. The diva has also been understood as a female star in opera, film, theatre or popular music, who transgresses boundaries of normative womanhood in the transformation of her personal suffering into art, which enables her to be a source of inspiration and identification for her audience (Bradshaw, 2008; Doty, 2007). O'Neill (2007) explains the importance of audience identification within the spectacle of the diva performance, arguing that the relationship between diva and diva audience is a symbiotic one: while the diva depends on the adoration of her audience (historically, at least, understood to be largely male and gay), the audience can look up to the diva as an arbiter of taste, as inspiration and guidance on how to live a life that goes beyond conventions of gender or sexuality. Particularly for minority or marginalised audiences, the diva offers spectators:

a compelling brass standard that has plenty to say to women, queer men, blacks, Latinos, and other marginalized groups about the costs and the rewards that can come when you decide both to live a conspicuous public life within white patriarchy and to try and live that life on your own terms. (Doty, 2007: 2)

And while the diva uses her own, usually troubled, biography as spectacle and performance, it is the audience that makes sense of it, and uses it to shape and make sense of their own life narratives (O'Neill, 2007). Jones' appeal as disco diva to queer and black audiences is well documented (Guzman, 2010; Lobato, 2007; Royster, 2012). She is often championed for 'her seamless presentation of the multitude of roles that are available to individuals in contemporary society' (Guzman, 2010: 80) during the disco era and beyond – as evidenced by her successful comeback and her ability to mobilise her fans even after a 19-year break from recording and releasing music.

Similar connections between Grace Jones and the diva myth can be made with regards to the diva's life trajectory: the story goes that the diva is a talented underdog who overcomes the obstacles in her life and transforms these experiences into art and fame, all while forgoing or sacrificing normative womanhood in the exchange for commercial success. With success comes stardom and the difficulties of maintaining stardom, so the 'star inevitably dims, either through tragedy or ageing; diva dies alone' (Bradshaw, 2008: 71). Many of these elements can be found in Jones' biography: uprooted from her native Jamaica as a child, she continued to struggle with her parents' religious and strict way of raising her until (and arguably after) moving to New York and Paris to work as a model, and later as a performance artist and musician. Always an eccentric and hedonistic character, her career took a hit in the late 1980s, and after a drug bust in 1989 and bankruptcy in 1992, her star image did begin to dim and fade, although nostalgia amongst her admirers ensured that her musical legacy continued (Lobato, 2007). However, where Jones breaks this prescribed diva destiny is with her comeback in 2008.

2008's *Hurricane*: the comeback as disruption of the diva myth

Grace Jones' comeback in 2008 with the release of *Hurricane* constituted a disruption of the diva trajectory in itself. The album (and the ensuing concerts and promotional appearances) signified the end of a 19-year musical hiatus, in which Grace Jones nearly faded into obscurity. According to the usual diva life narrative, a lonely and secluded death would be the inevitable end to Grace Jones' biography. Yet Jones' reappearance on the popular music stage at the age of 60 was met with critical acclaim, even though, as noted above, the media coverage predominantly focused on her supposedly 'ageless' body (Gardner, 2012). This, in many ways, contrasts with the negative and often punitive judgements made about the ageing of the *white* female celebrity body, as circulates ubiquitously in the popular press, magazines and online gossip blogs. This invocation of the black female body as apparently less prone to the vicissitudes of ageing – of ageing as being a challenge or 'problem' more acutely felt by and rendered on the bodies of white women – is arguably commonplace in popular culture (Gilleard and Higgs, 2013). In an analysis of press accounts covering her comeback in general and her performance at the 2008 Meltdown Festival in particular, Gardner (2012) notes that the descriptions of Grace Jones' corporeality often strayed into very problematic territory. The 'ageless' black body was often also portrayed as 'scary' or 'other', as historically racist animal metaphors were adopted to describe her physicality: her buttocks, for example, became her 'hindquarters', which she 'shakes and wiggles in the face of the photographers' (Gardner, 2012: 72), inviting comparisons to a performing show horse rather than an influential disco icon.

Furthermore, her seemingly ageless body (and the performances and promotional material which showcased this body) signified 'her refusal to comply with an accepted trajectory of decay and decrepitude' (Gardner, 2012: 71), which seemed remarkable and worthy of both wonder and scrutiny. This sense of astonishment nurtured the perception of Grace Jones as 'well-preserved', effectively turning her into an artefact. Her status as 'well-preserved' was emphasised through a repetition of descriptive terms that aligned her with works of art, placing her outside the realms of 'the human' and instead turning her into an *object*, of art or otherwise. Both framings – as either artefact or animalistic – employ racist codings and historical associations of the black body as 'other' and non-human. Moreover, the focus on her body is not only problematic with regard to discourses of racial coding, but also it entailed a neglect of the actual musical output that constituted her comeback. As I will argue, the lyrical content of *Hurricane* subverts notions of both agelessness and diva performance in its chronicles of the *maternal*, which is a performance of femininity not commonly associated with the diva. Furthermore, my focus on the lyrics – her 'voice', so to speak – here becomes a political strategy that counteracts the obsessive focus on her body and the objectification this engenders. Because ageing is largely understood in corporeal and visual terms, an engagement with the lyrics complicates Jones' aged embodiment and opens the space to read her comeback in more explicitly political terms. Indeed, in the songs and stories of older black women, Holloway and Demetrakopoulos (1997) identify a protection of both history and future in their narrations of the experience and survival of racial oppression on the one hand, and a passing on of traditions and histories of origin on the other. Through an engagement with lyrics and performance, it becomes evident that Jones' diva comeback functions as an act of (queer) aged black female storytelling of (queer) survival and possibility, and it is her position as an ageing diva that enables such storytelling.

Hurricane's narratives of motherhood and the maternal

Hurricane (2008) is the first album in Jones' long career to deal extensively with her family background and history (Sawyer, 2008). What becomes evident in its lyrical narratives is a repeated engagement with and negotiation of the maternal, either through narrations of (biological) reproduction, or through the retelling of her mother's biography, or dramatisation of Jones' relationship with her mother.

The title track of *Hurricane* ('Hurricane') begins with English trip hop artist Tricky repeating 'From cradle to grave' six times, lyrically setting the song up for the exploration of life, death and life creation. Grace Jones continues Tricky's introduction with 'I am woman, I am sun / I can give birth to she / I can give birth to son!', going on to assert that 'I can scheme, I can lie / I'll take care of you, til the day you die'. The latter lyrics mark a break with the diva's perceived rebellion against a caring, self-sacrificing traditional femininity, as the song proudly proclaims Grace Jones' capability to care and take care. Unlike the comeback's press coverage, which often painted her as a non-human animal or artefact, the lyrics emphasise Jones' humanity through the repeated act of caring for another. Furthermore, the lyrics explicitly link female gendered subjectivity to the ability to reproduce and give birth. This notion of fertility is, for example, emphasised through the lines 'I can hold brush, I can push broom / When I walk by, flowers will bloom', which at the same time recall images of a very domestic femininity. This is the exact same femininity against which the diva is supposed to rebel in her quest for fame and which is at odds with the androgyny that was so central to the image Jones consolidated early in the 1980s. Here, her feminine body is directly linked to fertility: Jones' mere appearance can nurture flowers into bloom.

The rather conventional equation of femininity with fertility becomes surprisingly queer when one considers her age. As a postmenopausal (and therefore presumably no longer fertile) woman, Jones' proclamation of her fertile prowess positions her outside or beyond the age narrative of infertility, bodily failure and mortality. It also gives the perception of her as 'ageless' an interesting twist: not only is her body 'ageless', but so are its reproductive abilities. In the context of her reception, the lyrical images of normative womanhood serve a subversive purpose, as they function to renegotiate the image of Grace Jones as 'scary' artwork on the one hand, and complicate the notion of her as 'ageless' on the other.

However, the topic of reproduction is not foreign to Grace Jones and her pre-comeback body of work. With regards to 1982's *A One Man Show* and its performance of 'Demolition Man', which included several Grace Jones doppelgangers, Maria Guzman (2010) states: 'In a truly inspired nod to both the sexual and the industrial revolutions, Jones becomes the antithesis of natural reproduction (giving birth), and it never looked so good!' (Guzman, 2010: 84). Both technology and reproduction are present in *Hurricane* (2008), as evidenced by the lyrics discussed and by the track 'Corporate Cannibal', in which Jones performs the Robo-Diva with mechanical precision, toying with anxieties about black women and technology (James, 2008) (declaring 'I'm a man-eating machine'). Conjoining images of Jones' postmenopausal fertility and her cyborg 'man-eating machine' subjectivity indeed position her as 'the antithesis of natural reproduction', and indirectly within the concept of 'queer time'. Halberstam defines queer time as 'specific models of temporality that emerge within postmodernism once one leaves the temporal frames of bourgeois reproduction' (2005: 6). Jones' visions of reproduction depend neither on human corporeality nor the temporality of the heteronormative life cycle that is structured around (female) fertility and its decline (Halberstam, 2005). These images defy the linearity of natural reproduction, as fertility and reproduction are not contingent on the young female fertile body. While this presents a lyrical subversion of normative concepts of aged femininity, reproduction and time, Jones turns to more conventional perceptions of these categories on the same album.

Less queer is Jones' engagement with and portrayal of the maternal when singing about her own mother and their changing relationship. Here, the lyrics function to simultaneously disrupt the diva persona carefully constructed through Grace Jones and her audience, and through the media reception that dehumanised her with admiration.

But the lyrics also constitute a transgression of the transgression: if the diva transgresses ideals of normative womanhood through the absence of (often idealised) motherhood, then a focus on Grace Jones as maternal – and the expression of a fond engagement with her mother – is a spectacular use of the personal in performance (an established diva strategy), as well as a transgression of what the diva is supposed to be. This becomes particularly evident in the song 'I'm Crying (Mother's Tears)', which portrays the relationship between Jones and her ageing mother, where the parent-child caretaker relationship is shown as in flux. The song chronicles 'Little memories of our past', where Grace Jones 'Bathed in the water [her mother] ran every morning', and talks of having had night terrors when, 'in the middle of a scare, she's there'. The lyrics progress towards a point where Jones proclaims, 'I'm now all grown up', and at an age where she is compelled to take care of herself and her mother, a prospect many face in an ageing society. The lyrics chronicle experiences that typically only come with ageing, and these stand in sharp contrast to the perceived agelessness of Grace Jones and the queering of temporality. But this does not mean that Grace Jones has turned away from the spectacular diva life that made her famous and she has now dedicated her life to the fulfilment of expectations of normative womanhood. On the contrary, the music video to the single 'Williams Blood' (2009) effectively reinstates Jones as the eternal disco diva.

Diva-becoming and diva-being in 'Williams Blood' (2009)

It has been suggested that Grace Jones developed her distinctive, often provocative style and performance persona partly as a reaction to her conservative religious upbringing (Guzman, 2010; Anderson, 1993). Indeed, Jones herself confirms that '[t]here was nothing else to see but the church. But that's what charged my imagination' (Sawyer, 2008). As outlined above, the overcoming of struggles and the artistic influence of the biographical are integral parts of the diva myth. Whether or not Grace Jones 'truly' consciously constructed her performances as a reaction to her childhood is almost irrelevant, as the discussions of her early life seem to form an integral part of discussions of her, therefore directly feeding into her personal diva myth. Considering this, the lyrics and music video to 'Williams Blood' can be read as a re-emphasising of this myth on the one hand, and a playing with it on the other. The lyrics chronicle the continuous struggle with her father and her father's family regarding her career, while the music video effectively illustrates Grace

Jones' current (and past) diva-being in its performative recalling of her disco past. Both the narrations of inter-familial conflict and the visual reassurance of her diva status function not only as personal accounts or public recreations of her disco image, but they also place Jones in the role of the old black woman and their 'spiritual/political significance as foremothers' (Holloway and Demetrakopoulos, 1997: 177) who embody survival, wisdom and memory.

Hurricane's lyrical narratives not only deal with the maternal lineage and its influence, implicitly recalling images of the black matriarch, but also explore the concept of the paternal. While 'the maternal' influence on *Hurricane* constitutes an almost sentimental reflection on growing up, ageing and caring, 'Williams Blood' offers a more critical account of her family history and influence, in particular the influence stemming from her father's side. Jones described her relationship with her father as complicated, stating that 'I hated my dad, he was so strict. But now I love him, because they didn't make him bishop for a long time because of me' (Sawyer, 2008). This is a conflict that is evident in 'Williams Blood' throughout, interwoven and contrasted with her mother's biography and the influence she has had on Jones.

The impact her father's religious background had on her life is outlined in the song lyrics. 'Williams Blood' begins with 'You can't save me, you can't save a wretch like me', a distortion of the line '...That saved a wretch like me' from the hymn 'Amazing Grace', early on establishing the link between her religious background and her fraught and complicated relationship with its ideologies. It also functions as an overarching summary of Grace Jones' diva-becoming: although her religious family has at times distanced themselves from her and were not supportive of her career, this could not tame or 'save' her, nor prevent her rise to stardom as a queer disco diva.

The first verse is followed by 'She's so happy (I don't want to keep up I can't keep up)', a line in which the narrative perspective changes from third to first person within the same line. This change of perspective blurs the lyrical boundaries between her mother's account of her early marriage and Jones' own subjective account and understanding of her upbringing, as the latter part indicates a discomfort and desire to break out from her traditional family life. Through the switching between narrative positions, Jones' history becomes lyrically intertwined with that of her mother, reinforcing the bonding that is expressed throughout the song. The lyrical queering of the narrator's voice constitutes a passing on and influence of the maternal not only through blood lineage, but also through the stories that are told and passed down through generations.

Contrary to the affirmatively positive relationship that is portrayed with her mother, her relationship with her father has always been strained. In this context, the repeated 'I've got the Williams blood in me' – 'Williams' being her mother's maiden name – highlights her maternal blood line and emphasises her maternal heritage as an influence on her musical and performance art career. Similarly, the aforementioned interlude, 'She's so happy (I don't want to keep up I can't keep up) / She's so happy, keeping up (I don't wanna keep up, keeping up with the Joneses)' creates a claustrophobic atmosphere that works as a catalyst for Grace Jones' diva-becoming. The said claustrophobia generates the desire to break away from her, at times, oppressive family environment and is expressed as a necessity. This necessity of overcoming, and the successful overcoming, make this narration a story of black female survival, told by one of the 'older black women whose very conditions make the politics of their survival a lesson for us all' (Holloway and Demetrakopoulos, 1997: 185). The inclusive 'for us all' becomes particularly evident when one reads Jones' comeback in general, and the diva performance in 'Williams Blood' in particular, as a story of queer survival.

If the lyrics serve as an introduction to and explanation of Jones' diva-becoming, the music video to 'Williams Blood' shows Grace Jones at her best diva-being. The video is a live performance video, consisting of moments from her comeback 2008 Meltdown Festival performance. Jones is seen on stage, performing for an enthusiastic, adoring audience. She is wearing predominantly androgynous outfits like capes, coats and sparkling bowler hats twinned with high heels – all of them showcasing her long, trademark legs as she struts round the stage. These outfits convey the idea of Jones as 'ageless', as they cover body parts (such as upper arms) that could 'expose' signs of ageing, and they highlight the parts (most prominently her legs) that could easily belong to someone 30 years younger. Here, Jones becomes truly 'ageless', as it seems near impossible to determine her age based on visual clues alone.

Jones' sparkling bowler hat shines like a disco ball, visually reminding the viewer of her famous history as a disco diva. The stage is very much presented as her own, and there is a suggestion that it is shared with the audience on an 'invitation-only' basis. There is a clear spatial differentiation between her and her fans, with Jones at times standing on a platform, hovering above her audience. These sequences recall the linguistic origins of the word 'diva', the Italian word for female deity. But in true diva fashion, this spatial separation is later broken, when she is subsequently seen with a group of visibly excited fans, sharing the stage with Jones. The mythical construction of Jones as otherworldly being (Lobato,

2007) not only exemplifies the diva relationship to her adoring audience, but also conjures up her disco diva past. In this context, Jones' 'ageless' body becomes a canvas upon which both past and present can be painted. The 'disco coding' of her performance invokes a sense of nostalgia (Lobato, 2007) and history, as it visually transports the audience back to the aesthetics of the 1970s and implicitly recalls the queer struggles of that era. But as the song is a story of overcoming and survival, at the same time it invokes a sense of pastness, as struggles need to be left behind in order to be overcome. Indeed, the comeback itself becomes a temporal marker of overcoming, as Jones is old enough to have 'lived to tell the tale'. But at the same time, this oscillating between past and present contained within the music video is facilitated by the image of the 'ageless' Grace Jones, as her corporeality conveys no indication of time. Jones' aged 'ageless' body becomes a metaphorical visualisation of 'queer time', where time is both suspended and simultaneously past and present. But this does not mean that Jones shies away from exposing the signs of her ageing.

Exposing and queering the ageing black body: Grace Jones for *Dazed & Confused*

Just like 'Williams Blood', a Chris Cunningham photo shoot for British style magazine *Dazed & Confused*[1] strongly references past artistic performances and is framed as an anti-fashion shoot (Anon, 2008). But unlike 'Williams Blood', which effectively used fashion and lighting to portray Jones as an ageless disco diva, the photo shoot does not shy away from the exposition of the ageing body. The images show a naked Grace Jones, posing in various forms and poses of entrapment: we see her behind a glass or plastic panel in what can be interpreted as a cushioned box, as well as curled up draped in luminescent wire. These varied forms of containment can be read as a link to her earlier artworks with photographer Jean-Paul Goude that played with (and arguably even 'created') Jones' body as malleable on the one hand, and as a take on Grace Jones' current objectified artefact status on the other. As Jones herself confirms, '[h]e's shooting me like art' (Anon, 2008), making her the object of the artistic gaze that appreciates and utilises Jones' 'malleable' photogenic qualities.

One image shows a nude Grace Jones in an environment reminiscent of a padded cell. Her distorted posture manages to showcase her long, 'ageless' legs, and emphasises a sense of entrapment, while her facial expression can be read as either conforming to the cell's connotations of insanity, or as an expression of defiance. Jones gleefully sticking out her tongue reproduces a gesture primarily associated with children, which alongside the nudity, marks her behaviour as 'improper' for a woman of her age. As responses to Madonna's later career have shown, the media and general public do not generally react kindly to (post) menopausal women who show signs both of ageing and active sexuality (Gorton and Garde-Hansen, 2013). In a media culture where female pop stars are only allowed to age if they 'pass' as youthful with the help of airbrushing, artful clothes and make-up, Jones' nudity is remarkable in its untouched and outright simplicity. While the images are digitally manipulated to alter Jones' bodily shape, they leave signs of ageing untouched in the process. Bodily signifiers of ageing, like stretch marks (which are also visible reminders of Jones' status as a mother), uneven skin and loosening connective tissue are not desirable qualities in a postfeminist media and celebrity culture that champions youth and passing as youthful (Gorton and Garde-Hansen, 2013). Yet they are very evident here, and their cheerful exhibition on a nude 60-year-old (whose body is simultaneously framed as 'art') arguably counters the perception of 'the ageing female body as unappealing and abject' (Martin, 2012: 102).

Similarly 'unappealing' by ageist, sexist and normative standards is the image of Grace Jones pressing her body against a glass panel. This image follows the theme of entrapment present in most of the photos, heightened by the shadow of a hand behind Jones, as if it is chasing or grabbing her. But visually more dominant, and more relevant to the content of this chapter, are Grace Jones' own hands, which are placed on her crotch. Together with her potentially ecstatic facial expression, this image invites us to read it as a stylised portrayal of masturbation. Alongside the obvious subversion of what constitutes 'proper' behaviour for a woman her age, this image further advances Jones' history as a queer and queering performer. Jones appears here as self-desiring, and perhaps somehow outside of a heterosexual matrix (Butler, 1990) which situates women in relation to a public (male) gaze that is loaded with 'fear, loathing and shame [and that] actively construct[s] what women can and cannot do with their bodies as they grow older' (Gorton and Garde-Hansen, 2013: 295). In this context, these images are subversive both in their portrayal of the ageing female body as a site of pleasure and in that they do not attempt to hide the signs of ageing, while the autoerotic connotations function as a reminder of Jones' queer diva status.

Performing the aged and ageless queer diva

In conclusion, a closer engagement with the actual artistic output of Jones' comeback reveals that, contrary to popular perception,

Grace Jones has indeed aged; not only this, she has made modes of (female black) ageing the subject of her comeback. In her lyrics, she both invokes an almost normative ageing femininity in conjunction with explorations of 'the maternal' and a subversion of that femininity through queer modes of reproduction. Similarly complex, the music video to 'Williams Blood' builds on this queering of ageing and time in its narratives of survival that are both personal and political. Finally, the photo shoot with Chris Cunningham unravels notions of her ageless body – the body with which public opinion has been so preoccupied – while her body is queered through the exploration of ageing female sexuality. In her diva performances, age becomes the queering factor: it is through her simultaneous enactment of ageing and agelessness that normative notions of ageing femininity are subverted.

But her queering of what ageing means for the female pop star is also a queering of the diva trope itself. Jones demonstrates that 'the diva' is indeed a successful performance strategy for the ageing female pop star, but she does so by reconfiguring what it means to be a diva in one's 60s. With her queering of the maternal she transgresses the gender transgression of the diva by partially embracing normative womanhood, but the images this conjures up serve a subversive purpose: they reconstruct Jones' humanity in her later years, drawing on discourses which have previously been negated in her public construction and circulation. Furthermore, the subversion of popular perceptions about her through a complex, momentary return to normative womanhood functions as a queering of the diva myth and its gendered expectations. The 'Williams Blood' music video serves as a visual reminder of Jones' disco diva past and institutes her diva present, which is enriched by moments of nude vulnerability in *Dazed & Confused* that dismantle the myth of the 'ageless' diva. This complex interplay between the diva myth or trajectory and Jones' adaptation of it, alongside her various negotiations of ageing and her ageing body both through the visual and the lyrical, effectively demonstrate that although it is not necessarily foreseen by the myth itself, the diva trope can indeed be a successful performing strategy for ageing female pop stars. Indeed, perhaps it is even necessary to queer the diva myth in order to enhance one's pop music career. And with another album in the process of being recorded at the time of writing (October 2014), Grace Jones seems still living proof of the longevity and appeal of the diva, both for fans and performers.

Note

1. Images available online at http://www.dazeddigital.com/artsandculture/article/1273/1/chris-cunningham-photographs-grace-jones-for-dc

References

Anderson, C.G. (1993) 'En Route to Transnational Postmodernism: Grace Jones, Josephine Baker and the African Diaspora', *Social Science Information*, 32 (3), pp. 491–512.

Anon (2008) 'Chris Cunningham Photographs Grace Jones for D&C', *Dazed & Confused*, available at http://www.dazeddigital.com/artsandculture/article/1273/1/chris-cunningham-photographs-grace-jones-for-dc

Bradshaw, M. (2008) 'Devouring the Diva: Martyrdom as Feminist Backlash in *The Rose*', *Camera Obscura*, 23(1), pp. 69–87.

Butler, J. (1990) *Gender Trouble: Feminism and the Subversion of Identity* (London: Routledge).

Doty, A. (2007) 'Introduction: There's Something about Mary', *Camera Obscura*, 22(2), pp. 1–8.

Gardner, A. (2012) 'Framing Grace: Shock and Awe at the Ageless Black Body', in R. Jennings and A. Gardner (eds) *Rock On: Women, Ageing and Popular Music* (Farnham: Ashgate Publishing Ltd), pp. 65–83.

Gilleard, C. and Higgs, P. (2013) *Ageing, Corporeality and Embodiment* (London: Anthem Press).

Gorton, K. and Garde-Hansen, J. (2013) 'From Old Media Whore to New Media Troll: The Online Negotiation of Madonna's Ageing Body', *Feminist Media Studies*, 13(2), pp. 288–302.

Guzman, M. J. (2010)'"Pull Up to the Bumper": Fashion and Queerness in Grace Jones's One Man Show', in C. E. Henderson (ed.) *Imagining the Black Female Body: Reconciling Image in Print and Visual Culture* (Basingstoke: Palgrave Macmillan), pp. 79–93.

Halberstam, J. (2005) *In a Queer Time and Place: Transgender Bodies, Subcultural Lives* (New York: New York University Press).

Holloway, F. C. and Demetrakopoulos, S. (1997) 'Remembering Our Foremothers: Older Black Women, Politics of Age, Politics of Survival as Embodied in the Novels of Toni Morrison', in M. Pearsall (ed.) *The Other Within Us: Feminist Explorations of Women and Aging* (New York: Perseus), pp. 177–195.

James, R. (2008) '"Robo-Diva R&B": Aesthetics, Politics, and Black Female Robots in Contemporary Popular Music', *Journal of Popular Music Studies*, 20(4), pp. 402–423.

Jennings, R. (2012) 'It's All Just a Little Bit of History Repeating: Pop Stars, Audiences, Performance and Ageing – Exploring the Performance Strategies of Shirley Bassey and Petula Clark', in R. Jennings and A. Gardner (eds) *Rock On: Women, Ageing and Popular Music* (Farnham: Ashgate Publishing Ltd), pp. 35–51.

Lobato, R. (2007) 'Amazing Grace: Decadence, Deviance, Disco', *Camera Obscura*, 22(2), pp. 134–139.

Kershaw, M. (1997) 'Postcolonialism and Androgyny: The Performance Art of Grace Jones', *Art Journal*, 56(4), pp. 19–25.

Martin, R. (2012) 'Outrageous Agers: Performativity and Transgression: Take One', in E. Tincknell and J. M. Dolan (eds) *Aging Femininities: Troubling Representations* (Newcastle: Cambridge Scholars), pp. 97–112.

O'Neill, E. R. (2007) 'The M-m-mama of Us All: Divas and the Cultural Logic of Late Ca(m)pitalism', *Camera Obscura*, 22(2), pp. 11–37.

Royster, F. T. (2012) *Sounding Like a No-No?: Queer Sounds and Eccentric Acts in the Post-Soul Era* (Ann Arbor: University of Michigan Press).

Sawyer, M. (2008) 'State of Grace', *The Observer*, 11 October 2008. Available at http://www.theguardian.com/music/2008/oct/12/grace-jones-hurricane

Sedgwick, E. K. (1994) *Tendencies* (London: Routledge).

Springer, K. (2007) 'Divas, Evil Black Bitches, and Bitter Black Women: African American Women in Postfeminist and Post-Civil-Rights Popular Culture', in: Y. Tasker and D. Negra (eds) *Interrogating Postfeminism: Gender and the Politics of Popular Culture* (Durham, N. C.: Duke University Press), pp. 249–276.

7

From the Woman Who 'Had It All' to the Tragic, Ageing Spinster: The Shifting Star Persona of Jennifer Aniston

Susan Berridge

In a montage episode of *Friends* (NBC, 1994–2004), 'The One Where They All Turn 30' (7.14), Rachel (Jennifer Aniston) sits down to a birthday breakfast with her friends and 24-year-old boyfriend, surrounded by colourful balloons. Dressed in a plain white T-shirt and pyjama bottoms, with shoulder-length bobbed hair and wearing a child's birthday crown, her youthful girlishness is highlighted. Yet, while the episode underlines Rachel's youth, it simultaneously suggests that she is at an inappropriate life stage in relation to her age. Rachel's narrative in the episode revolves around her anxieties about getting older without having achieved any of her self-imposed life goals – goals that include meeting a man, getting married and having children. Reinforcing the idea of Rachel as in a state of arrested development, she is currently living in Joey (Matt LeBlanc) and Chandler's (Matthew Perry) former apartment, a space that connotes immaturity in the series more widely – connected as it is with bachelor and often childish lifestyles. In keeping with the generic conventions of the sitcom, Rachel's response to turning 30 is portrayed as a comedic overreaction. Yet, the narrative ultimately culminates with Rachel splitting up with her boyfriend to concentrate instead on her realising her long-term aims. In doing so, the episode clearly articulates some of the central tenets of postfeminist discourses of ageing and 'time crisis', which measure success through the attainment of particular life goals such as marriage and motherhood (Negra, 2009).

What is striking about the episode is the disjuncture between Rachel's life and Aniston's life at the time that it aired. The episode was broadcast for the first time in early 2001, at a point when Aniston was 31 and newly married to A-List film star Brad Pitt. Thus, at the same time that Rachel fretted over her 'temporal failure', Aniston was arguably the poster girl for 'having it all' – the envied haircut, the highly successful television career, the youthful girl-next-door good looks, the dream husband, and with it, implicitly, the prospect of 'starting a family'. Significantly, this was reversed just a few years later. Rachel ended up by the finale of *Friends*, broadcast in 2004, with her 'happy ending', having reunited with the father of her daughter and long-time on-off love interest Ross. In contrast, Aniston was facing an imminent separation from Pitt, amidst rumours of his affair with Angelina Jolie. Accordingly, her star image suddenly and dramatically shifted from the girl to aspire to, to the doomed and ageing singleton, all while she was still in her (early) 30s.

Currently, in the landscape of female celebrity, Aniston constitutes one of the most important discursive sites for anxieties around gender, age and chronological propriety. It is difficult to think of equivalent female celebrities who have remained unwed and childfree into their 40s and been such permanent fixtures on the front covers of celebrity gossip and women's magazines as Aniston. As Diane Negra notes, 'In postfeminist culture the single woman stands as the most conspicuously time-beset example of contemporary femininity, her singlehood encoded as a particularly temporal failure and a drifting off course from the normative stages of the female lifecycle' (2009: 61). Despite now being engaged to be married to Justin Theroux, at the time of writing in late 2014, Aniston continues to be positioned as a high-profile exemplar of precisely this 'temporal failure' outlined by Negra. Examining interviews conducted with the star in women's magazines as well as coverage of Aniston in celebrity gossip and entertainment magazines from both the UK and US, and focusing predominantly on the period following her split with Pitt in 2005, this chapter will explore Aniston's shifting star persona in more depth, situating this discussion in relation to postfeminist discourses of ageing. I argue that Aniston can be seen as emblematic of how the ageing, unwed and childfree woman has been treated by popular culture at a particular moment in time at the start of the new millennium and thus, offers a crucial case study to explore the powerful and punishing ways in which gender intersects with critical discourses of ageing.

Ageing, Celebrity Studies and feminism

Su Holmes and Negra foreground the gendered differences in the media treatment of male and female celebrities, particularly when they 'fall from grace', arguing that there is a heavy emphasis on policing inappropriate or 'out of bounds' behaviour in women in the current media climate (2011: 2). Significantly, this idea of 'out of bounds' behaviour is inextricably linked to gendered notions of temporal propriety, and yet in both feminist and Celebrity Studies, age has been less carefully attended to than other forms of identity. The relative lack of scholarship that considers the relationship between ageing, gender and stardom is all the more surprising given what is at stake, particularly for 'older' female celebrities who typically lose visibility as they age.

As Holmes and Negra note, Celebrity Studies and feminist studies have not traditionally been seen as 'natural bedfellows', partly due to the way in which celebrity culture often focuses on the intense scrutiny and judgement of the physical appearance of female celebrities (2011: 14). Moreover, contemporary feminist studies of stardom have tended to focus on *young* female stars, reflecting the way in which celebrity culture itself privileges youth. Celebrity culture and Western culture more widely are marked by a fear of ageing, which is typically constructed as a kind of 'trauma', 'linked to a prevailing but increasingly, if problematically, contested understanding of age primarily in terms of decline and disintegration rather than accumulation and growth' (Wearing, 2007: 280).

Yvonne Tasker and Negra suggest that 'the ambivalence about aging that strongly characterizes such fictions is also extended to feminism itself. As postfeminism has raised the premium on youthfulness, it has installed an image of feminism as "old" (and by extension moribund)' (2007: 11). This is not necessarily a new phenomenon. Kathleen Woodward argues that 'ageism is entrenched within feminism itself', using the 1980s example of lesbian feminists feeling alienated by the women's movement due to their older age (1999: xi). That said, the notion or construction of second-wave feminism as outdated and redundant has certainly become increasingly pronounced in more recent years with the rise of postfeminist culture.

Notably, there is no common consensus over what the term 'postfeminism' entails. It can be interpreted in vastly different ways depending on a particular scholar's political beliefs, with some criticising the term for implying that the goals of feminism have already been achieved and others viewing the term more positively as a useful descriptor for recent changes in the media representation of women (Gill, 2007). Importantly, generational difference becomes central to these debates. There may be no common agreement on what postfeminism entails, but it is nevertheless differentiated from second-wave, or 'older', feminism. Charlotte Brunsdon explains that second-wave feminism often becomes the other

of postfeminist women, who falsely demonise this earlier, older generation for repressing all sense of difference between women and for being
excessively hostile (2006: 43).

In her analysis of screen representations of 'older' women, Sadie
Wearing questions connections between the '"aging" of feminism and
culturally authoritative narratives and anxieties over age more generally' (2007: 280). Wearing's chapter is one of a number of more recent
feminist studies examining the links between gender and age in relation
to older female celebrities (see also Tally, 2008; Morley, 2011; Jermyn,
2011, 2012a). This growing interest in ageing is further evidenced by the
2012 special issue of *Celebrity Studies*, introduced by Deborah Jermyn and
entitled 'Back in the Spotlight: Female Celebrity and Ageing' (2012b).
Many of the women discussed in this scholarship – including stars such
as Diane Keaton and Meryl Streep – are notably older than Aniston by a
few decades, pointing to the importance of recognising the subjectivity
of ageing and what constitutes an 'older woman' (Jermyn, 2012b). Age
is not a fixed category but is instead constantly shifting, particularly
in recent years as postfeminist culture has given license, and indeed
made it aspirational, for women to be youthful and girly at an older age
(Jermyn, 2012b: 1). And yet, despite the fact that Aniston is younger
than many of the female stars discussed in this emerging academic criticism, it remains striking that media coverage of the star still repeatedly
draws attention to her age and holds her age-accountable in ways that
equivalent male stars are not. Thus, Aniston is a vital example to use to
develop this recent scholarship further. This chapter will pay particular
attention to the way in which extratextual discourses of the star intersect with (gendered) discourses of ageing.

Acting your age, looking your shoe size

Postfeminist media culture is characterised by an intense preoccupation
with the body, particularly the female body, and underpinned by themes
of self-surveillance, monitoring and discipline (Gill, 2007: 6). This is no
more evident than in the celebrity gossip industry, which focuses on
the scrutiny and judgement of the female celebrity, examining these
stars in order to discern how effectively they have managed to evade the
physical signs of ageing and thus conform to normative postfeminist
constructions of youthful beauty (Fairclough, 2012: 90). This scrutiny is
motivated by a fetishisation of youth where ageing is 'imagined less as
an inevitable, natural process than as a moral failing' (Wearing, 2007:
287). In postfeminist culture, the onus for maintaining a youthful

appearance lies firmly with the individual female, with extended girl-hood offered as a fantasy for everyone regardless of their age (Tasker and Negra, 2007: 18).

Reflecting this contemporary obsession with youth, articles on Aniston commonly begin by mentioning her age and include discussions of her appearance as is typical with female celebrities of all ages, most often praising her youthful looks and positioning her as someone to aspire to. An interview with the star in *Elle* notes that, 'In flip-flops, snug Generra jeans, and a black T-shirt stamped with a skull sticking a red tongue out at the world, Aniston, 36, doesn't look old enough to drink. She has smooth, tawny skin, and thick, caramel-color hair pin-streaked with blond frames her small face' (Milea, 2005). While this article was written in 2005, the celebration of Aniston's youthful appearance persists a decade on. A relatively recent interview with Aniston and Paul Rudd in *GQ* starts by noting that 'both look astonishingly the same as they did two decades ago' (Martin, 2012). *GQ* featured another article on Aniston a year later, heralding her as 'Woman of the Week' and noting that Aniston seems 'to be living in some alternate universe where time stands still', illustrating the piece with three images of Aniston at 36, 40 and 43 years old (Clark, 2013).

This aspirational praise of Aniston's youthful appearance is often coupled with criticism of how much she spends to achieve this look, pointing to a key paradox at the heart of celebrity and postfeminist culture. Kirsty Fairclough (2012) highlights the precarious balance that must be achieved by female celebrities between maintaining youthful beauty and not appearing to try too hard for fear of seeming desperate. Fairclough identifies the 'desperate' as a category constructed by the gossip industry and applied to celebrities over 40 who are 'configured as desperate to remain youthful in order to suspend time and reclaim their once glittering careers and images, but are often constructed as failing at both' (2012: 97). With this failure, these celebrities tend to be maligned in the popular press, their attempts at maintaining a youthful appearance via cosmetic surgical procedures taking precedence over their actual work (ibid.). Similarly, Wearing argues that, 'A very familiar double standard seems to be in operation in a culture that finds the signs of age in female bodies grotesque, laughable, and fearful (and makes a spectacle out of them) but equally mistrusts the efforts to efface those signs' (2007: 290).

While Aniston is typically seen to be ageing well and in 'acceptable ways', she nonetheless faces denigration for not being fully transparent in her efforts to evade the ageing process (Fairclough, 2012: 98). In 2014,

InTouch ran a piece which noted incredulously the price Aniston pays to maintain her youthful demeanour ('Say What?!: Jennifer Aniston Spends $8K a Month on Beauty Treatments to Keep Justin Theroux'), adding that she has 'been secretly spending thousands of dollars to stay looking young' and promising to reveal her secrets (Cooper, 2014). The use of the word 'secretly' here evokes the sense of mistrust and deceit around the efforts used to remain looking young. More significantly, the article positions Aniston as someone who *must* stave off the signs of ageing in order to *keep her man*. This reflects the way in which post-feminist culture evokes anxieties around ageing, suggesting that not maintaining a youthful appearance will result in romantic rejection and drawing heavily upon discourses of personal responsibility. Here, the onus for defying ageing is firmly placed on Aniston, containing any broader discussions of gendered inequalities.

This example speaks to one of the central contradictions in the way that discourses of ageing are evoked in media coverage of Aniston's star persona, particularly following her separation from Pitt. Aniston is widely praised for maintaining the physical signs of youth – with articles mentioning her smooth, unblemished skin, shiny hair and taut body – but at the same time, she is also frequently positioned in the popular press as a high-profile exemplar of the dangers of not achieving particular gendered life goals by a certain age. While postfeminism may offer fantasies of 'age-transcendence' in terms of *looking* young, there are simultaneously strict limits imposed on temporal propriety and, specifically, on matching women's age with the appropriate (and highly gendered) life stage (Negra, 2009: 14). As Negra identifies, 'one of the signature attributes of postfeminist culture is its ability to define various female life stages within the parameters of "time panic"', as evidenced in the aforementioned *Friends* episode (Negra, 2009: 47). Postfeminist culture suggests that the solution to this time crisis lies in becoming more feminine, by finding a (heteronormative) romantic partner and having a baby, thus 'forcefully renewing conservative social ideologies centering on the necessity of marriage for young women and the glori-fication of pregnancy' (Negra, 2009: 47). Although postfeminist culture celebrates the notion of choice and empowerment for women, these choices are deeply constrained and limited.

While Aniston has not been subject to quite the same degree of public scrutiny, in relation to whether she has or has not had cosmetic surgery, as other 'older' female stars, she is nevertheless often on the receiving end of a different kind of 'biological' scrutiny, with near constant speculation over her (in)fertility. This emphasis on Aniston's (in)fertility highlights further the gendered nature of ageing celebrity discourses, drawing attention to the way that female stars are expected to account for their age and equivalent life stage in ways that male stars need not. Even before Aniston separated from Pitt, there was frequent media speculation about whether she was pregnant yet and, if not, why not (cf. the covers of numerous *UsWeekly* magazines from the early 2000s which reveal a near constant obsession with Aniston's fertility, asking of Pitt and Aniston in 2002 'will they ever have babies?' and stressing the couple's baby struggles two years later as a reason for their split). Similarly, a 2002 article in *Time Europe*, albeit mocking the media obsession with Aniston's fertility, nonetheless began by stating that Aniston and Pitt were not yet trying for a baby (Cagle and Won Tesoriero, 2002).

The media's obsession with Aniston's fertility has intensified as she has moved into her 40s. For example, a recent issue of *UsWeekly* focuses on new rumours about whether Aniston is pregnant with Theroux's child (Lee, 2014). Reflecting upon the sexist and ageist logics that underpin contemporary celebrity culture, Holmes and Negra maintain that, 'When female celebrity life choices and personal circumstances do not fit (or no longer fit) within a "family values" script, one option is for them to be cast in the mode of another postfeminist archetype, the "sad singleton"' (2011: 8). They directly cite Aniston as an example of such a celebrity who is treated with dismay. Where marriage and motherhood are equated with full womanhood, postfeminist culture perpetuates the notion that unwed, childless women's lives are somehow lacking and/or not yet underway.

In media coverage of the star following her separation from Pitt, she is overwhelmingly cast as a victim, someone to be pitied. While it is widely accepted that Pitt instigated their split, in discussions of Aniston's love life prior to her engagement to Theroux, there is little sense that singleness and/or childlessness (childfree-ness) might be an active or desirable choice on her part. Interviews directly following her separation frequently adopt a sentimental and mournful tone. Exemplifying this, her famous 2005 interview with *Vanity Fair* – the first interview she gave following the break up – includes the line: 'a testament to both [Pitt's] passion for architecture and the couple's hopeful vision of their shared future, the beautiful old house awaited only a baby in a bassinet to complete a picture-perfect existence... Instead of the joyful announcement many had anticipated from the Pitts, there was only silence'(Bennetts, 2005), again echoing the notion of normative, gendered life stages.

Gossip magazines similarly position Aniston as someone to be pitied. *UsWeekly* covers in the years immediately following her separation have repeatedly emphasised Aniston's inability to find a new romantic partner, almost always positioning her as a victim in each new relationship: an issue from 16 October 2006 talks about 'why Vince left Jen', referring to her relatively brief relationship with fellow actor Vince Vaughn, while 25 December 2006's issue announced that 'Jen Suffers Another Humiliating Split'. An issue dated 30 July 2007 aligned Aniston with Jessica Simpson and Cameron Diaz, asking 'Why Can't They Find Love: Beautiful, Rich and Alone', while later issues focus on Angelina Jolie 'torturing' and spreading 'nasty rumors' about Aniston (19 November 2008 and 23 November 2009, respectively). The notion of Aniston as victim in her own love life has decreased slightly since her engagement to Theroux, yet even now, gossip magazines frequently suggest that their relationship might be troubled. For example, the cover of 13 December 2013's issue of *Grazia* announced: 'Jen and Justin: Split Rumours Hot Up' (Amer, 2013).

Paradoxically, while Aniston is cast as the victim in these discussions suggesting a lack of agency and control, at the same time, this is accompanied by suggestions that it was her career-minded attitude that cost her her marriage to Pitt and any subsequent children. The implication here is that Aniston mismanaged her timings. By allowing herself to be distracted from the imperative to start a family at the sanctioned point in the timetable of normative femininity, she is now seen to be paying the price years later. At times, Aniston has attempted to highlight the inherent sexism underpinning the notion that she was to blame for her break up, arguing in *Elle* that 'a man divorcing would never be accused of choosing career over children' (Hahn, 2009). But almost in the same breath, she then reaffirms heteronormative life goals such as motherhood, stating: 'I've never in my life said I didn't want to have children. I did and I do and I will!...I've always wanted to have children, and I would never give up that experience for a career. I want to have it all' (Hahn, 2009).

Notably, victimhood is the antithesis of postfeminism, as it exposes the failure to take advantage of possibilities of empowerment – of 'having it all' – supposedly available to women in the contemporary era, regardless of their age. Aniston emphatically rejects the term, arguing in *Vanity Fair* that 'to live in a victim place is pointing a finger at someone else, as if you have no control' (Bennetts, 2005). Instead, she commonly positions herself as someone to be *empathised* with, rather than sympathised with. This is clearly evidenced in a 2009 interview in *Elle* in which she argues that, 'I support women, men, anybody who is in a place that's not their strongest and who is ready to push forward. So if

I'm the emblem for *this is what it looks like to be the lonely girl getting on with her life*, so be it...Don't we all have days when we feel lonely...?' (Hahn, 2009, original emphasis). Her use of the term 'we' here works to align her with any person who has experienced heartache, thus underlining the universality of her situation. Aniston's star image more widely is predicated on the notion of her being accessible, and this accessibility notably hinges on connotations of authenticity and youthfulness. Aniston positions herself as the inherently low-maintenance, girl next door, reinforced by her preference for simple (albeit expensive, designer) outfits and 'natural', low-key (yet highly groomed) styling when at red carpet events.

Paradoxically, further emphasising her accessibility and ordinariness, her similarity to Rachel Green in *Friends* is also often emphasised in interviews, thus capitalising on the domestic, intimate nature of the television medium and the intense forms of identification it can promote (Ellis, 1982). Her *Vanity Fair* interview includes the line '"I haven't been feeling emotional lately, really I haven't," she wails, fluttering her hands like Rachel Green in distress' (Bennetts, 2005). Parallels between Aniston and Rachel persist to the current day. For example, when Aniston sported a shorter haircut in 2013, *UsWeekly* ran a nostalgic article about 'The Rachel', her iconic layered haircut that she debuted in *Friends* back in 1994 (Eggenberger, 2013). As these analogies to Rachel evoke a period when Aniston was in her mid-20s to early 30s, they arguably add to the sense of chronological failure underpinning contemporary discussions of the star. With the closure of *Friends* in 2004, Rachel remains perpetually 35, with a daughter and partner, in stark contrast to the route that Aniston's life has taken since. If *Friends* encouraged viewers to root for Rachel's eventual romantic union with on-off love interest Ross (David Schwimmer) over the series' ten seasons, then it is interesting to consider whether this long-term investment in Rachel's love life has been transposed onto Aniston following the series' end.

Significantly, the shift in Aniston's star persona from the girl who 'had it all' to the ageing, pitiful singleton coincided with the end of her hugely popular portrayal of Rachel and a move from television towards film roles, many of which draw thematic parallels to her personal life. Arguably, the success of Aniston's films pales in significance to extratextual discussions of her private life, a pattern that is true of many female stars (Geraghty, 2000). Articles that purport to promote one of her upcoming films frequently detour into discussions of her previous relationship with Pitt, her rivalry with Jolie, her love life and/or her (in)fertility. Yet Aniston's private and professional lives cannot be read as entirely separate. Richard Dyer notes that traditionally 'the roles and/ or the performance of a star in a film were taken as revealing the personality of the star' (1979: 22 cited in Jermyn, 2006: 73).

Arguably, Aniston is most well-known for her roles in romantic comedies, which several scholars have identified as a particularly conducive genre for representing 'older' women (Tally, 2008; Wearing, 2007; Jermyn, 2011, 2012a; Morley, 2011). Negra argues that temporal anxiety is a common feature of contemporary romantic comedies, noting that in these films, management of the ageing process and, specifically, achieving the 'appropriate' postfeminist life goals – falling in love, getting married, having children – are positioned as key to personal fulfilment (Negra, 2009: 53). Many of Negra's examples prominently feature Aniston as the central love interest, including *Along Came Polly* (Hamburg, 2004) and *Bruce Almighty* (Shadyac, 2003), as well as *Picture Perfect* (Gordon Caron, 1997).

Picture Perfect offers an interesting example of how Aniston's fictional roles embody the same fears around temporal failure as the extratextual discourses surrounding her personal life. Even though this was her first starring film role, released in 1997 when Aniston was 28 years old, and before she met Pitt, it still emphasises temporal anxieties. Aniston plays Kate, an independent, single woman working at a successful advertising firm. While she is vocal about her enjoyment at being single and self-sufficient, she finds herself struggling to progress at work due to the fact that she has not yet attained any of the key markers of maturity – her own car, house, a husband, children – while her mother (played by Olympia Dukakis) constantly pressures her to get married and give her a grandchild.

In Aniston's later roles, particularly her roles following her split from Pitt, this sense of urgency around achieving key life goals 'in time' increases. In 2006, she starred in *The Break-Up* (Reed, 2006) with her real-life-boyfriend-at-the-time, Vince Vaughn, followed by *He's Just Not That Into You* (Kwapis, 2009) in which she plays a woman longing for her reluctant boyfriend to propose; *The Switch* (Gordon and Speck, 2010, co-produced by Aniston), in which she plays an unmarried 40-year-old desperate for a baby; and *We're the Millers* (Thurber, 2013), which features Aniston as an ageing, single stripper who becomes a surrogate mother to two teenagers. Interviews with the star often identify the parallels between her personal life and professional roles. For example, 'she deserves better than getting-the-guy flicks. Aniston can tell you all about getting the guy. She deserved better than that, too.' (Milea, 2005). Aniston herself did the same in a humorous speech delivered at the 2009

Women in Film Awards where she traced connections between her life offscreen and her film titles, ending by joking, 'If any of you have a project called "Everlasting Love with an Adult Stable Male", just go to my table'.

If these roles all feature Aniston playing women who are longing for romantic commitment and children as they grow older, the flipside to this are her roles as a predatory, older single woman in the films *Horrible Bosses* (Gordon, 2011) and *Horrible Bosses 2* (Anders, 2014) as well as in her 2008 guest role in the television sitcom *30 Rock* (NBC, 2006–2013) in which she plays a wild, unhinged party 'girl', made an object of disgust because she is now too old for such an irresponsible, chaotic lifestyle (3.03 'The One with the Cast of *Night Court*'). In these latter roles she is less interested in commitment than in, respectively, casual sex and desperately clinging to the lifestyle of her youth. What all these roles have in common, regardless of whether Aniston's characters are portrayed as longing for romantic monogamy or simply looking for no-strings-attached sex, is an emphasis on chronological decorum (or lack of it). The humour in her roles in *Horrible Bosses* and its sequel as well as in *30 Rock* partly derives from the age-inappropriateness of her behaviour, thereby reaffirming the normativity of postfeminist life stages.

As Rebecca Williams notes in her insightful analysis of Drew Barrymore's shifting star persona, generic expectation can undermine the idea of the star as author of their own image (2007: 117). In Aniston's case, while she frequently and emphatically rejects the construction of herself as a romantic 'victim' and, more recently, has been outspoken about how much she enjoys being in her 40s, her ability to construct her star image on these terms could be seen to be restricted by the kinds of roles she plays. However, I hesitate to suggest that Aniston has no agency in the way that her persona has been constructed. For example, it is difficult to know with certainty whether these are the only roles she is offered, or conversely, whether she actively chooses to play these kinds of parts. Arguably, her 'unlucky in love' image reinforces her commercial interests, illustrated by the close parallels between her film roles and star persona and her enduring presence on the front covers of women's and gossip magazines, many of which have close ties with the film industry and its promotional needs. It is not as simple, then, as the press constructing an image of Aniston as someone to be pitied and Aniston then challenging this reading. Although Aniston rejects the victim role, at the same time, she often reaffirms the hegemonic equation of personal fulfilment with heteronormative marriage and motherhood.

However, even if Aniston does play a part in the way that her star image is constructed, what does this say about the kinds of choices offered to single women of a particular age in Hollywood? Aniston may have remained firmly in the public sphere following her divorce, but this has been accompanied by near constant judgement of her appearance and life choices, particularly her lack of children. As Negra asserts, 'postfeminism might be seen as particularly punishing in its relation to single women, having raised their cultural profile though without any corresponding enlargement of their status/options' (2009: 10).

The simultaneous celebration/repudiation of the older, single woman reflected in Aniston's film roles and extratextual discourses surrounding the star is emblematic of a postfeminist sensibility which both fetishises youth and offers promises of age-transcendence, while at the same time measuring success in relation to strict temporal management. Aniston's 'temporal failure' is variously positioned in gossip and women's magazines as beyond her control and as her responsibility, highlighting the contradictions and complexities underpinning postfeminist culture, which both celebrates women's empowerment and the notion of choice while at the same time cautioning against female autonomy by implying that independence may lead to emotional isolation (Tasker and Negra, 2007). Just as postfeminism embraces the notion of choice, at the same time, it individualises these choices, suggesting that the responsibility for 'having it all' lies firmly with the individual woman. This implication, in turn, obscures any broader discussions of gendered inequalities (Gill, 2007: 12). It is worth noting that there is no equivalent emphasis on ageing and 'time crisis' circulating around male celebrities; George Clooney's unmarried and childless status up until 2014, for example, was configured in the media not as failure but as evidence of his still being engagingly footloose, even into his 50s.

It is important to recognise that Aniston's star image is open to polysemic interpretations. Hers is also a dynamic persona that is subject to change, particularly at the present moment in light of her current engagement. More detailed research needs to be undertaken into how audiences engage with the extratextual discourses surrounding the star. Yet, nevertheless, through looking at a range of women's, gossip and entertainment magazine coverage of the star from both the UK and US, important patterns begin to emerge. These patterns point to the way in which female celebrities have become a key site upon which anxieties about ageing and femininity, and particularly in Aniston's case marriage and motherhood, are played out (Fairclough, 2012: 90–91). Looking at the extratextual discourses surrounding Aniston reveals that postfeminist culture intersects powerfully with representations of singleness in a way that limits the kinds of stories being told about single women (Taylor, 2012). For all the rhetoric of 'choice' that underpins postfeminism, remaining unwed and childless/childfree beyond a certain age does not appear to be one of them.

References

Amer, C. (2013) 'Jen and Justin: Split Rumours Hot Up', 13 December, *Grazia* online, available at http://www.graziadaily.co.uk/LatestIssue/in-this-weeks-issue – jen – -justin-split-rumours-hot-up-plus-the-latest-on-nigellas-court-drama [accessed October 29 2014].

Anon (2002–2014) 'Jennifer Aniston's *UsWeekly* Covers', available at http://www.usmagazine.com/celebrity-news/pictures/jennifer-anistons-us-weekly-covers-201382/28166 [accessed 21 October 2014].

Bennetts, L. (2005) 'The Unsinkable Jennifer Aniston', September, *Vanity Fair* online, available at http://www.vanityfair.com/culture/features/2005/09/aniston200509 [accessed 6 May 2013].

Brunsdon, C. (2006) 'The Feminist in the Kitchen: Martha, Martha and Nigella', in J. Hollows and R. Moseley (eds) *Feminism in Popular Culture* (Oxford and New York: Berg), pp. 41–56.

Cagle, J. and Won Tesoriero, H. (2002) 'Oh-So-Sunny in Friends, Aniston Gets Serious in Her New Film', 18 November, *Time Europe*, 160(21), p. 66.

Clark, D. (2013) 'Woman of the Week: Jennifer Aniston', 15 February, *GQ* online, available at http://www.gq.com/blogs/the-feed/2013/02/woman-of-the-week-jennifer-aniston.html [accessed 20 October 2014]

Cooper, D. (2014) 'Say What?! Jennifer Aniston Spends $8K a Month on Beauty Treatments to Keep Justin Theroux', 31 March, *InTouch* online, available at http://www.intouchweekly.com/posts/jennifer-aniston-spends-8k-a-month-on-beauty-treatments-to-keep-justin-theroux-36656 [accessed 20 October 2014].

Dyer, R. (1979) *Stars* (London: BFI).

Eggenberger, N. (2013) 'Jennifer Aniston Would Rather Shave Her Head Than Have "The Rachel" Cut Again', 13 August, *UsWeekly* online, available at http://www.usmagazine.com/celebrity-beauty/news/jennifer-aniston-would-rather-shave-her-head-than-have-the-rachel-cut-again-2013138 [accessed 10 December 2014].

Ellis, J. (1982) *Visible Fictions: Cinema, Television, Video* (London: Routledge).

Fairclough, K. (2012) 'Nothing Less Than Perfect: Female Celebrity, Ageing and Hyper-scrutiny in the Gossip Industry'. *Celebrity Studies*, 3(1), pp. 90–103.

Geraghty, C. (2000) 'Re-examining Stardom: Questions of Texts, Bodies and Performance', in S. Redmond and S. Holmes (eds) *Stardom and Celebrity: A Reader* (London: Sage), pp. 98–110.

Gill, R. (2007) 'Postfeminist Media Culture: Elements of a Sensibility', *European Journal of Cultural Studies*, 10(2), pp. 147–166.

Hahn, K. (2009) 'Jennifer Aniston: Hollywood's Sweetheart Reveals the Calm Behind the Storm the Tabloids Have Created', 4 August, *Elle (UK)* online, available at http://www.elle.com/pop-culture/cover-shoots/jennifer-aniston-361331 [accessed 6 May 2013].

Holmes, S. and Negra, D. (2011) (eds) 'Introduction', in *In the Limelight and Under the Microscope: Forms and Functions of Female Celebrity* (New York and London: Continuum), pp. 1–16.

Jermyn, D. (2006) 'Bringing out the ! in You': SJP, Carrie Bradshaw and the Evolution of Television Stardom', in S. Holmes and S. Redmond (eds) *Framing Celebrity: New Directions in Celebrity Culture* (Oxon and New York: Routledge), pp. 67–85.

Jermyn, D. (2011) 'Unlikely Heroines?: "Women of a Certain Age" and Romantic Comedy', *Cineaction*, pp. 26–33.

Jermyn, D. (2012a) '"Glorious, Glamorous and That Old Standby, Amorous": The Late Blossoming of Diane Keaton's Romantic Comedy Career', *Celebrity Studies*, 3(1), pp. 37–51.

Jermyn, D. (2012b) '"Get a Life, Ladies. Your Old One Is Not Coming Back": Ageing, Ageism and the Lifespan of the Female Celebrity', *Celebrity Studies*, 3(1), pp. 1–12.

Lee, E. (2014) 'Jennifer Aniston Is Not Pregnant with Justin Theroux's Baby: Sources Debunk New Rumour', 2 May, *UsWeekly* online, available at http://www.usmagazine.com/celebrity-news/news/jennifer-aniston-not-pregnant-with-justin-therouxs-baby-sources-say-201425#ixzz373TbBrKQ [accessed 20 October 2014].

Martin, B. (2012) 'I Love You, Wo-Man', 14 February, *GQ* online, available at http://www.gq.com/entertainment/movies-and-tv/201203/jennifer-aniston-paul-rudd-gq-march-2012-cover-story [accessed 6 May 2013].

Milea, H. (2005) 'The Better Girl: Jennifer Aniston Dishes on Vince, Clive and Her "Sexy Little House"', 3 October, *Elle (UK)* online, available at http://www.elle.com/pop-culture/cover-shoots/the-better-girl-19474 [accessed May 6 2013].

Morley, A. (2011) 'Grotesquerie as Marker of Success in Aging Female Stars', in S. Holmes and D. Negra (eds) *In the Limelight and Under the Microscope: Forms and Functions of Female Celebrity* (NY and London: Continuum), pp. 103–124.

Negra, D. (2009) *What a Girl Wants? Fantasizing the Reclamation of Self in Postfeminism* (Oxon and New York: Routledge).

Tally, M. (2008) 'Something's Gotta Give: Hollywood, Female Sexuality and the "Older Bird" Chick Flick', in S. Ferriss and M. Young (eds) *Chick Flicks: Contemporary Women at the Movies* (New York: Routledge), pp. 119–131.

Tasker, Y. and Negra, D. (2007) (eds) 'Introduction: Feminist Politics and Postfeminist Culture', in *Interrogating Postfeminism: Gender and the Politics of Popular Culture* (Durham, NC: Duke University Press), pp. 1–25.

Taylor, A. (2012) *Single Women in Popular Culture: The Limits of Postfeminism* (Hampshire and New York: Palgrave Macmillan).

Wearing, S. (2007) 'Subjects of Rejuvenation: Aging in Postfeminist Culture', in Y. Tasker and D. Negra (eds) *Interrogating Postfeminism: Gender and the Politics of Popular Culture* (Durham, NC: Duke University Press), pp. 277–310.

Williams, R. (2007) 'From *Beyond Control* to In Control: Investigating Drew Barrymore's Feminist Agency/Authorship', in S. Redmond and S. Holmes (eds) *Stardom and Celebrity: A Reader* (London: Sage), pp. 111–125.

Woodward, K. (1999) (ed.) 'Introduction', in *Figuring Age: Women, Bodies, Generations* (Indiana: Indiana University Press), pp. ix–xxix.

Filmed

Along Came Polly. Directed by John Hamburg. US, 2004.
The Break-Up. Directed by Peyton Reed. US, 2006.
Bruce Almighty. Directed by Tom Shadyac. US, 2003.
Friends. Created by David Crane and Marta Kauffman. US: NBC, 1994–2004.
He's Just Not That Into You. Directed by Ken Kwapis. US, 2009.
Horrible Bosses. Directed by Seth Gordon. US, 2011.
Horrible Bosses 2. Directed by Sean Anders. US, 2014.
Picture Perfect. Directed by Glenn Gordon Caron. US, 1997.
The Switch. Directed by Josh Gordon and Will Speck. US, 2010.
30 Rock. Created by Tina Fey. US: NBC, 2006–2013.
We're the Millers. Directed by Rawson Marshall Thurber. US, 2013.

8

'Don't Wear Beige – It Might Kill You': The Politics of Ageing and Visibility in *Fabulous Fashionistas*

Deborah Jermyn

When I was little, a witch lived on our road. At least, that is what some of the children on our road said. This witch was an old lady who lived in the basement flat of a house on the corner, and my friend Lizzie told me that she had been going past her window one evening and could see straight into her house and she was clearly a witch. What Lizzie had actually seen through the window remained uncertain. But the proof that our neighbour was a witch was most definitely visually evident. The children knew she was a witch because of the way she dressed. She did not look like other old ladies. She dressed to be seen, even though she was old.

Some of the details of this are hazy in my mind now. I *seem* to remember dramatic flowing scarves and a pair of big glasses. But I do remember bright red hair – hair that was clearly dyed, framing an old lady's face, hair that could never have passed as 'natural' at any age. Old ladies were not meant be this way. They were meant to have grey perms, set at the hairdressers, and uniforms of neutral polyester. As Julia Twigg has noted, 'Fashion and age sit uncomfortably together. Fashion inhabits a world of youthful beauty, of fantasy, imagination, allure ... Age by contrast is perceived as a time of greyness, marked by retirement from display or engagement with the erotic and style-conscious' (2013: 1). The old lady who lived on our street was not like that and therefore, the children had pronounced, she was a witch.

Many years down the line, watching Sue Bourne's documentary *Fabulous Fashionistas* broadcast in September 2013, memories of this neighbour came to mind. Shown as part of Channel 4's prestigious *Cutting Edge* series in the UK (1990–), the film explores six women subjects with

a striking *joie de vivre* and an average age of 80, each of whom still maintain a strong sense of individual style and relish the sartorial world. As
children, we had already been able to distinguish our neighbour's 'difference' because, like a number of Bourne's subjects, she had maintained
a distinctive aesthetic presence, an air of splendour that 'regular' old
ladies were not meant to have. We had demonised her because we could
not understand her, because she had not kept to the script of growing
old. I reflected that if I passed her in the street today I would still notice
her, but now, I would want to catch her eye and give her a conspira-
torial nod: I'd want to silently congratulate her, for *not* sticking to the
script. How wonderful and gratifyingly provocative it would seem now,
to see her remaining flamboyant, colourful, and individual – to remain
visible – in later life, in a culture where many older women recurrently
speak about the disquieting, disempowering sensation of becoming
invisible as they age. For it was this kind of delight I felt during *Fabulous
Fashionistas* as I watched, and the stories and styles of Jean, Bridget,
Gillian, Daphne, Sue and Baroness Trumpington unfolded.

I was not alone in my response to the film. During its broadcast the
hashtag #fabfashionistas began trending all over the UK, with *Guardian*
journalist Hadley Freeman and fashion diversity activist Caryn Franklin
both tweeting that this one-off doc merited a whole TV series. 'I can't
remember the last time I saw a documentary as inspiring as *Fabulous
Fashionistas*', enthused Rachel Cooke in the *New Statesman* review
(Cooke, 2013), while Rebecca Nicholson in *The Guardian* called it 'a
delightful, delicate documentary... It's style *and* substance, and it's
lovely' (Nicholson, 2013). Evidently *Fabulous Fashionistas'* depiction of
ageing women as still vibrant, engaging, and refusing to disappear into
the background in the manner in which our culture typically compels
them to do ('Getting old doesn't have to mean going into a care home
and sitting in a circle with one's mouth open and teeth falling out and
all that stuff', as Bridget observes in the film), had struck an important
social chord.[1]

In this chapter, I want to begin to 'uncloak' *Fabulous Fashionistas* and
its seeming cultural impact more closely, as a significant addition to
the limited repertoire of films examining women's experience of ageing.
To do so I draw on reviews, textual analysis, existing scholarship from
fashion and ageing studies, and interviews with the director Sue Bourne
and two of her subjects, Sue Kreitzman and Bridget Sojourner. In doing
this, one of the significant interventions I wish to make, albeit in a
modest fashion, is to challenge the absence of older women's own voices
in what little work exists in the field to date, even while recognising

that the voices that make it to the page here have inevitably undergone mediation, be it via Bourne's edit or my own. I am interested in part here in thinking about some of the cultural afterlife of the film in terms of how it worked to bring its women subjects into the public eye. At the onset of the film the women's pre-existing connections to the world of celebrity are rather different, as I will outline. But following the broadcast, as a result of the film all of them experienced either a renewal of or introduction to public recognition and 'celebrity' – and at precisely the time in their lives when, by virtue of their age and gender, as 'old ladies' they might expect to have the least presence, the least visibility in the public domain, of any major demographic group. I ask, *can the success of the film be entirely embraced as a progressive outcome for older women?* That is, did its positive reception speak, perhaps, to a culture finally ready for more diverse, more affirmative accounts of ageing femininities than our history of delimited and well-worn stereotypes of older women, and the very limited available repertoire of older female celebrities, has allowed? Or was it a reminder that women can only hope to court attention and recognition – throughout the life course – primarily in terms of how they look? In fact, as I will demonstrate and as the women subjects themselves and Bourne argue persuasively, the implied frivolity of the title 'Fabulous Fashionistas' functioned as a kind of culturally acceptable ruse to bring images and narratives about women and ageing that popular culture has rarely facilitated into the public domain.

'Six very different women, six very different wardrobes...': the *Fabulous Fashionistas*

Sue Bourne is one of the UK's leading observational documentary filmmakers, the director and producer of close to 20 documentaries, including the award-winning *My Street* (2009) and *Mum and Me* (2008). Working virtually exclusively through her own production company, Wellpark Productions, her website describes her style of filmmaking as 'almost a brand', and notes 'while [her films] capture the essence of life in contemporary society, in her gentle, thoughtful way Bourne has repeatedly managed to find the "extraordinary in the apparently ordinary"' (Wellpark Productions, n.d.). *Fabulous Fashionistas* has proved to be Bourne's biggest film to date, drawing huge international audiences after it was uploaded to the Internet following the Channel 4 screening.[2] As Bourne tells it, 'Someone somewhere put it up on YouTube, about a million people watched it worldwide before I even realised it was out there. So it became a phenomenon' (2014), while in interview, Sue Kreitzman reflected on how, following the film, 'Anywhere we are in the world, people come up to me. It's a British film, British TV. I'm *astounded* by how many people have seen it' (2015). In conversation, Bourne also explained how the original project that led to *Fabulous Fashionistas* was initially envisaged as a feature film in alliance with renowned US 'Advanced Style' photographer and blogger Ari Seth Cohen. Cohen's website, dedicated to images of the arrestingly debonair older women he spots and photographs around New York, had garnered a massive following and led to a beautifully produced book, also called *Advanced Style* (Cohen, 2012).[3] But after months developing the project and raising funding, problems emerged and 'The access collapsed, which was a bit of a blow. So Channel 4 said, "Why don't you do the film in Britain?"' (Bourne, 2014).

The film is structured round individual profiles of each of the six subjects, featuring Bourne in voice-over narration, while she is also the film's (unseen) interviewer. She tells us a little bit about each subject's back story and biography, asking them about their style, filming them in their regular lives (Jean working in a local boutique and out running; Bridget gardening and practicing tai-chi) and inviting all of them to share some of the contents of their wardrobe. Jean, we learn, met her husband at the age of 15 and had been recently widowed after 56 years together, prompting her to go out and get a job in her 70s whereupon she was hired on the spot by Gap (becoming their oldest employee); Bridget is a former charity health worker, who now campaigns on ageism and diversity (the film shows her challenging a series of model agencies to hire her and end their proclivity for nubile teenagers), who manages to maintain her style on a state pension by frequenting charity shops; Gillian is a highly acclaimed dancer and choreographer (of *Cats* and *Phantom of the Opera* fame), still working at nearly 90, and happily married for decades to a man 27 years younger than she; Daphne is 'the fashion world's go-to older model', who restarted her long dormant modelling career at aged 70 after being widowed; Sue was once a highly successful food writer and TV cook, who abandoned that career to become an artist and curator of folk-style 'outsider-art'; Baroness Trumpington, a former Mayoress of Cambridge, sits in the House of Lords and became an Internet sensation in 2011 after being caught on camera sticking two fingers up at Lord King. Bourne described how the recruitment of her subjects was a long and laborious task, in part because 'style' had to be inscribed as an important aspect of their identity, but also because she insisted they all be 70+ (2014). However, in enforcing this criteria she ensured her film really was about women in the 'advanced' life stages which go so particularly under-represented in popular culture, since

Figure 8.1   Sue Bourne in a media masterclass screening of *Fabulous Fashionistas* at University of Roehampton, 2014

Source: Photo by Toby Shaw

where 'older' women do feature on our screens, it is very often 'only in terms of a kind of extended middle age' (Jermyn, 2012: 2).

The women fit neatly within the terms of Marshall and Rahman's research on the older people's magazine, *Zoomer*, where they argue, 'The promotional and aspirational role of celebrity creates a new pedagogy of the ageing self – a shift from ageing as a trajectory of decline towards a vision of older age as, subject to the right choices, full of possibilities and, above all, agency' (2014: 2). All of them talk about the importance of work and staying active and interested in the world as one ages (as Gillian observes, 'I think, to retire is dangerous'). Quite aside from anything viewers might feel about their individual styles, they are all aspirational visions of 'ageing well'; Daphne, Gillian, Jean and Bridget each speak passionately at one time or another about maintaining health through exercise and are filmed undertaking this, with Gillian and Daphne advocating rigorous morning stretching, yoga and Pilates routines (indeed Gillian has subsequently released a fitness DVD, *Longevity Through Exercise* (2014)). Since the film aired, they have been subject to an endless round of interviews and invitations, from academic conferences ('Mirror Mirror: Representations and Reflections on Age and Ageing' at the London College of Fashion, 2013) to cultural festivals ('Women of the World', The Royal Festival Hall, 2014) to tabloid fashion spreads (Styles, 2013). They have become recognisable cultural commentators in the UK speaking out against ageism, functioning as celebrities, at an age when already-established women celebrities more often than not have disappeared from the public eye. But as their brief biographies above demonstrate, the women subjects hold varying relationships to celebrity and visibility at the start of the film. Gillian, Daphne, Sue and Baroness Trumpington were all formerly or currently public figures before becoming part of *Fabulous Fashionistas*. Only Jean and Bridget were really 'ordinary' subjects at the outset in this respect, who can bear witness, therefore, to the uncommon experience of becoming recognised 'public figures' as *older women*, following the film's broadcast. In other words, at precisely the time in their lives that women are expected to forego their (already delimited) voice and any claim to being a subject of interest in the public world, they have seemingly demonstrated there is an audience for them as 'new' exemplars of articulate, experienced, vital and individual older women.

Jean, in particular, has gone on to become a successful model (somewhat ironically given Bridget's thwarted efforts to be hired as a model in the film). She appears regularly in *The Guardian's Weekend* magazine, while a portrait of her was exhibited at the National Portrait Gallery in London, winning second prize in the BP Portrait Award in 2014.

Furthermore, in January 2015, Sue had an installation at London's flag-ship Selfridges department store, including her own window display in one of the premier shopping sites in the world, as one of the featured artists taking part in the 'Bright Old Things' initiative celebrating the work of older designers. As the store announced, 'In a twist on our

Figure 8.2   Sue Kreitzman's window display at Selfridges, featuring a Sue-styled mannequin, London (2015)

Source: Photo by Deborah Jermyn

annual Bright Young Things campaign, this year we're celebrating the retirement renaissance and 14 inspiring individuals who've embraced a new vocation later in life' (Selfridges, 2014) – another cultural text, then, which in its small way seems to speak to a changing tide in attitudes to ageing, acknowledging the enduring energy and imagination of these older creative talents, with Kreitzman colourfully leading the way.

In the film she explains how her flamboyant custom-made kimono-style jackets and jewelry are sourced using fabrics from flea markets and junk stores wherever she goes and that her clothes are an extension of her art (made at that time by Lauren Shanley). As part of the Selfridges exhibition, one could buy Kreitzman's artwork on notebooks and bags, a version of the 'Zeitgeist' necklace she wears in the film, another featuring her face and, most intriguingly of all, her own words immortalised on a pendant. One of the most celebrated moments in the film, repeatedly returned to by amused reviewers, was the sequence where Sue admits she hates beige and believes it is the colour of death; 'Don't wear beige – it might kill you', she warns viewers. Such was the impact of this maxim and its petition to avoid the insipid invisibility of stereotypical old age that hip East London jewelry designers Tatty Devine inscribed it onto a

Figure 8.3 "Don't wear beige' – Sue's celebrated adage fashioned into a Tatty Devine pendant and for sale in Selfridges, London

Source: Photo by Marina Vorobieva

necklace, so that Sue's *bon mots* could travel with her devotees always for £30 ('It's like being a sort of elderly female Oscar Wilde', as Kreitzman observed in interview (2015)).

'Not quite respectable': fashion, feminism and ambivalence

But what other experiences of ageing and visibility are missing in all this; what perspectives were not acknowledged in the overwhelmingly positive reception of *Fabulous Fashionistas*, and the strident anti-ageist viewpoints expressed in the film itself? Stepping away from the beguiling testimonies of countless viewers' claims to have been moved and inspired by *Fabulous Fashionistas*, is there not sometimes a nagging sense of something simultaneously retrograde or regressive in the film too? While commentators across the media (and social media) celebrated the fact of older women finally being given a dedicated space on national TV, what had earned these older women that platform? The contents of their wardrobes.

Rather than 'advancing' representation somehow, then, was the film instead just transposing older women into the trappings and judgemental hierarchies that confine younger women, who can expect to be appraised, elevated or relegated alongside one another according to how they look on a daily basis. As John Berger put it in *Ways of Seeing* 40 years ago, girls soon learn that much of their value is inscribed in how they look (i.e., to others) and in being looked at – they learn to be both the surveyed and the surveyor of themselves (1972). Decades down the line from their girlhoods, were these women still moving through the world in this way, still party to this deeply gendered 'way of *being*'? For example, Bridget's anti-ageist protest in the film focuses on the world of modelling, and a challenge to the youth-oriented women's magazine market to hire her; in essence, one could say she demands the right of older women to remain object of the gaze. In this sense, her actions speak to the contradiction at stake in such campaigning where it could be argued that this kind of activism, in seeking to promote older fashion models, is at one level fighting for the right to women's enduring passivism. In the film Bridget refers to her campaign as 'a political statement', but are there not other, arguably more pressing political matters this energy might be more meaningfully focused on? In this respect, Elizabeth Wilson points to the troubled status of fashion in our culture, and 'our feeling that a love of fashion is not quite respectable. Halfway between hobby and ritual it is indulged in the "privacy of the home", yet flaunted in the public world, is stigmatized by its uncertain status as not quite art, yet certainly not really life' (Wilson, 1985: 229).

Ageing activists' and scholars' calls to address the manner in which older women are rendered culturally invisible is undoubtedly a pressing political issue. But in addressing this, there is arguably a need to conceptualise a notion of female visibility that is not, paradoxical though it may seem, primarily or merely invested in their appearance. Any 'visibility' for older women that can only operate and be earned within the same restrictive, judgemental constraints as that which delimit younger women – which also, of course, compel them to make a rolling investment in clothes, cosmetics, accessories and other accoutrements of femininity – is perhaps not something worth campaigning for. *Fabulous Fashionistas* and its reception invoke a world which largely embraces and admires ageing women who continue to seek out the pleasures of individual dress and style and/or 'feminine' consumption. But, in fact, as Kirsty Fairclough has shown, those older women celebrities that do remain in the public eye and continue to abide by this regime can expect to be subjected to a ceaseless media 'hyper-scrutiny' as a result, where 'they are examined in terms of how effectively they lock into prescribed notions of post-feminist beauty norms of which the invisibility of ageing is a fundamental component' (2012: 90). Furthermore, in another countercurrent to the film's position, there is an established thread running through some feminist accounts of ageing which speaks of the *freedom* that 'invisibility' can bring women, of some women's relief at no longer having to expect, or negotiate, constant judgement about how they look and what they wear, since older age effectively removes them from this spectrum. As Germaine Greer has put it, 'It is quite impossible to explain to younger women that this new invisibility, like calm and indifference, is a desirable condition' (1991: 430). Rather than offering new and innovative representations of ageing femininities, then, was the film merely championing the prolonging of a punishingly gendered regime?

At certain moments the film reveals what might be called a neo-liberal discourse at work. Gillian tells us, for example, in a line that could have come straight from a L'Oreal Age Perfect advert, 'I think you have to *pit* yourself, if you like, against the ageing process and you just mustn't allow it in', drawing, then, on the idiom of the beauty industry's anti-ageing discourses that encourage consumers to see ageing as the enemy they must battle against. As noted, a number of the subjects are seen enacting their regular fitness regimes, which viewers are seemingly meant to admire all the more when, we are told, they persevere with doing so in the face of a knee replacement (Jean) or a body that hurts every morning (Gillian). These are women who seem in some ways, then, to have adopted the rhetoric of postfeminism as conceptualised by Ros Gill, enacting what she identifies as an 'emphasis upon self surveillance, monitoring and discipline' as well as 'a focus upon individualism, choice and empowerment' (Gill, 2007). Postfeminism has of course been critiqued also for a preoccupation with *young women* as its primary subjects, facilitating a generationalism between women that undermines feminism, and yet we see here how the rhetoric of 'ageing well' addressed to older women borrows the very same discourses (and, in fact, the directive to 'age well' commences when women are barely out of their teens). Furthermore, just as postfeminism has been understood also to speak to and of a white subject, all the women here are white (a lack of diversity that speaks, too, to the whiteness of the fashion industry broadly). Indeed, most of them have also maintained palpably lithe bodies that deny the physiological changes that ageing generally brings with it for women; Jean and Daphne's success as 'senior' models is as much to do with still having bodies that fulfill the industry's 'clothes hanger' ideal, one far removed from post-menopausal physiognomy, as it is to do with their striking bone structures.

Further, an endless cycle of consumerism still lies at the heart of the women's pleasure in clothes, even if that consumption is not always predicated on wealth or spending great sums of cash. While, like a flash-forward to *Sex and the City*'s (HBO, 1998–2004) Carrie Bradshaw's future self, Gillian may mischievously reveal she had 'one indiscretion recently' as she pulls out a pair of new black patent pumps ('They're Prada. I need say no more, we all know what that means'), her gratification is no greater or lesser than Bridget's as she rifles through a box of sunglasses in a charity shop ('Look at them all! Ahh!'), or Baroness Trumpington's pride in a £20 suit from a catalogue ('I think it's a catalogue called "Chums"'). The pitch of Bourne's voice-over seems to lend itself as well to investment in postfeminism's familiar makeover paradigm when, reflecting on Jean's story, she tells us, 'Maybe old age doesn't have to be so bad after all. Instead of your horizons shrinking, you could even find yourself with a brand new career'. As the neo-liberal regime would have it, the potential for the reinvention of self here is never complete.

'I just sort of pretended, really, that it was about style': ageing 'under the wire'

When all these issues are stacked up together in this way, *Fabulous Fashionistas* might start to seem a rather less progressive call to arms than its feisty mode of address suggests. However, any easy dismissal of the film as being irredeemably compromised by the seemingly prescriptively gendered agendas outlined above arguably fails to understand the 'real' place of fashion in this film. Because for Bourne, this *was never* a film about fashion or 'fashionistas'. In interview, she revealed her impetus for making the film was a personal one centred on trying to conceive of her own future ageing, which came from, 'looking for a template for the next 30 years... that was my starting point, looking for role models', at a socio-historical moment where, she believes, baby boomers are 'pioneers' who are 'redefining' the ageing process. She explained:

> But I knew if I went to any broadcaster in Britain and went 'I want to make a film about these wonderful, older, feisty women, they would tell me to take a hike, they would not be interested at all... so I had to come up with some clever way to conceal the fact that I was talking about age... and I just sort of pretended, really, that it was about style, but it isn't. It was just snuck in under the wire, which is what you have to do. (Bourne, 2014)

For Bourne, then, fashion was only 'the hook', or as Sue Kreitzman described it in interview, 'a McGuffin to talk about ageing and life' (2015). The film was always about capturing the 'attitude and spirit' of vibrant older women, in Bourne's words (2014) and fashion merely the angle that enabled her to get a commission. Indeed, it is important to remember here that there is a significant critical distinction between 'style' and 'fashion'. Apart from Gillian's Prada shoes and Bridget's vintage Yohji Yamamoto catsuit, designer labels are not in attendance, and there is no interest in the affairs of the high street. Sue even makes the point in the film that her array of custom-made jackets are so simple to wear and coordinate that 'they release me from the tyranny of fashion', removing herself quite consciously from the values implied by the title 'Fabulous Fashionistas'. In interview, Bourne also described how after meeting Baroness Trumpington she was exasperated that she would be able to include her in the film because the 'style' criteria did not fit. Then she found out about her weakness for catalogues, 'And I thought, "This is it!"', that is, the penchant for catalogue shopping was the 'cover' that enabled Bourne to credibly incorporate this disarmingly frank, humorous, erudite 91-year-old within the terms of her film's pitch. The 'snuck in' agenda, as Bourne put it, is there in her voice-over in the film when, as Bridget takes on the women's magazine industry for their ageism, Bourne observes that, 'What was becoming clear was that for all six women, their style and attitude was *not just about the clothes they wore* ... They all share a quality, a spirit, that keeps them going' (my emphasis); and it was this, as much as any of their outfits, that viewers responded to so warmly. Importantly, too, Bridget explained in interview that her magazine campaign was not enacted solely for the camera and in fact predated the film, though making the film had brought with it access to a meeting with *Vogue*. And she was insistent that for her, targeting the world of fashion in this way was important because of the heightened role it plays in perceptions of who and what warrants cultural visibility – as with Bourne, this was her 'way in' to making a larger intervention: 'The thing that I want to emphasise is that younger people's vision has been so limited... [I wanted to] expand it a little by recognising, you know, over 40, you're not deteriorating necessarily and you can have very interesting lives' (Sojourner, 2015).

Bourne was also well aware of the film's lack of diversity and frustrated by it, describing the enormously difficult struggle she had in finding her subjects. In interview, I noted it was encouraging to see there was some breadth of class identities in the film, to which she responded, 'You can see what it's lacking. It's got absolutely no racial or ethnic diversity whatsoever and I was absolutely hammered for that', before she went on to lament its regionalism, noting it was 'embarrassing' that most of her subjects came from London. She had found no solution for this though, and could only tell me, falling back in frustration, that, alongside the 'style' criteria, having decided she wanted all the women to be at least 70+, this benchmark had shrunk her pool of potential subjects smaller still, so that to have stipulated cultural diversity in addition ultimately seemed unworkable: 'It was hard enough simply finding them at 70, 80 and 90'. In addition, we might say that, while the film is lacking in respect of racial diversity, it arguably opens up some potentially queer spaces; there are only two male voices in the whole of the film, and while there are heterosexual narratives inscribed for some of the participants by way of images of their wedding albums and tales of (mostly deceased) husbands, this is not the case for all of them. Only Gillian is placed as being in a (straight) relationship currently, opening up the possibility of lives that do not adhere to the heteronormative standard and that might lend themselves to what Greer evokes as the female world of older women (1991: 436–437). Indeed, in interview, Sue Kreitzman relished the fact that, 'I've become a kind of gay icon. I love that. A regular Barbara Streisand, without the talent [laughs]. It's fabulous!' (Kreitzman, 2015). Furthermore, while the film notes that a number of the women are mothers, grandmothers and great-grandmothers it refreshingly steers clear of making this fact central to their (feminine) identities; there are no familiar images of smiling grannies doting on contented little ones here.

Bourne's account of how the film is not really about fashion is persuasive. Nevertheless, it is very possible that a feminist reading of *Fabulous Fashionistas* may end up unravelling when confronted with the ways in which it seemingly depicts an aspirational future for ageing women as one where they still manage to court the gaze. But this conflict simply crystallises the 'problem' fashion has historically held for feminism; on one side of the debate, pleasure in the superficialities of dress, cosmetics and appearance is a poisoned chalice that curtails and delimits the ways women function in the world; and on the other, fashion is a feminine realm that brings with it, as the film captures very adroitly despite Bourne's protestations above, the possibility of creativity, escapism and self-expression. As Paulicelli and Wissinger put it, condensing the dilemma into two effective questions: 'Can a woman who loves clothing and cares about the way she looks still be politically and intellectually engaged and, most importantly, taken seriously? Are fashion and feminism a contradiction in terms?' (2013: 14).

Bridget's continued activism undoubtedly provides an affirmative answer to Paulicelli and Wissinger's first question. Using the film as a platform to enrich her lobbying, she now incorporates *Fabulous Fashionistas* into this work – in interview, she explained she has adopted the film as an educational tool in the ageism workshops she runs with schools and care workers, underlining the sense that *Fabulous Fashionistas* makes some weighty social commentary from behind a seemingly frivolous title. She believed that showing extracts from the film in her ageism-awareness sessions was helping instigate a change in attitudes; 'I notice when I do the workshops – in the "before" brainstorm and "after" brainstorm – their perception changed, even if just for a short while' (Sojourner, 2015). In relation to Paulicelli and Wissinger's (2013) second question, 'feminism' is not mentioned explicitly in the film. But as a documentary about six women, made by a woman director, which (superficially at least) examines the contentious 'feminine' world of fashion and focuses on older women generally rendered absent in popular culture, it is certainly one which begs to be examined through a feminist lens. It deftly travels between the conflictual positions outlined above, never solving the ambivalence fashion signals for feminism, but going some way to demonstrate Elizabeth Wilson's passionate insistence that 'fashion is one among many forms of aesthetic creativity which make possible the exploration of alternatives. For after all, fashion is more than a game; it is an art form and a symbolic social system' (1985: 245). This is a sentiment at the heart of Sue Kreitzman's perspective, as a woman who quite literally turns her art into her wardrobe; as she put it in interview, 'I just love art, and wrap myself up in it every day' (2015). One must suppose that all the women are happy to be the focus of attention or object of the gaze: after all, they have all willingly submitted to featuring in a documentary where their style will be scrutinised. Sue and Bridget admit to this freely in the film, while in interview both of them spoke about the *pleasure* of being recognised in public (Kreitzman, 2015; Sojourner, 2015). But importantly this is harnessed to a repeated pronouncement by the subjects in the film that they 'couldn't give a damn' about what anyone thinks of how they look, and that they dress for *themselves*.

Looking for the language of ageing

In conclusion, it is important to note here that just as we lack an ample repertoire of images of ageing and older women, be they celebrities or 'civilians', so, too, have scholars and cultural commentators lamented the lack of a sufficient lexicon to speak about ageing – a result, in part, of the critical neglect this arena has seen in so many disciplines. In a *New York Times* blog, for example, Judith Graham polled a number of leading figures working in ageing studies or research for their views on what terminology should be adopted; to which Harry Moody, 67, director of academic affairs for AARP shrewdly observed, 'What's going on is we have a problem with the subject itself. Everyone wants to live longer, but no one wants to be old' (cited in Graham, 2012).

Sadie Wearing's important discussion of the complex process of 'rejuvenation' seen among some media representations of older women in recent times (2007) has been widely cited in subsequent work in this area, and this term is sometimes adopted to point to a seemingly tentative shift towards more optimistic or animated representations of older women than have typically been evident in popular culture. Hence I want to revisit the term 'rejuvenation' at this time and unpack its use in this way, asking whether we might more helpfully adopt the term 'reinvigoration' in some circumstances. Both words speak to the notion of re-embracing 'aliveness'. But to be 'reinvigorated' is not, as 'rejuvenated' is, to reclaim youth; Oxford Dictionaries online notes that the origin of the word 'rejuvenate' springs from the 'early 19th century: from re- "again" + Latin *iuvenis* "young"' (Oxford Dictionaries, n.d.). Thus when critics and commentators suggest that these older women's vibrancy is evidence of *rejuvenation* we risk the (continued) fetishisation of youth, and the conflation of youth with aliveness; an entanglement we need to move away from if we are to foster more diverse perceptions of 'aspirational' ageing. 'Youth' (or the illusion of it) is not the thing sought after by the subjects or filmmaker in *Fabulous Fashionistas*. As Bridget says in the film, 'How I look is to do with my identity, and the fun of it, it's nothing to do with looking younger, because I don't think I make myself look younger by the clothes I wear'. Similarly, Bourne was not prompted to make the film because she was looking for expert insights into how to look young but because, as noted, she was searching 'for role models' as she looked ahead to later life herself (2014); indeed her voice-over explicitly states at one point in the film, 'It's not about money, *it's not about looking younger*. For all these women it's about individual style and attitude' (my emphasis). In contrast to 'rejuvenate', then, the Oxford Dictionaries online defines 'reinvigorated' as: 'give new energy or strength to' (Oxford Dictionaries, n.d.), without any recourse to situating 'energy' and 'strength' as the province of the young.

But perhaps even this term may not suffice as we continue to struggle to find a language for ageing femininities, since to adopt 'reinvigoration' points to women's later-life accomplishments as being borne of a kind of reawakening, pointing to the desirability of a 'second wind' in older age and perhaps creating new cultural pressure to undergo such a (potentially neo-liberal) process. This sense of a later-life revitalisation is indeed how *Fabulous Fashionistas* consciously constructs the narratives of Daphne and Jean in particular. Both describe how, unexpectedly, they potently reimagined their lives after being widowed in retirement; in Jean's words, 'I'm leading, really, to be truthful, it is a different life. I suppose it's more adventurous'. But of course this 'second wind' is not only predicated on maintaining good health (a challenge the film recognises); it also becomes more readily attainable with a certain degree of financial health, though the fact is that older women are more likely to live in poverty than older men. For some older women, too, it may be more appropriate to draw on or find a language which points to how they have maintained vibrancy, curiosity, activity *throughout* the life course; as with Gillian, for example, who has worked solidly as a dancer and choreographer well into her eighth decade, or Sue, who describes how she segued from a successful career as a food writer into a new passion for art and curating without pause. Such an outlook also challenges the binarism of age Kathleen Woodward has spoken of, where dominant, delimiting cultural discourses have encouraged us to think only of the life course as divided into 'youth' and 'old age', rather than as a continuum, as she calls for (1999). Indeed, this is exactly the critical point Michele Hanson's review of the film made in *The Guardian*, noting, 'Channel 4 has got its social groups wrong. They're dividing us up in the wrong way, as usual, with a line between young and old. It should be between dull and vibrant' (2013).

Finally, one of the striking accomplishments of *Fabulous Fashionistas* is not just that it managed to extend the mainstream visual lexicon of ageing femininities, but that it managed also to explore ageing in an affirmative fashion without circumventing 'the d-word'. For all its inspiring narratives and images of vibrancy in later life, death is still a presence in the film and this is a significant aspect of the work it performs, since the shift towards more positive images of ageing very often means evading the prospect of death. It is there not just in the women's reflective contemplations on death at the end, where Bourne has clearly asked them directly if they think about dying. Rather it is there from the start in the stories of loss, grief and widowhood – perhaps most memorably Jean's moving account of telling her husband she loved him for the final time, and in Gillian's account of her brush with mortality, the unexpectedly severe bout of pneumonia that brought a 'death rattle' at night. One of the most memorable moments in the film, then, has nothing to do with fashion at all, but comes instead in the final scenes where Bridget reflects, 'As you get older you are realising that it is about letting things go … yeah, dying … it will be OK'. The acknowledgement and acceptance of death articulated here is rarely seen, astonishingly simple and yet enormously powerful; so unusual have the film's images of older women outside of culturally dominant images of either dependency, fragility or care facilitator proven that its subjects did indeed, in moments like these, become Bourne's hoped for 'role models'. And indeed death is there also in *Fabulous Fashionistas'* most cited, most recalcitrant moment: Sue's now celebrated adage, 'Don't wear beige – it might kill you' – a pithy rallying call for ageing women to resist the pressure to fade into invisibility and a slogan for 'ageing well' that carries with it, too, a reminder that since death lies ahead for all of us, we should live colourful lives for as long as we possibly can.

Acknowledgements

I am greatly indebted to my interviewees – Sue Bourne, Sue Kreitzman and Bridget Sojourner – and photographers Toby Shaw and Marina Vorobieva for giving up their time so generously to help in the production of this chapter.

Notes

1. Only one columnist I encountered, Michele Hanson in *The Guardian*, expressed real reservations about the film, noting she found the voice-over annoying and misguided; the subjects weren't interesting because they were old, Hanson argued, they were just interesting (Hanson, 2013).
2. *Fabulous Fashionistas* remains available online at the time of writing on Channel 4 on-demand/4-oD at http://www.channel4.com/programmes/fabulous-fashionistas/on-demand [accessed 3 February 2015] and is also on sale via the Wellpark Productions website.
3. The *Advanced Style* film, directed by Lina Plioplyte and funded through a Kickstarter campaign, was eventually released in 2014.

References

Berger, J. (1972) *Ways of Seeing* (London: Penguin).

Bourne, S. (2014) Personal interview held at University of Roehampton with Deborah Jermyn, Centre for Research in Film and Audiovisual Cultures Media Masterclass, London, 19 November.

Cohen, A. S. (2012) *Advanced Style* (New York: Powerhouse Books).

Cooke, R. (2013) 'Love Songs in Age: Fabulous Fashionistas', *New Statesman*, 26 September, available at http://www.newstatesman.com/tv-and-radio/2013/09/love-songs-age-fabulous-fashionistas [accessed 25 September 2014].

Fairclough, K. (2012) 'Nothing Less Than Perfect: Female Celebrity, Ageing and Hyper-scrutiny in the Gossip Industry', *Celebrity Studies*, 3(1), pp. 90–103.

Gill, R. (2007) 'Postfeminist Media Culture: Elements of a Sensibility', *European Journal of Cultural Studies*, 10(2), pp. 147–166.

Graham, J. (2012) 'Elderly No More', *New York Times* online, available at http://newoldage.blogs.nytimes.com/2012/04/19/elderly-no-more/?_r=0 [accessed 5 February 2015].

Greer, G. (1991) *The Change: Women, Ageing and the Menopause* (London: Hamish Hamilton).

Hanson, M. (2013) 'What *Fabulous Fashionistas* Doesn't Understand about Older Women', *The Guardian*, 23 September, available at: http://www.theguardian.com/lifeandstyle/2013/sep/23/fabulous-fashionistas-older-women [accessed 3 February 2015].

Jermyn, D. (2012) 'Get a Life, Ladies. Your Old One Is Not Coming Back': Ageing, Ageism and the Lifespan of Female Celebrity', *Celebrity Studies*, 3(1), pp. 1–12.

Kreitzman, S. (2015) Personal interview with Deborah Jermyn, London, 13 February.

Marshall, B. L. and Rahman, M. (2014) 'Celebrity, Ageing and the Construction of "Third Age" Identities', *International Journal of Cultural Studies*, 3 June, doi:10.1177/1367877914535399, pp. 1–17.

Nicholson, R. (2013) Review of *Fabulous Fashionistas*, *The Guardian*, 18 September, available at http://www.theguardian.com/tv-and-radio/2013/sep/18/fabulous-fashionistas-tv-review [accessed 25 September 2014].

Oxford Dictionaries online (n.d.) available at http://www.oxforddictionaries.com/definition/english/rejuvenate [accessed 20 April 2015]

Paulicelli, E. and Wissinger, E. (2013) 'Introduction' (special issue on 'Fashion'), *Women's Studies Quarterly*, 41(1–2), pp. 14–27.

Selfridges (2014) 'Bright Old Things', 18 December, available at http://www.selfridges.com/content/article/bright-old-things [accessed 3 February 2015].

Sojourner, B. (2015) Personal interview with Deborah Jermyn, London, 10 February.

Styles, R. (2013) 'The 87-Year-Olds Who Wear Doc Martens and Mini-skirts: World's Most Glamorous Pensioners Revealed in New Documentary', *The Daily Mail*, 17 September, available at http://www.dailymail.co.uk/femail/article-2422328/The-80-year-olds-wearing-Doc-Martens-mini-skirts-Worlds-glamorous-pensioners-unveiled-new-documentary.html [accessed 3 February 2015].

Twigg, J. (2013) *Fashion and Age* (London and New York: Bloomsbury).

Wearing, S. (2007) 'Subjects of Rejuvenation: Aging in Postfeminist Culture', in Y. Tasker and D. Negra (eds) *Interrogating Postfeminism: Gender and the Politics of Popular Culture*, Durham and London: Duke University Press, pp. 277–310.

Wellpark Productions (n.d.) http://www.wellparkproductions.com/ [accessed 3 February 2015].

Wilson, E. (1985) *Adorned in Dreams: Fashion and Modernity* (London: I.B.Tauris) (new edition, 2003).

Woodward, K. (1999) (ed.) 'Introduction', in *Figuring Age: Women, Bodies, Generations* (Bloomington and Indiana: Indiana University Press), pp. ix–xxix.

Filmed

Advanced Style. Directed by Lina Plioplyte. US, 2014.

Cutting Edge. UK: Channel 4, 1990–.

Fabulous Fashionistas. Directed by Sue Bourne. UK, 2013.

Mum and Me. Directed by Sue Bourne. UK, 2008.

My Street. Directed by Sue Bourne. UK, 2009.

Sex and the City. Created by Darren Star. US: HBO, 1998–2004.

9

The Best Exotic Graceful Ager: Dame Judi Dench and Older Female Celebrity

Melanie Williams

As the essays in this collection attest, celebrities can offer powerful designs for living; models of how to embody different identities successfully. This includes the highly fraught proposition of how to age and, caught in the middle of both misogyny and gerontophobia, women's negotiation of the ageing process presents particular challenges. It is therefore unsurprising that there should be a thirst for aspirational female role models; those women in the public eye who are seen to have 'aged well', neither resisting the bodily changes that ageing brings nor giving into them too easily and 'letting oneself go'. This pertains to many prominent women, from politicians to musicians, television presenters to sportswomen, but star actresses provide a particularly rich panoply of public images of ageing, from those culturally deemed successful to those designated failed or flawed. They therefore offer especially rich terrain for an examination of discourses of female ageing.

This essay examines one particularly prominent contemporary older female star, Dame Judi Dench, designated 'British acting royalty' in a recent interview (Finney, 2015: 23), a typically regal frame of reference for the multi-award-winning actress fêted for her work across theatre, television and, more latterly, film. However, Dench's acting prowess will not be the primary focus of attention in this analysis. Instead her status as celebrity will be foregrounded, and more specifically her embodiment of what Dolan and Tincknell describe as the 'graceful ager' (2012: xi). Making use of extensive coverage of the star across a range of media, as well as salient details from her onscreen appearances playing a range of older female characters, this exploration of Judi

Dench's celebrity persona will demonstrate some of the ways in which, as Deborah Jermyn rightly argues, 'the figure of the ageing woman star remains a heavily contested site' (Jermyn, 2012b: 49). In particular, the chapter examines how Dench's star image manages to combine elements of the respectability of damehood and 'national treasure' status with being acclaimed in more demotic terms as 'badass' and 'nothing short of awesome' (Freeth, 2013) – appellations not usually applied to an 80-year-old woman.

As Jermyn notes, 'Hollywood has long stood as a kind of exemplary instance of popular culture's erasure of older women' (Jermyn, 2012a: 3), and yet as she observes elsewhere there has been some notable change in this regard over the last decade, with the flourishing of Hollywood rom-coms featuring older protagonists such as *Something's Gotta Give* (Meyers, 2003), *It's Complicated* (Meyers, 2010) as well as the remarkably commercially successful *Mamma Mia!: The Movie* (Lloyd, 2008) (see Jermyn, 2011; Jermyn, 2014). Looking at British cinema over the same period, a parallel pattern of renewed interest in older people's emotional travails can be observed (see *Last Orders* (Schepisi, 2001), *The Mother* (Michel, 2003), *Calendar Girls* (Cole, 2003), *Ladies in Lavender* (Dance, 2004), *The Best Exotic Marigold Hotel* (Madden, 2011), *Song for Marion* (Williams, 2012), *Quartet* (Hoffman, 2012) and others), but with the important caveat that this national cinema's emphasis on heritage film had already made it a more obviously hospitable place for older actresses (Geraghty, 2002). Indeed, one of Judi Dench's first notable film roles was in the foundational British heritage film, *A Room with a View* (Ivory, 1985), playing the romantic novelist Eleanor Lavish who befriends Maggie Smith's Charlotte Bartlett. Dench's international breakthrough in a starring role came with another heritage film, *Mrs Brown* (Madden, 1997), playing Queen Victoria in the low-budget production originally intended for television, but then picked up and given high-profile publicity and international distribution by Harvey Weinstein, leading to the actress's Oscar nomination. Although she did not win, her brief appearance as Elizabeth I in *Shakespeare in Love* (Madden, 1998) brought her a compensatory award as Best Supporting Actress the following year. Oscar-nominated several times since for titles such as *Chocolat* (Hallstrom, 2000), *Iris* (Eyre, 2001), *Mrs Henderson Presents* (Frears, 2005), *Notes on a Scandal* (Eyre, 2006) and *Philomena* (Frears, 2013), Dench also became an increasingly prominent 'M' in the James Bond franchise, from her debut in *Goldeneye* (Campbell, 1995) to her dramatic demise in *Skyfall* (Mendes, 2012).

Dench among her peers

The obvious cross-reference that springs to mind in considering Judi Dench's celebrity identity is that enjoyed in parallel by another British Dame, Helen Mirren, who also won an Oscar for playing a monarch, and enjoyed an unexpected later-career boost as a film star (after being previously more strongly associated with prestigious stage and television work). The highly prominent international success of both Mirren and Dench in recent years conveys a sense of the older women's new cultural visibility, and an implicit advocacy for post-middle-age life as equally dynamic and fulfilling as the years that came before. As Helen Mirren remarks in her 2015 L'Oreal advertising campaign: 'Age is just a number!'. However, despite their numerous similarities, Mirren and Dench present quite different forms of celebrity embodiment. They are over ten years apart in age (at the time of writing, Mirren is 69 while Dench has just recently celebrated her 80th birthday), and Mirren's public image – perhaps because of this gap – is much more obviously entangled with discourses of sexuality than Dench's. As commentators have noted, Mirren is 'framed as explicitly desirable' (Wearing, 2012: 149), and perpetually presented as 'hot Helen' (Fairclough-Isaacs, 2014). When Mirren's 'bikini body' was captured by a paparazzi photographer in 2008, her remarkably nubile figure became a media *cause célèbre* (Anon, 2008). On the strength of incidents like this and her numerous glamorous red carpet appearances (far more than for the roles she actually plays on film), the star has become ubiquitous as a model of positive, sexy but still 'graceful' ageing (Dolan and Tincknell, 2012). By comparison, the older Dench presents a more approachable gamine image, a feminine type more strongly redolent of boyish youthfulness than outright sexiness, exemplified by her trademark pixie haircut. Judi Dench is also, as Sadie Wearing notes, firmly associated with the celebrity persona of 'the theatrical dame' wherein 'discourses of hard graft and professionalism are often explicitly disassociated from "glamour"' (Wearing, 2012: 151). In this category, her most noticeable peers would be actresses such as Vanessa Redgrave (see also Jennings and Krainitzki in Chapter 11 of this collection) and Dame Maggie Smith. But here, too, there are some interesting distinctions to be observed between Dench and her contemporaries. After film success which came to her much earlier in life, Maggie Smith has also enjoyed a late career boost through her celebrated role as the Dowager Countess in the popular television series *Downton Abbey* (ITV, 2010–). Her character's acid asides have spawned an online meme cult (as documented by Marghitu, 2013), and yet it is important to note that this form of online celebrity is for Maggie Smith *in character* rather than as herself. If Smith features at all here it is surely within the strict realms of 'star-as-performer' in which attention is focused on 'the work of acting, so that, in a reversal of the celebrity category, it is performance and work which are emphasised' (Geraghty, 2000: 192). In spite of Smith's stylish and soignée offscreen appearance, she does not seem to function as a celebrity in quite the same way as Judi Dench or Helen Mirren. Both of these have been elevated, I would argue, to a level of stardom beyond their onscreen performances alone, however admired and lauded and central to their images those performances might be. As Richard Dyer famously surmised, 'we're fascinated by stars because they enact ways of making sense of the experience of being a person' (Dyer, 2004: 15), and both Mirren and Dench exert a fascination through their inspirational – and aspirational – embodiments of female later life. Yet although Mirren's image has been treated to visible analysis in the growing corpus of scholarship on media representations of older women (see Dolan, 2012; Wearing, 2012; Fairclough-Isaacs, 2014), Dench's celebrity persona, while equally culturally visible, has been neglected in previous analyses. So what are the ways in which her image as successful older woman is distinctive and how does it fit with existing paradigms of female ageing?

Graceful or rebellious ageing

Having crossed the threshold age of 80, Judi Dench might be seen as moving beyond the so-called 'third age' and towards the gerontological category of the 'fourth age', into what sociologist Julia Twigg describes as 'the more challenging territory of deep old age' (quoted in Jermyn, 2012a: 2). But even prior to her landmark birthday in December 2014, Dench had directly addressed, both in her onscreen appearances and in her offscreen publicity, some of the challenges endemic to ageing. A number of her roles deal either indirectly or more directly with the losses or aftermath of widowhood, as in *Mrs Brown, As Time Goes By* (BBC, 1992–2005), *The Last of the Blonde Bombshells* (BBC, 2000), *Mrs Henderson Presents, The Best Exotic Marigold Hotel,* and *Esio Trot* (BBC, 2014), and Dench herself was sadly widowed in 2001 after a long and happy partnership with actor Michael Williams, with whom she had frequently co-starred. However, the trauma of bereavement is often linked to a kind of rebirth in many of Dench's films. This includes taking on new professional roles, as in *Mrs Henderson Presents* in which her character takes over a theatre, or *The Best Exotic Marigold Hotel* in which she plays a woman who has never had a paid job before and who becomes a cultural consultant for an Indian call centre, and although not a widow, Dench's Matty Jenkyns in *Cranford* (BBC, 2007–2009) starting a business in later life. Widowhood can also enable new romantic entanglements for the characters she plays, with Bill Nighy's character in *The Best Exotic Marigold Hotel*, or Billy Connolly's Scottish gillie in *Mrs Brown*. Dench's onscreen roles communicate a vision of the older female protagonist as, to use Jermyn's formulation, 'active, vital, still passionate about life and new experiences' (Jermyn, 2012a: 1). As one character remarks of sex in *The Best Exotic Marigold Hotel* (although the comment has much wider ramifications): 'It's never over'.

However, this positivity in depicting later-life stages is counterbalanced by a number of other roles in which ageing is cast in terms of decline, decrepitude and irrecoverable loss. The biopic *Iris* focuses on its subject's harrowing one-way journey into dementia, contrasting the bright eloquent young Iris with the numbness of the older and much diminished iteration. Both *Ladies in Lavender* and *Notes on a Scandal* deal with the problematics of the unreciprocated sexual desire felt by Dench's characters towards younger people. Beyond her screen roles, the actress has also spoken out publicly about her own struggles with loss of sight caused by macular degeneration and, in broader terms, what she sees as the failings of care for the elderly in contemporary Britain, borne of a deep-seated gerontophobia: 'We're not good at dealing with old age in this country. We shove people in a room and leave them sitting round a television' (Anon, 2012). Indeed, the whole premise of *The Best Exotic Marigold Hotel* is that the labour of caring for older people could be outsourced to the Indian subcontinent, in parallel with call centre work (although the only character in the ensemble who really requires extensive care is Maggie Smith's Muriel who is recovering from a hip replacement operation).

Yet in spite of the challenging markers of ageing with which Dench's star persona is imbricated, the longevity of her acting career and its sudden stratospheric success in the medium of film, offers a powerfully contrasting narrative of positive ageing. Rather than old age seeming to represent a dwindling of one's powers, as so often suggested particularly of postmenopausal women, Judi Dench suggests the possibility of later life as a period of unparalleled success, capitalising on the accumulated wisdom and skill that comes from years of life experience: as the narration for a recent television documentary on Dench insisted, 'She just gets better and better' (*Talking Pictures*, 2014). But interestingly, this idea of welcoming and enjoying the experience of ageing is something the star herself problematises and sometimes actively repudiates in interviews: 'I don't embrace ageing, I think it's hideous…I don't let the word "old" happen in my house' (Freeth, 2013). The rhetoric of transcending age by ignoring it (echoing the advertising slogan in Mirren's L'Oreal advert) figures in other interviews with Dench: 'Age is a number. It's something imposed on you…You are only as old as you feel. It's not to do with age; it's something to do with inside. It's the engine' (Rahman, 2014). In such remarks, we can see how chronological notions of age are overridden by a more subjective approach, corresponding with Sadie Wearing's observations on how ageing in postfeminist culture frequently entails 'a fantasy of escaping (or evading) time', or of maintaining a state of perpetual girlhood despite one's biological age (Wearing, 2007: 278). It is interesting to note how Dench's publicity often details the star's engagement with activities more readily associated with younger demographics. For instance, her knowledge of texting acronyms like 'YOLO' provides the title for *Good Housekeeping*'s 2015 article on Dench, an article in which the star also reports that she is considering getting a permanent tattoo. (She had a temporary one on her bottom with Harvey Weinstein's name on it – to thank him for securing *Mrs Brown*'s theatrical release (Finney, 2015)). She delighted in being shown how to smoke a joint convincingly for her role in Sally Potter's film *Rage* (2009), and enthusiastically took up drinking Starbucks' Caramel Macchiatos and riding a micro-scooter while filming *The Shipping News* in 2001 (Hallstrom) (Miller, 2003: 323), all activities and pursuits more readily associated, however erroneously, with younger people. Even when she does adopt a hobby which is seen as more culturally befitting of an older woman, it is presented as having a surprising twist, as actor Matthew MacFadyen observed of Dench on the set of *Pride and Prejudice* (Wright, 2005):

> She makes these like needlework embroideries on set in the tedium of filming…but they are all: 'You Are a Cunt'. And she gives them as presents. And it's Dame Judi Dench. And she is doing this beautifully, intricate, ornate (work). You kind of see the work materializing as the shoot goes on. Like: 'You Are a Fucking Shit'. (Shah, 2014)

Details like these, as well as recurrent comments in profiles and biographies about Dench's unruly sense of humour, and her participatory appearances on cheeky comedic chat shows such as *The Graham Norton Show* (BBC, 2007–), provide some unexpected connections between her ostensibly sedate celebrity image and the raucous 'ladette' culture of postfeminism (see Jackson and Tinkler, 2007). Less subject to the criticisms faced by younger women who adopt 'ladette' behaviours, Dench's privileged position in terms of seniority, class identity and professional status enables her to use culturally loaded signifiers like tattoos and swearing to complicate the stuffy reputation commonly bestowed upon theatrical dames and so-called 'national treasures'. Instead of compromising her damely dignity, they arguably give a fuller sense of a well-rounded individual which runs counter to the usual (rather restrictive) cultural logic of what is appropriate for women over 60, and perhaps women of her particular class milieu especially.

In a truly fascinating coda, Judi Dench even became an inadvertent participant in British youth culture when her surname was adopted as an acclamatory adjective by the rapper Lethal Bizzle, a phenomenon met with understandably bemused broadsheet commentary (Wolfson, 2011). When Dench was interviewed for Greg James' BBC Radio One show in October 2012 – a remarkable event in itself, given its generally youth-oriented tone – she agreed to pose in Bizzle's 'Stay Dench' merchandise, striking a pose in a baseball cap emblazoned with her unexpectedly repurposed surname. Her approval, in turn, galvanised sales of Bizzle's clothing line, as the rapper later recounted:

> 'I pulled over to the side of the road when she came on the radio and she really smashed it. When she started saying in her posh voice that her grandchildren wore T-shirts saying "Denchgang" on them it had me in stitches. I'll send her a Christmas card and send her whole family some Denchgang stuff'.
>
> Speaking about his sales since Judi Dench wore the cap, he said: 'They have gone mental. I'll wake up and I'll get random sales at 3am from Australia. We've been talking to Selfridges for a while but the reaction from Judi hurried up the deal. They took loads of caps. They were like, "We can't ignore this". It sealed the deal'. (Eames, 2012)

It may have started off as coincidence that Bizzle's synonym for 'cool' happened to be the same as the surname of one of Britain's foremost actresses (and the source of much 'culture clash' hilarity in the press). But the way in which that random connection then developed and flourished through Dench's participation provides further evidence of her engagement with youth and youthfulness, as well as consolidating her status as a 'good sport' who does not take herself too seriously; perhaps one of the highest accolades in British culture.

Judi Dench: style icon

Central to Dench's embodiment of 'graceful ageing', the star's style of dress, hairstyle and make-up have been the subject of extensive laudatory commentary in the press and in online fora. Tellingly, the star features regularly in the UK *Daily Mail*, in both its print and online iterations. Recognised as an important site of debates around contemporary female identity, due to both its appeal to women readers as well as its frequently paradoxical strictures around what constitutes 'acceptable' femininity, the *Daily Mail*, as Railton and Watson suggest, offers 'a blueprint for how to grow old(er) and how to be old(er) as a woman as well as a set of guidelines for how to put this into practice. Indeed, the paper frequently identifies and celebrates "role models" for the older woman, figures in the public eye who are deemed to have aged well', among them Joan Collins, Twiggy, Jerry Hall and the inevitable Helen Mirren (Railton and Watson, 2012: 199). And yet, as they note, this newspaper regulates successful ageing in terms which are so narrow and so self-contradictory as to border on the uninhabitable:

> So, women should diet, but do so 'sensibly'; exercise, but 'in moderation'; dye greying hair, but to a 'natural' shade; wear make-up, but not appear 'gaudy'; look 'sexy', but not act sexually. Indeed, the watchwords of attractive older femininity are apparently decorum, poise, elegance and grace. (Railton and Watson, 2012: 200)

It is noteworthy therefore that Dench is held up by the *Daily Mail* as an exponent of attractive older femininity, balancing perfectly those contradictory demands. For example, a picture of her red carpet appearance in a long dress with split skirt at the 2013 Venice Film Festival was captioned 'Elegant: The distinguished actress shows her younger counterparts how to flash the flesh and still maintain dignity' (Anon, 2013), invoking unspecified inelegant younger women flashing too much flesh in order to boost Dench's prestige, in a 'slut-shaming' move typical of the *Mail*'s commentary.

It is fair to say that Judi Dench, despite not having fashion model provenance like the aforementioned Twiggy and Jerry Hall or being a 'well-maintained' former sex symbol like Joan Collins, has managed to achieve the status of style icon. One of *The Guardian*'s most stylish over-50s (Cartner-Morley, 2013), with Pinterest pages established in her name ('Judi Dench, style icon') and fashion bloggers eulogising her prescient sense of style ('she rocked the pixie long before Anne

Hathaway', according to McGowan, 2012), Judi Dench has also earned the acclaim of *Elle* magazine as an example of 'timeless glamour'. Among a company of women as diverse as Catherine Deneuve, Iris Apfel, Yoko Ono, Jane Fonda, and Barbra Streisand, Dench garners special praise for 'perfect[ing] the art of red carpet dressing later, rather than earlier, in life. We learned everything we know about dress coats from her' (Millar, 2014). Presented with a lifetime achievement award by *Harper's Bazaar* in 2011, two years later the magazine's chief fashion and beauty editor Avril Graham lavished praise on the star's personal style, which she hailed as 'never froufrou. She possesses an innate elegance, but is comfortable and is a touch bohemian'. Noting that Dench 'does not have (and never has had) a designated stylist', Graham concluded: 'Let's be real here: this is a lady of a certain age and an actress who is about her craft. She doesn't need a style agenda' (Shapiro, 2013). Thus stylishness is best served by not being attended to over-assiduously and 'effortless' style depends upon the appearance, at least, of a lack of contrivance, a concern with other higher matters. This belies the degree of effort and, it is worth stating, expenditure that goes into the maintenance of such casual elegance. Avril Graham's commentary on Dench's style credentials reveal how far designer brands lie behind the star's glamorous appearance, with mention of 'a Donna Karan black v-neck gown', a 'relaxed black Eileen Fisher ensemble', 'a dusty blue kurta and white trousers by the Linen Press (an English company that operates out of a former Cumbrian farmhouse)' and 'Indian designers Abu Jani and Sandeep Khosla [who] have a shop on Beauchamp Place right around the corner from Harrods'. Dench's look may appear artless, but its air of bohemianism conceals the expenditure that makes it less accessible and harder to emulate than it may initially appear. This was demonstrated when one *Daily Telegraph* reader wrote to the newspaper's fashion editor Hilary Alexander, planning a mother-of-the-bride outfit and using Dench as a possible template:

> I feel a special effort is called for and so have been investigating the MOB possibilities in magazines and on the net. Most are awful! I realise I am 60 and not as slim as I once was, but I do not want to look either frumpy or shiny! What I would really like is something akin to the jewelled/beaded coats which Dame Judi Dench has worn to many film premieres. (Alexander, 2010)

Dench is cited as a potential template for the average-sized older woman, a role model for successfully navigating the challenges of appearing glamorous (not 'frumpy') while avoiding gaudiness (or being too 'shiny'). The advice that follows is revealing:

> Judi Dench's coats are indeed like something from 1,001 Nights – but they are expensive. ... the cost for off-the-peg coats is between £1,500 and £6,000. For made-to-measure sharwanis, as they are called, try Daminis, Green Street ... £2000 for the more detailed ... A cheaper alternative, worth exploring, is one of the devoré (burnt-out) velvet coats from Hampstead Bazaar, St Christopher's Place, London ... in velvet with metallic gold thread, £175; matching scarf, £45. (Alexander, 2010)

Even the cheapest option listed here is by most people's standards expensive, with the top-of-the-range coats worn by the star herself costing significantly more, thereby making the emulation of that look on a regular basis economically impossible for many women. As Joanne Garde-Hansen observes, 'reinvention of the aging self may be costly and unsustainable' (Garde-Hansen, 2012: 163) and likewise, Dench's much-admired signature hairstyle ('Judi Dench haircut' is one of the most popular Internet search terms associated with her name), despite its short casual appearance, is perfected through the kind of precision cutting and carefully applied sparkly silver and ash blonde highlights that do not come cheaply.

Judi Dench is often praised for her rejection of cosmetic procedures and surgical interventions and her mature acceptance of the wrinkles and lines that 'natural ageing' brings, and the courage of this stance is not to be taken lightly given the cultural pressure on older women in the public eye to 'refresh' their appearance periodically. It seems like a mixture of pride and trepidation that motivated Dench to write in her diary on the eve of the 1998 Academy Awards: '<u>Countdown to the Oscars!</u> or Will I be the only unlifted face in Hollywood?' (quoted Miller, 2003: 292). 'Unlifted' but still making it in Hollywood over 60, Dench acts as a powerful endorsement of the ageing woman's continuing 'radiance' (a word often applied to the star) and a repudiation of the idea that an acceptable embodiment of older femininity necessarily entails intervention. Indeed, some commentators have explicitly juxtaposed what they see as more generous European approaches to women's ageing with the dynamic of denial which they conflate with the American attitude:

> One cannot enjoy the abundant offerings of our current film and TV landscape without noticing the distinct differences between the faces of our counterparts across the various ponds and the sinewy,

panicked faces over here. Watching 'Downton Abbey' with Maggie Smith's delightfully craggy face and the aging – and ageless – women who make up both the upstairs and 'down'...Dame Judi Dench in... anything...Here in the States? We have men and women who clearly hate their faces so much that when any hint of age makes itself known, it's cut away like so much loathsome debris. Perfection is the goal; age is the cancer. (Wilke, 2014)

But this celebration of 'accepting' age should perhaps be tempered with an awareness of the cultural capital possessed by the likes of Judi Dench which makes this rejection of artificial rejuvenation not only possible but much more acceptable. Dench acknowledges the appeal of erasing the ravages of age: 'I'd love to go right now and come back with completely smooth skin. . . . it's not that I don't mind the lines, because I do, but just not enough to do anything' (Finney, 2015: 26). However, she then goes on to imply that a combination of being 'squeamish' and of not wanting to compromise her ability to act, and indeed her niche in the industry, may have prevented her: 'My agent would go barmy. I'd do myself out of the parts for old people' (Finney, 2015: 26). And the star's rejection of the quick, easy rejuvenation of surgery or cosmetic fillers does not preclude her ability to benefit from the less culturally derogated youth-giving properties of an expensive hairstyle and bespoke tailoring. Those watchwords of appropriate ageing identified by Railton and Watson – 'decorum, poise, elegance and grace' – and the avoidance of anything overly sexy or 'gaudy', have obvious connotations of class, with a strong bias towards a subtlety of self-presentation implicitly understood to be middle class (see Skeggs, 2003). As Jermyn suggests of Jane Fonda, '"successful" ageing is explicitly tied to her consumerism and use of the right products' (Jermyn, 2012a: 2), and despite Judi Dench's somewhat different star image, there are obvious connections to be made to Dench's own highly 'classed' star image, her purchase of the correct accoutrements, and what is widely regarded as her graceful negotiation of ageing.

Conclusion: stay Dench

Judi Dench's onscreen and offscreen appearances are usually quite distinct from each other, with the actress most frequently appearing either in period dress (*Ladies in Lavender, Pride and Prejudice, Cranford*) or in more dowdy contemporary guise (*Notes on a Scandal, Philomena*), in contrast with her more glamorous 'red carpet' appearances or her casual elegance 'off duty'. However, Dench's images converge in the sleeper box-office hit, *The Best Exotic Marigold Hotel*, in which her character Evelyn Greenslade wears clothes virtually indistinguishable from the actress's own signature wardrobe of tunics and loose trousers, accessorised with draped patterned scarves, and the same gamine cropped hairstyle. As mentioned earlier, this film directly concerns itself with the indignities and difficulties of old age experienced by its ensemble of characters as well as reflecting upon (while also shoring up) India's magical status as a realm in which the British are able to 'find themselves'. Evelyn begins the film newly widowed, closeted and befuddled by aspects of modern life ('Is wireless the same as broadband and what on earth does that have to do with wifi?') before reinventing herself as a foreign traveller, adventurer, blogger and financially independent woman with a fulfilling job. In its final sequences, her fond friendship with Douglas (Bill Nighy) tentatively blossoms into romance and the closing shots of the film visually link the film's triumphantly reunited young couple riding on their motorbike (with Dev Patel's Sonny up front while Tena Desae's Sunaina clings onto him riding pillion), and the older couple who strike exactly the same pose on their own motorbike, eliding any distinctions along the lines of age: romance is romance, regardless of how old the couple might be. Nighy's cobalt blue and white patterned shirt contrasts beautifully with Dench's flowing turmeric and saffron coloured tunic and scarf, as their bike zips along the busy street. The overall impression of this moment is very much akin to what Jermyn discerns in certain moments in *Something's Gotta Give*, 'which, however clumsily, give subjectivity, visibility and the sense of a *future* to these older women' (Jermyn, 2012b: 48). For all the class-bound impediments to any simple notion of identification with Dench, such a vibrant portrayal of an older woman *still* remains a relative rarity despite the evident thirst for such a thing, with a 2011 UK film council survey finding that 69% of women aged 50–75 felt their group was significantly under-represented (cited in Jermyn, 2012b:48).

In an essay on representations of older women, Rosy Martin asked about where we might 'look for images of "average" middle-aged, or older women when the media concentrate upon a heroine/victim dichotomy showing older women as either super-fit marathon runners or shivering in lonely pensioner poverty, whilst radical make-over, under-the-knife, prime-time entertainment reinforces the desirability of looking ten years younger' (Martin, 2012: 99). I would argue that something resembling this kind of middle ground might be found in the celebrity persona of Dame Judi Dench, doing the utopian work of stardom identified by Richard Dyer of magically resolving societal contradictions: both aspirational and down-to-earth, 'real' and glamorous, dignified and raucous, acknowledging age while managing to disavow the conventional wisdom that it necessarily entails dilapidation and 'a process of dispossession' (Woodward, 1991: 149). The apparent resolutions provided to that series of contradictions are, of course, largely illusory. But at the same time it would feel ungenerous to do anything other than agree with one blogger's assessment of the star's remarkable achievement as an older female celebrity: 'Pretty badass don't you think?' (McGowan, 2012).

References

Alexander, H. (2010) 'Ask Hilary: Where Can I Find a Judi Dench Evening Coat?', *Daily Telegraph*, 23 August. Available at http://fashion.telegraph.co.uk/article/TMG7954089/Ask-Hilary-Where-can-I-find-a-Judi-Dench-evening-coat.html [accessed 14 February 2015].

Anon (2008) 'Helen Mirren the Bikini Queen Reigns Supreme at 63', *Mail Online*, 21 July. Available at http://www.mailonsunday.co.uk/tvshowbiz/article-1035510/Helen-Mirren-bikini-queen-reigns-supreme-63.html [accessed 14 February 2015].

Anon (2012) 'Meet the Very British Cast of *The Best Exotic Marigold Hotel*', *Radio Times Online*, 24 February. Available at http://www.radiotimes.com/news/2012-02-24/meet-the-very-british-cast-of-the-best-exotic-marigold-hotel [accessed 14 February 2015].

Anon (2013) 'Still Stunning at 78! Dame Judi Dench Wows at Venice Film Festival in Elegant Ivory Gown... as She Shows How to Elegantly Flash a Leg', *Mail Online*, 1 September. Available at http://www.dailymail.co.uk/tvshowbiz/article-2408128/Dame-Judi-Dench-wows-Venice-Film-Festival-elegant-ivory-gown – shows-elegantly-flash-leg.html [accessed 14 February 2015].

Cartner-Morley, J. (2013) 'The 50 Best-Dressed over-50s – in Pictures', *The Guardian*, 29 March. Available at http://www.theguardian.com/fashion/gallery/2013/mar/29/50-best-dressed-over-50s [accessed 14 February 2015].

Dolan, J. (2012), '*The Queen*, Aging Femininity, and the Recuperation of the Monarchy', in A. Swinnen and J. A. Stotesbury (eds) *Aging, Performance and Stardom: Doing Age on the Stage of Consumerist Culture* (Zurich and Berlin: LIT Verlag), pp. 39–53.

Dolan, J. and Tincknell, E. (2012) (eds) *Aging Femininities: Troubling Representations* (Cambridge: Cambridge Scholars Press).

Dyer, R. (2004) *Heavenly Bodies: Film Stars and Society*, 2nd edition (London: Routledge).

Eames, T. (2012) 'Lethal Bizzle Thanks Judi Dench for Sales of Clothing Brand', *Digital Spy*, 11 December. Available at http://www.digitalspy.co.uk/showbiz/news/a444466/lethal-bizzle-thanks-judi-dench-for-sales-of-clothing-brand.html#~p59Z3FaqxjGKdW [accessed 14 February 2015].

Fairclough-Isaacs, K. (2014) 'Mature Meryl and Hot Helen: Hollywood, Gossip and the "Appropriately" Ageing Actress', in I. Whelehan and J. Gwynne (eds) *Ageing, Popular Culture and Contemporary Feminism: Harleys and Hormones* (London: Palgrave Macmillan), pp. 140–154.

Finney, J. (2015) 'You Don't Have to Tell Me What YOLO Means!', *Good Housekeeping*, March, pp. 22–26.

Freeth, B. (2013) 'Now THIS Is Why Dame Judi Dench Is Nothing Short of Awesome', *Marie Claire*, 9 December. Available at http://www.marieclaire.co.uk/blogs/545057/now-this-is-why-dame-judi-dench-is-nothing-short-of-awesome.html [accessed 14 February 2015].

Garde-Hansen, J. (2012) 'The Hip-Op Generation: Re-presenting the Ageing Female Body in Saga Magazine', in J. Dolan and E. Tincknell (eds) *Aging Femininities: Troubling Representations* (Cambridge: Cambridge Scholars Press), pp. 161–170.

Geraghty, C. (2000) 'Re-examining Stardom: Questions of Texts, Bodies and Performance', in C. Gledhill and L. Williams (eds) *Reinventing Film Studies* (London: Arnold), pp. 183–201.

Geraghty, C. (2002) 'Crossing Over: Performing as a Lady and a Dame', *Screen*, 43(1), pp. 41–56.

Jackson, C. and Tinkler, P. (2007) '"Ladettes" and "Modern Girls": "Troublesome" Young Femininities', *Sociological Review*, 55(2), pp. 251–272.

Jermyn, D. (2011) 'Unlikely Heroines?: "Women of a Certain Age" and Romantic Comedy', *CineAction*, 85, pp. 26–33.

Jermyn, D. (2012a) 'Introduction: "Get a Life, Ladies. Your Old One Is Not Coming Back": Ageing, Ageism and the Lifespan of Female Celebrity', *Celebrity Studies*, 3(1), pp. 1–12.

Jermyn, D. (2012b) '"Glorious, Glamourous and That Old Standby, Amorous": The Late Blossoming of Diane Keaton's Romantic Comedy Career', *Celebrity Studies*, 3(1), pp. 37–51.

Jermyn, D. (2014) '"The (un-Botoxed) Face of a Hollywood Revolution": Meryl Streep and the "Graying" of Mainstream Cinema', in J. Gwynne and I. Whelehan (eds) *Harleys and Hormones: Ageing Popular Culture and Contemporary Feminism* (Basingstoke: Palgrave Macmillan), pp.108–123.

Marghitu, S. (2013) 'Violet, Dowager Countess of One-Liners: Maggie Smith in *Downton Abbey* and Internet Stardom', unpublished paper presented at Exploring British Film and Television Stardom conference, Queen Mary, University of London, 2 November.

Martin, R. (2012) 'Outrageous Agers: Performativity and Transgression: Take One', in J. Dolan and E. Tincknell (eds) *Aging Femininities: Troubling Representations* (Cambridge: Cambridge Scholars Press), pp. 97–112.

McGowan, A. (2012) 'Judi Dench Style Evolution: She Rocked the Pixie Long Before Anne Hathaway', *Huffington Post*, 7 December. Available at http://www.huffingtonpost.com/2012/12/06/judi-dench-photos-2012_n_2251608.html [accessed 14 February 2015].

Millar, L. (2014) 'Timeless Glamour', *Elle UK*, 23 May. Available at http://www.elleuk.com/fashion/celebrity-style/timeless-glamour-fashion-icons-joan-collins-judi-dench-jane-fonda#image=6 [accessed 14 February 2015].

Miller, J. (2003) *Judi Dench: With a Crack in her Voice* (London: Orion).

Rahman, A. (2014) 'Judi Dench Is Tired of People Saying She Is Too Old to Act', *The Hollywood Reporter*, 12 November. Available at http://www.hollywoodreporter.com/news/judi-dench-is-tired-people-748698 [accessed 14 February 2015].

Railton, D. and Watson, P. (2012) '"She's So Vein": Madonna and the Drag of Aging', in J. Dolan and E. Tincknell (eds) *Aging Femininities: Troubling Representations* (Cambridge: Cambridge Scholars Press), pp. 195–206.

Shah, Y. (2014) '5 Things We Love about Judi Dench on Her 80th Birthday', *Huffington Post*, 5 August. Available at http://www.huffingtonpost.com/2014/12/08/judi-dench-birthday_n_6277764.html [accessed 14 February 2015].

Shapiro, B. (2013) 'Judi Dench of *Philomena*: In Real Life, Dressing the Part', *New York Times*, 20 December. Available at http://www.nytimes.com/2013/12/22/fashion/Judi-Dench-Philomena-Red-Carpet-Fashion-.html?_r=2& [accessed 14 February 2015].

Skeggs, B. (2003) *Class, Self, Culture* (London: Routledge).

Wearing, S. (2007) 'Subjects of Rejuvenation: Aging in Postfeminist Culture', in Y. Tasker and D. Negra (eds) *Interrogating Postfeminism: Gender and the Politics of Popular Culture* (Durham: Duke University Press), pp. 277–310.

Wearing, S. (2012) 'Exemplary or Exceptional Embodiment? Discourses of Aging in the Case of Helen Mirren and *Calendar Girls*', in J. Dolan and E. Tincknell (eds) *Aging Femininities: Troubling Representations* (Cambridge: Cambridge Scholars Press), pp. 145–160.

Wilke, L. D. (2014) 'Why American Women Hate Their Faces and What They Could Learn from the Brits', *Huffington Post*, 4 March. Available at http://www.huffingtonpost.com/lorraine-devon-wilke/why-american-women-hate-their-faces_b_4897336.html [accessed 14 February 2015].

Wolfson, S. (2011) 'Judi Dench: A New Street Icon?', *The Guardian*, 6 December. Available at http://www.theguardian.com/culture/shortcuts/2011/dec/06/judi-dench-street-icon [accessed 14 February 2015].

Woodward, K. M. (1991) *Aging and Its Discontents: Freud and Other Fictions* (Bloomington, Indiana: Indiana University Press).

Filmed

As Time Goes By. BBC Television. UK, 1992–2005.
The Best Exotic Marigold Hotel. Directed by John Madden. UK, 2011.
Calendar Girls. Directed by Nigel Cole. UK, 2003.
Chocolat. Directed by Lasse Hallstrom. US/UK, 2000.
Cranford. BBC Television. UK, 2007–2009.
Downton Abbey. ITV. UK, 2010–.
Esio Trot. BBC Television. UK, 2014.
Goldeneye. Directed by Martin Campbell. US/UK, 1995.
The Graham Norton Show. BBC Television. UK, 2007–.
Iris. Directed by Richard Eyre. UK, 2001.
It's Complicated. Directed by Nancy Meyers. US, 2010.
Ladies in Lavender. Directed by Charles Dance. UK, 2004.
The Last of the Blonde Bombshells. BBC Television. UK, 2000.
Last Orders. Directed by Fred Schepisi. UK, 2001.
Mamma Mia!: The Movie. Directed by Phyllida Lloyd. US/UK, 2008.
The Mother. Directed by Roger Michel. UK, 2003.
Mrs Brown. Directed by John Madden. UK, 1997.
Mrs Henderson Presents. Directed by Stephen Frears. UK, 2005.
Notes on a Scandal. Directed by Richard Eyre. UK, 2006.
Philomena. Directed by Stephen Frears. UK, 2013.

Pride and Prejudice. Directed by Joe Wright. UK, 2005.
Quartet. Directed by Dustin Hoffman. UK/US, 2012.
Rage. Directed by Sally Potter. UK, 2009.
A Room with a View. Directed by James Ivory. UK, 1985.
Shakespeare in Love. Directed by John Madden. UK/US, 1998.
The Shipping News. Directed by Lasse Hallstrom. US, 2001.
Skyfall. Directed by Sam Mendes. US/UK, 2012.
Something's Gotta Give. Directed by Nancy Meyers. US, 2003.
Song for Marion. Directed by Paul Andrew Williams. UK, 2012.
Talking Pictures: Judi Dench. BBC Television. UK, 2014.

10

'I'm Not Past My Sell By Date Yet!': Sarah Jane's Adventures in Postfeminist Rejuvenation and the Later-Life Celebrity of Elisabeth Sladen

Hannah Hamad

Introduction

At apparent odds both with what has been highlighted as 'the cultural invisibility of the aged' (Wearing, 2007: 279) and with Matt Hills' observation that 'age and aging don't seem to play well' in the BBC's rebooted iteration of iconic science fiction series *Doctor Who* (Hills in Jenkins, 2009), British television actor Elisabeth Sladen became one of the biggest stars of UK children's television in her 60s. Reprising the iconic role of the Doctor's investigative journalist companion Sarah Jane Smith that she first played in 1973, and in which she was once regularly seen by audiences numbering in excess of 11 million (Chapman, 2006: 99), Sladen experienced a quite remarkable career renaissance and resurgence of her celebrity during her seventh decade. This was such that at the time of her death in 2011, she had the distinction to be playing the longest running (albeit not continuously) character performed by the same actor on British television outside of soap opera (Mulkern, 2011: 143). Frequently during its initial broadcast run from 2007 until 2011, when the fifth and final series was unavoidably curtailed due to Sladen's untimely and unexpected death from cancer, the *Doctor Who* spin-off *The Sarah Jane Adventures* (hereafter, *SJA*), in which she starred in the title role as an alien-fighting journalist assisted by a small group of local teens, was the highest rated show on its host channel, CBBC.[1] This was routinely the case for the episodes that comprised the first two series in 2007 and 2008, when each one topped the Broadcasters' Audience Research Board's lists of the highest rated shows for that channel in its respective week of broadcast (BARB, 2015). Furthermore, after an apparent dip in its CBBC primacy during the third series,[2] it continued to be the case for the entire run of the fourth series, and the partially completed (and posthumously broadcast) fifth series.

In the decades that followed her run in the original series from 1973– 1976, she was remembered by audiences and fans as the best loved of the *Doctor Who* companions (Tulloch and Alvarado, 1983: 212; Garner, 2010: 161). Nevertheless, she subsequently became only a marginal and intermittent presence on British television, a common fate for the young female actors that flanked the Doctor over the years. As Sladen attested just two years after her departure from the series, 'the television people didn't want me' (Pratt, 1978: 9). After the revivification of her television career, prompted by her appearance in the *Doctor Who* episode 'School Reunion' in 2006, and the subsequent commissioning and success of *SJA*, Sladen's persona was renegotiated into the public sphere through carefully 'managed' (Negra, 2009: 77) discourses of ageing femininity, in line with the imperatives of the postfeminist media culture in which it was now operating. She was thus positioned as an example of what Wearing describes as the postfeminist 'subject of rejuvenation' (2007: 277), for example, as 'the ageless Elisabeth Sladen' (Anon, 2007; Whitelaw, 2008), who was 'young on time travel', having 'rolled back the years [and] found the secret of eternal youth' (Keal, 2009: 27). Her re-entry into the public sphere as an ageing female subject was thus negotiated in a manner commensurate with the imperative to police the ageing of the older female body in postfeminist culture.

This chapter explores Sladen's status as a symptomatic figurehead for what Wearing calls 'the "aging" of feminism' (2007: 280), tracking her celebrity from the time of her run as Sarah Jane in the original *Doctor Who*, when she was introduced as a conscious response to the rise of the UK women's movement, through the latter-day resurgence of her celebrity in millennial postfeminism, and the attendant problematic of negotiating her 30 years of ageing, as it intersects with postfeminist norms of femininity. But it will also consider the fact of Sladen's death at the height of this renewal of her fame and what it brings into view so clearly: that ageing 'well' and warding off the physical signs of ageing so abjected in media culture are ultimately unable to evade the final outcome of ageing. There is a range of illuminating scholarship that deals with the relationship between celebrity and death, and death and visual media. Steve Jones and Joli Jensen, for example, interrogate the phenomenon of 'posthumous fame' in the realm of popular music celebrity in their collection *Afterlife as Afterimage* (2005), which explores fan cultures and processes and practices of mourning and remembrance for popular musicians whose celebrity is enhanced and transformed after death. Elsewhere, in her monograph *Dead Matter*, Margaret Schwartz conducts a materialist analysis of the complex mediation of the figure of the iconic corpse in culture (forthcoming 2015). Nonetheless, discussions of death and dying as the unavoidable endpoint of the ageing process often remain curiously absent from much of the extant work on mediated ageing, and celebrity and ageing. In the case of Elisabeth Sladen, her untimely death at the height of her resurgent later-life celebrity emphasises a need to acknowledge and discuss the place of death in discourses and narratives of ageing celebrity. This chapter will therefore culminate in a look at how the narrative of Sladen's celebrity, and the trajectory of her mediated ageing, were forced to accommodate her relatively sudden death into its discourse.

'There's nothing "only" about being a girl': Sarah Jane Smith and second-wave feminism

It is widely acknowledged and recorded that the character of Sarah Jane Smith, a 23-year-old journalist, was introduced to *Doctor Who* in 1973 to be the Doctor's new companion in direct response to the perceived cultural currency of the second-wave feminist women's movement of the 1960s and 1970s. She was intended, as Patrick O'Neill writes, to be 'the first of a new breed of companions for *Doctor Who*: bright, independent women, not just screamers' (O'Neill, 1983: 28). Underscoring the fact that the determination to challenge the apparent 'passivity' of the female companion was a conscious undertaking, Jonathan Bignell and Andrew O'Day note that writers were specifically instructed to make the characterisation of Sarah Jane 'stronger' (2004: 169). Speaking in the early 1980s, then producer Barry Letts attests to this:

> Speaking personally, I'm very much in favour of women's lib. I don't like the great extremists who would like to castrate all men and throw them in the nearest ocean...I think that's bloody stupid. But I honestly do think that women have been conditioned to second class status and I think that's a very bad thing, and I'm pleased it's being changed. So when Sarah Jane Smith came into the programme we were pleased that it fitted in...with the idea that we wanted a

> *Doctor Who* assistant who would strongly initiate things. (Tulloch and Alvarado, 1983: 182)

This passage is indicative of much that is troubling about the excessive assignation of feminism to the character of Sarah Jane, not least due to her (male) originator's easy alignment of feminism with misandry. But what it does show is a clear intention on the part of the programme makers (however flimsily followed through in the ensuing years) to grant narrative agency to the assistant character, and at a time when feminism was high on the cultural agenda. Then script editor Terrance Dicks similarly confirms that the decision to experiment with the levels of agency afforded to the assistant upon Sarah Jane's introduction was taken in response to changing audience mores with respect to roles for women in the series:

> One of the perpetual criticisms we got about the female lead... *from* women was that they never did anything except stand around screaming and wait for the Doctor to come and rescue them. And it was becoming increasingly obvious...that you could no longer get away with that kind of thing, that people didn't want it anymore. They very much wanted a heroine who was stronger...She wouldn't think the Doctor was wonderful, and she would argue...She always tended to stand up for herself and go off and do things by herself. (Tulloch and Alvarado, 1983: 183)

To whatever degree Sarah Jane's characterisation was intended to embody feminism, such intentions clearly came from a limited understanding of its discourse. The character was at this stage being wholly shaped by masculine subjectivities, determinants and understandings of feminism, at manifest odds with the goals of the second-wave feminist project. Thus, and notwithstanding the extent to which she initially served successfully as a reference point for contemporary social events pertaining to the women's movement, the limitations of Sarah Jane's potential as a politically charged figure for feminism must thus be understood within these masculine contexts of production and authorship. Sladen herself acknowledged as much, writing retrospectively toward the end of her life:

> After a long line of supposedly subservient female companions, Sarah Jane Smith was intended as the show's nod towards the nascent Women's Lib movement. I didn't want to make a big thing of this,

though, assuming the Doctor to be a more liberal thinker than 1970s Britons. As the only girl running around UNIT's military set-up, Sarah Jane needed to make herself heard, but I figured this could be achieved simply by making her a strong character. Of course the writers occasionally had other ideas. In 'The Monster of Peladon' for example, the Doctor actually orders Sarah Jane to give the Queen the full 'Women's Lib' lecture, no punches pulled. The irony of male writers getting a male character to 'order' a woman to talk about feminism wasn't lost on me. (Sladen and Hudson, 2011: 83)

The so-called '"Women's Lib" lecture' to which Sladen refers comes as part of 'The Monster of Peladon', a serial much discussed by scholars for both its direct reference to the women's movement, and its allegorical treatment of the contemporaneous miners' strike of 1974; and therefore of its conscious attempt to resonate with contemporary social issues (Tulloch and Alvarado, 1983: 52–54, 182–183; Tulloch and Jenkins, 1995: 30–32, 58, 109–113, 130–131; Chapman, 2006: 94–95). The Doctor, having become embroiled in a dispute between the working-class miners and the power elite of the alien planet Peladon, entreats Sarah Jane to raise the feminist consciousness of the young Queen: 'Sarah, why don't you…stay and have a few words with the Queen? I have an idea you could give her some good advice'. Her reticence to assert herself stems, she professes, from her feeling of gender inferiority at being 'only a girl'. Sarah Jane responds with a characteristically reductive explanation of feminism:

'Women's liberation', your Majesty. On Earth it means…well, very briefly, it means that we women don't let men push us around. There's nothing "only" about being a girl, your Majesty. Never mind why they made you a Queen, the fact is you *are* the Queen, so… just you jolly well let them know it!

Further highlighting the limitations of Sarah Jane's political charge as an embodiment of the values of second-wave feminism in the 1970s was the contemporaneous construction of Sladen's celebrity persona elsewhere in the media, which unsurprisingly operated more straightforwardly as a form of sexual objectification. For example, announcing her forthcoming appearance in the series in June 1973, a number of national newspapers, including *The Daily Mirror*, ran the story accompanied by a purposely taken glamour shot of the actress. Sladen is posed perched upon a concrete bollard, smiling broadly and running her fingers through her hair, dressed in minuscule cut-offs and a scoop-necked gypsy top (Anon, 1973: 2). Following her departure from *Doctor Who*, the same image would go on to be used to illustrate news media items that announced her appearance as the presenter of *Stepping Stone*, a children's programme for the under-fives (Anon, 1977: 16). Such constructions of femininity as a sexual spectacle were of course entirely in step with the gender discourse pertaining to female celebrity as it was mediated in UK tabloid newspapers at the time (and still), which routinely published nude glamour shots of famous women; but it was manifestly at odds with both the values of the second-wave feminism that the character was created (by men) to embody, and with her semiotic signification in her early appearances in the series.

With respect to this, Tulloch and Alvarado point to the fact that Sarah Jane was consciously divested of some of the semiotic trappings of sexualised femininity (e.g., mini-skirts) that had marked her predecessor Jo Grant (Katy Manning) via her costuming; such as her Robin Hood-style Lincoln green in 1973's 'The Time Warrior', her leather jacket in 1974's 'The Monster of Peladon' and her overalls in 1976's 'The Hand of Fear'. Such costuming, they argue, was intended to appear 'tomboyish' (1983: 101), going on to describe it as 'women's lib gear', asserting that her clothes 'were designed in accordance with the dominant media representations of feminists', and citing intentionality in this regard from Barry Letts (1983: 102). James Chapman likewise aligns what he reads as Sarah Jane's 'masculine' attire with an attempt to 'assert the character's feminist credentials' (2006: 80), as does Sladen herself, who notes that the 'smart brown trouser suit and white, wide-collared shirt' in which she was dressed for her inaugural appearance as Sarah Jane was a deliberate move away from the 'dolly-bird outfits' of previous assistants, and connoted the character's identity as a 'strong feminist journalist' (Sladen and Hudson, 2011: 109). Thus, as one *Times* journalist wrote in their obituary for Sladen in 2011, Sarah Jane 'was hardly the archetype for a new feminist superwoman that some commentators have suggested' (Anon, 2011: 82).

Compounding the dissonance between Sarah Jane's purported feminism and the reality of Sladen's experience as a female celebrity, the downward trajectory of her career following her departure from the series, as she aged, and especially following the birth of her daughter, was symptomatic of the entrenched culture of what Jermyn describes as 'the under-representation of older women on television' (2012: 6). As Sladen concurs in her memoirs, 'the [television] industry can be pretty cold to women of a certain age', and after having withdrawn from the public sphere in her late 30s following the birth of her daughter, the 'door swung closed' on her television career (Sladen and Hudson, 2011: 289). This only underscores the extent to which the latter-day renewal of her television stardom, following what was initially intended to be an isolated guest appearance on the rebooted *Doctor Who* was an extraordinary occurrence for a 60-year-old woman with a defunct acting career. All the same, as the next section illustrates, it was necessary to negotiate her return through familiar, and troublingly persistent, cultural scripts of postfeminist femininity.

Postfeminist discourse, toxic intergenerationality, and the return of Sarah Jane Smith

Postfeminist anxieties and cultural scripts, as well as familiar tropes of ageing femininity, infuse the character dynamic, structure the narrative, and underpin the central conceit of 'School Reunion'. This was to reinsert the now 56-year-old (by the show's timeline, since Sladen herself was 60) journalist back into the world of the Doctor after a 30-year estrangement, notwithstanding the re-pairings that took place in special episodes in the 1980s and 1990s, but which go unacknowledged in this episode. A much longed for reunion was thus staged, giving rise to reflections on what life after the Doctor holds for his abandoned former friends. Furthermore, this came at a time in the show's lifespan when the actor embodying the Doctor was becoming increasingly younger.[3]

When Sarah Jane happens upon the TARDIS (the Doctor's time-travelling spaceship) while investigating strange goings-on at a London school, she is shocked – not only to find herself confronted with the Doctor again, but also to find that his appearance is noticeably younger than before. She tells him 'You look... incredible'. Standing under a shaft of light, she herself appears to glow; this underscores the paradox by which she has both visibly aged in the decades since they last met, yet how she still bears a striking resemblance to the Sladen/Sarah Jane familiar from the mid-1970s, having apparently enacted the necessary policing of the self, and performed the labour of youthful femininity (hair, make-up, etc.) required of women in neo-liberal postfeminism. As Whelehan and Gwynne write, summarising Sharon Hinchcliff (2014), 'while advancing age was once understood as an experience of freedom from societal pressures of physical desirability and a relaxation of body anxieties, postfeminism and neoliberalism has [sic] ensured that these concerns remain in sharp focus for women in midlife and even beyond' (2014: 8). So in order to successfully manage the process of ageing in step with the cultural imperative to negotiate the ageing female body, Sladen can be seen to have managed its visible signs, and her femininity can thus be easily located in relation to discourses of (the maintenance of) youth via the clear invitation of favourable parallels to be drawn with her younger self. Hence, rather than transcending the binary of young/old that persists in structuring our thinking about age and ageing, the extent to which Sladen appears to embody both past and present versions of herself by playing this character with such equivalence at points in her life 30 years apart, the semiotic and performative invocation of her younger self instead structures the meaning and negotiates the cultural viability of her older self.

When the Doctor affirmatively responds in kind with 'so do you', Sarah Jane's immediate response is to call attention to the thus far unspoken fact of her physical ageing and his, not just lack, but reversal thereof, with a shake of her head and a forthright assertion that 'I got old'. All the while her lighting, hair and make-up have been primed to invite favourable comparison with her younger self, and to showcase the extent to which she has managed her ageing 'successfully'. Hence, from their first exchange in the full knowledge of one another's identity, the terms of their relationship have been revised to account for and negotiate her ageing, and to situate this in contrast to his perpetual agelessness. This is despite the ironic fact that it is he who has become dramatically older – by approximately 150 years[4] – but instead of ageing as a result, he has become younger. The Doctor's ability to regenerate, and thus reverse the physical decline that comes with ageing, has of course been a central conceit of his characterisation since Patrick Troughton succeeded William Hartnell in the role in 1966. As Tennant's Doctor avers in 'School Reunion' in response to Rose's (Billie Piper) accusatory questioning about her status as the latest in a long line of young female friends destined for the 'abject singlehood' (Negra, 2009: 61) that Sarah Jane has shown comes following abandonment by him: 'I don't age. I regenerate. But humans decay. You wither and you die'. This irony hence does not belie the fact that the physical youth of the 900-year-old Doctor as embodied by a 34-year-old David Tennant, when contrasted with the openly self-shaming 56-year-old Sarah Jane, whose ageing appears to have nonetheless been successfully managed (i.e., resisted), is entirely symptomatic of what Susan Sontag canonically described as the gendered 'double standard of aging' (1972).

The main and most obvious way in which postfeminist discourses of ageing femininity manifest in 'School Reunion' is via the intergenerational 'catfight' that is staged between Sarah Jane and Rose. They each, in the first instance, adopt positions of intense defensiveness upon meeting each other, leading both, in light of this encounter, to revise the assumptions they had previously made about their respective relationships to the Doctor. An instantly vexed Rose looks Sarah Jane up and down with suspicion, asking 'Who's *she*?'. Sarah Jane's response is dripping with scornful sarcasm: 'Hiiii, nice to meet you', before she then anchors the emergent dynamic of toxic intergenerationality between herself as the relic of second-wave feminism, and Rose, a daughter of millennial post-feminism, with an aside to the Doctor: 'You can tell you're getting older, your assistants are getting younger'. Furthermore, in a neat nod to the fact that Rose, as a youthful subject of postfeminism lacks consciousness of the gains made by women of Sarah Jane's generation, she retorts with an affronted 'I'm not his *assistant!*'. Age difference and generational discord continue to structure their fractious exchange as Sarah Jane continues to belittle Rose for her youth, ignorance and naivety, and Rose expresses little but contempt for Sarah Jane's age, knowledge and experience: 'Where are you from? The dark ages?'.

Their swipes at one another are verbal, rather than physical, but they nevertheless reflect the persistent tendency of postfeminist culture to pit women against one another, especially across generational lines. The 'catfight' trope has of course long served as a means of articulating toxic discord between women in media culture. As Deborah Jermyn writes, 'a "generationalism" has emerged [in popular culture] in which older women, and the second wave feminism they stand for…feature primarily as outdated antagonists to this younger [postfeminist] generation', (2012: 2). This, as we have seen, is exactly the scenario that is played out in the initial encounter between Sarah Jane Smith and Rose Tyler.

As illustrated at the outset, publicity leading up to the broadcast of 'School Reunion' was striking for the extent to which it negotiated Sladen's return to the public sphere and reignited celebrity in post-feminist terms of 'successful' ageing, firmly locating her ageing femininity in relation to over-determined discourses of youth and agelessness. This phenomenon continued, following the commissioning of *SJA* and promotional activities undertaken to support it. For example, Sladen was profiled in a piece for Scottish newspaper *The Daily Record* under a headline asserting that the 63-year-old actor had been kept 'young on time travel', and 'rolled back the years' (Keal, 2009: 26). Elsewhere in the article she is referred to as a 'girl' and as 'Evergreen Elisabeth' (Keal, 2009: 26), while her 'successful' ageing is asserted more directly when Keal asserts that 'Elisabeth, 61 [sic], has scarcely changed from her Seventies heyday'. Most invidiously of all, Keal distils the essence of the postfeminist imperative for older women to continue to strive to embody normative femininity as idealised within a 'cult of youth' (Negra, 2009: 76), when he writes: 'As Dr Who's longest serving sidekick, Sarah Jane Smith, Elisabeth Sladen still looks slim, sexy and sensationally youthful' (2009: 26).

SJA liberated Sladen's character from the constraints of the gendered dynamic of the *Doctor Who* format that required her to play the passive sidekick to a hubristic, mercurial and paternalistic central male character. However, *SJA*, like 'School Reunion' before it, would prove highly symptomatic as a postfeminist media fiction of ageing femininity. It articulated many of postfeminist culture's most dominant tropes, including through its status as a 'narrative of adjusted ambition' (Negra, 2009: 95) in which Sarah Jane's life choice to remain a single, childless, public sphere professional is shown to have been erroneous, necessitating the recuperation of her commensurately abject femininity through a recidivist later-life re-uptake of a more normative mode of femininity – in this case: motherhood. The show initially seemed to offer the tantalising possibility that Sladen was going to take the starring role in a flagship series on national children's television playing a professional, economically independent single woman in her late 50s who is childfree by choice, and beloved of the teens in her local neighbourhood. However, the 2007 inaugural episode, 'Invasion of the Bane', quickly contrived a scenario to divest her of her singlehood and provide her with an adopted teenage son: Luke Smith, an 'archetypal' human created by an alien race.

The series establishes Sarah Jane as the personification of the kind of 'abject singlehood' (Negra, 2009: 61) that postfeminist culture has time and again offered up as a cautionary tale of 'miswanting' (Negra, 2009: 95), warning women of the pitfalls of prioritising life choices wrongly, lest they age into such abject singlehood in perpetuity. The following is an excerpted dialogue from 'Invasion of the Bane' that takes place between Sarah Jane and Mrs Wormwood (Samantha Bond), a recurring villain whose femininity is pitted against that of Sarah Jane, enabling them to stage a succession of spectacles of toxic sisterhood centred around their respective motherhoods or lack thereof:

Mrs Wormwood: 'I take it, Miss Smith, you're single?'
Sarah Jane: 'Yes.'
Mrs Wormwood: 'No children?'
Sarah Jane: 'No.'
Mrs Wormwood: 'Such a wasted life'

She is established in these terms temporarily in order to apparently (and subsequently) refute the logic of this scenario – that the childless postmenopausal woman is beloved and admired by the children of the neighbourhood who find her mysterious and alluring. By the conclusion of the episode, this apparent potential challenge to the status quo of media depictions of ageing femininity is offset by the renegotiation of hegemonic norms when her femininity is resituated in more conventional terms with the series-makers having contrived a scenario to give her a child, and thus begin the process of repositioning and recuperating her femininity to fulfil the cultural imperative of maternity.

Garner writes of *SJA*: 'the enigma that is central to Sarah Jane's character arguably concerns whether Sarah Jane will be able to continue balancing her responsibilities towards Luke with defending the Earth' (2010: 167). Although he does not situate this observation in terms of the postfeminist cultural politics of gender, he nonetheless positions Sarah Jane and what he identifies as the central conceit of her series alongside one of postfeminist culture's most enduring dilemmas of femininity: the ubiquitous work/life balance and the perpetual requirement to manage it according to the imperatives of the current cultural moment. He goes on to note 'the decision to make Sarah Jane a mother' determining that this 'results in the character occupying the recurrent position of the "good adult"' (Garner, 2010: 167). In fact, he reads her aforementioned work/life balance, her transition from lifelong childless singlehood to later-life motherhood, and her scuppered wedding and concomitant embodiment of the 'runaway bride' figure so ubiquitous in postfeminist media culture, only in terms of their respective narrative functions. But the stakes of these scenarios are raised considerably when considered intersectionally in terms of the cultural politics of ageing and femininity.

Postfeminist fears and anxieties about ageing femininity continue to structure and infuse the discourse of *SJA* throughout its run over the course of the ensuing five years. Instances range from asides by antagonistic minor characters whose pejorative references to Sarah Jane's age appear ostensibly to garner sympathy for our protagonist – for example, 'She's just an old woman with a funny lipstick. End of.' ('Revenge of the Slitheen – Part 2') and 'You're a tough old bird. I'll give you that.' ('Warriors of Kudlak – Part 2') – to larger narrative threads and structuring discourses that serve the more hegemonic function to negotiate her age. In a knowing reference to one of postfeminist culture's most iconic cautionary tales of abject singlehood and miswanting, *Fatal Attraction* (Lyne, 1987), Sarah Jane is referred to by the mother of one of the regular child characters as a 'bunnyboiler' ('Eye of the Gorgon – Part 2'). Later she is positioned as a 'child-snatching maniac' ('The Lost Boy – Part 2') in a narrative that sees her accused of abducting Luke from his 'real' parents on account of her deranged desire for a child in the face of her abjection as a single, childless postmenopausal woman – a scenario for which there are innumerable equally misogynist templates elsewhere in popular culture. The first series double episode, 'Whatever Happened to Sarah Jane?', is marked by its structuring discourse of 'toxic sisterhood' in a narrative that pits Sarah Jane against her childhood friend Andrea (Jane Asher), whose antipathy towards her former friend is positioned as envy of the extent to which she has aged 'successfully': 'Look at you. Scrubbed up well. You always did look younger than you were'. ('Whatever Happened to Sarah Jane? – Part 2'). Conversely, the third series double episode 'The Mad Woman in the Attic' is a cautionary tale of the perils of ageing 'badly', which stops just short of offering up Sarah Jane herself as the symptomatic example whose off-script life choices constitute a fate to be avoided. Sarah Jane's teenage neighbour and friend Rani (Anjli Mohindra) is afforded a glimpse of her own future of aged abject singlehood as 'The mad old woman of Bannerman Road', an epithet by which Sarah Jane had been known at the outset of the series. By this point in the series though, Sarah Jane has experienced a later-life recuperation of her second-wave feminist 'miswanting', the tragic outcomes of which – abject singlehood and solitary ageing – have been renegotiated to situate her in maternal terms, something viewed by programme makers as a straightforwardly happy outcome for the character. As Lynette Porter writes:

> The series' frequent scriptwriter Phil Ford reiterated at Gallifrey One that he believes there can be no better television ending for the series, or the adventures of Sarah Jane, than to show how pleased she is to have traveled the universe with the Doctor but, eventually, to find her greatest adventure is in having a family. The final episode leaves *Who* fans with Sladen's voice saying that the adventure goes on. (Porter, 201: 119)

The finality of this ending to the episode comes of course from the fact that it was posthumously broadcast following Sladen's death earlier that year. In what follows, the final section therefore considers the impact that this event had upon the negotiability of the discourse of ageing femininity she had heretofore embodied with such success for the currency of her celebrity.

'Goodbye… my Sarah Jane': the death of Elisabeth Sladen

Writing in reference to Madonna, and to her fans' affective engagements with her negotiated performance of ageing femininity, Joanne Garde-Hansen argues that there is a cultural imperative for the ageing process to be managed via the discourses of agelessness and anti-ageing outlined here in relation to the latter-day celebrity of Elisabeth Sladen, because if the beloved celebrity 'ages, we age, and thus we are reminded of our own mortality' (2011: 131). This was sadly brought into vivid view when, having re-established her heretofore dormant celebrity on precisely this kind of managed platform of ageless or 'successful' ageing, Sladen died of cancer on Tuesday, 19 April 2011, at the age of 65, to the unwitting surprise of fans and general audiences across the United Kingdom and beyond. On 23 April 2011, CBBC broadcast a short memorial programme to the recently deceased star of the channel's flagship series: 'My Sarah Jane: A Tribute to Lis Sladen'. Here we are confronted with image upon image, taken from archive footage of the original series, of Sladen's younger self, followed by those of her older self. It culminates in a montage of images and clips of Sladen in character as Sarah Jane that moves forward in time beginning with her first appearances in the series in 1973 through her time on the show in the ensuing years, and on into her starring appearances in *SJA* before closing with the now iconic moment that concluded 'School Reunion', in which Sarah Jane is granted the face-to-face goodbye with the Doctor that she was denied as a younger woman. In some ways, the postfeminist media fictions of anti-ageing and agelessness that so often accompany the negotiation of later-life celebrity for postmenopausal women were disrupted and belied by the necessity of confronting Sladen's death – the inevitable outcome of ageing for everyone – in the face of such a successful negotiation of Sladen's defiance of both the physical and discursive markers of age. But in other ways these discourses remain steadfast and persistent, and the unexpectedness of Sladen's death becomes a morbid means of underscoring and celebrating the extent to which she was seen and understood right up to the end of her life (and beyond) to have aged without ageing, to connote youth, vitality, and the corporeal norms of pre-menopausal femininity, and therefore to have aged 'successfully'. In this way, rather than giving truth to the postfeminist lie that female ageing can be reversed, evaded or halted, Sladen's death enabled her embodied negotiation of this discourse in the face of her imminent end to be celebrated as a triumph of a well-lived femininity.

Notes

1. CBBC is one of the BBC's two channels dedicated to serving child audiences. Programming on this channel is aimed at a 6 to 12-year-old viewership (DeBrett, 2010: 49).
2. A guest appearance by David Tennant as the Doctor across both parts of the double episode 'The Wedding of Sarah Jane Smith' provided a noteworthy ratings boost (BARB, 2015).
3. Christopher Eccleston who originated the role of the Doctor when the show was rebooted in 2005 was 41 years old at the outset of his tenure. His successor David Tennant, who stars alongside Sladen in this episode, was considerably younger at 34. While his successor Matt Smith, the final actor to play the Doctor alongside Sladen before her death, in the Series 4 double episode of *The Sarah Jane Adventures* 'Death of the Doctor', was younger still at 27.
4. The amount of time (in earth years) that has elapsed for the Doctor since he last saw Sarah Jane is 150 years.

References

Anon (1973) 'Dr Who's New Girl' *The Daily Mirror*, 27 June, p. 2.

Anon (1977) 'Mirror TV', *The Daily Mirror*, 8 November, p. 16.

Anon (2007) 'Last Night's TV', *The Times*, 25 September, available at http://entertainment.timesonline.co.uk/tol/arts_and_Entertainment/tv_and_radio/article2522908.ece [accessed 9 October 2009].

Anon (2011) 'Elisabeth Sladen', *The Times*, 21 April, p. 82.

BARB: Broadcaster Audience Research Board (2015) Available at http://www.barb.co.uk [accessed 26 January 2015].

Bignell, J. and O'Day, A. (2004) *Terry Nation* (Manchester: Manchester University Press).

Chapman, J. (2006) *Inside the Tardis – The Worlds of* Doctor Who: *A Cultural History* (London: I.B. Tauris).

DeBrett, M. (2010) *Reinventing Public Service Television for the Digital Future* (Bristol and Chicago: Intellect/University of Chicago Press).

Garde-Hansen, J. (2011) *Media and Memory* (Edinburgh: Edinburgh University Press).

Garner, R. P. (2010) '"Don't You Forget About Me": Intertextuality and Generic Anchoring in *The Sarah Jane Adventures*', in R. P. Garner, M. Beattie and U. McCormack (eds) *Impossible Worlds, Impossible Things: Cultural Perspectives on* Doctor Who, Torchwood, *and* The Sarah Jane Adventures (Newcastle-Upon-Tyne: Cambridge Scholars Publishing), pp. 161–181.

Hinchcliff, S. (2014) 'Sexing Up the Midlife Woman: Cultural Representations of Ageing, Femininity and the Sexy Body', in I. Whelehan and J. Gwynne (eds) *Ageing, Popular Culture and Contemporary Feminism: Harleys and Hormones* (Basingstoke and New York: Palgrave Macmillan), pp. 62–77.

Jenkins, H. (2009) 'Triumph of a Time Lord (Part One): An Interview with Matt Hills', available at http://henryjenkins.org/2006/09/triumph_of_a_time_lord_part_on.html#sthash.Wj3cPOBM.dpufhttp://henryjenkins.org/2006/09/triumph_of_a_time_lord_part_on.html [accessed 26 October 2009].

Jermyn, D. (2012) '"Get a Life, Ladies. Your Old One Is Not Coming Back": Ageing, Ageism and the Lifespan of the Female Celebrity', *Celebrity Studies*, 3(1), March, pp. 1–12.

Jones, S. and Jensen, J. (2005) *Afterlife as Afterimage: Understanding Posthumous Fame* (New York: Peter Lang).

Keal, G. (2009) 'Young on Time Travel', *The Daily Record*, 13 October, p. 26.

Mulkern, P. (2011) 'Elisabeth Sladen 1948–2011', *Radio Times*, 30 April – 6 May, p. 143.

Negra, D. (2009) *What a Girl Wants? Fantasizing the Reclamation of Self in Postfeminism* (London and New York: Routledge).

O'Neill, P. (1983) 'Elisabeth Sladen Returns to the TARDIS', *Starlog*, 6(7), pp. 28–29.

Porter, L. (2012) *The* Doctor Who *Franchise: American Influence, Fan Culture and the Spinoffs* (Jefferson: McFarland).

Pratt, T. (1978) 'Who'd Be a *Dr Who* Girl? – The Tardis Travellers Who Hit a Time-Lag in Their Careers', *The Daily Mirror*, 28 April 1978, p. 9.

Schwartz, M. (forthcoming 2015) *Dead Matter: The Meaning of Iconic Corpses* (Minneapolis: University of Minnesota Press).

Sladen, E. and Hudson, J. (2011) *Elisabeth Sladen: The Autobiography* (London: Aurum Press).

Sontag, S. (1972) 'The Double Standard of Aging', in M. Rainbolt and J. Fleetwood (eds) *On the Contrary: Essays by Men and Women* (Albany: State University Press of New York).

Tulloch, J. and Alvarado M. (1983) Doctor Who: *The Unfolding Text* (London: Macmillan).

Tulloch, J. and Jenkins, H. (1995) *Science Fiction Audiences: Watching* Doctor Who *and* Star Trek (London and New York: Routledge).

Wearing, S. (2007) 'Subjects of Rejuvenation: Aging in Postfeminist Culture', in Y. Tasker and D. Negra (eds) *Interrogating Postfeminism: Gender and the Politics of Popular Culture* (Durham: Duke University Press), pp. 277–310.

Whelehan, I. and Gwynne, J. (2014) 'Introduction: Popular Culture's "Silver Tsunami"', in I. Whelehan and J. Gwynne (eds) *Ageing, Popular Culture and Contemporary Feminism: Harleys and Hormones* (Basingstoke and New York: Palgrave Macmillan), pp. 1–13.

Whitelaw, P. (2008) 'Last Night's TV: *The Sarah Jane Adventures* BBC1', *The Scotsman*, 30 September, available at http://thescotsman.scotsman.com/topstories/Last-night39s-TV-The-Sarah.4539665.jp [accessed 9 October 2009].

Filmed

'Eye of the Gorgon – Part 2' (2007) *The Sarah Jane Adventures*, television programme, BBC, 8 October.

'Invasion of the Bane' (2007) *The Sarah Jane Adventures*, television programme, BBC, 1 January.

'The Lost Boy – Part 2' (2007) *The Sarah Jane Adventures*, television programme, BBC, 19 November.

'The Mad Woman in the Attic' (2009) *The Sarah Jane Adventures*, television programme, BBC, 23 October.

'The Monster of Peladon' (1974) *Doctor Who*, television programme, BBC, 23 March – 27 April.

'Revenge of the Slitheen – Part 2' (2007) *The Sarah Jane Adventures*, television programme, BBC, 1 October.

'School Reunion' (2006) *Doctor Who*, television programme, BBC, 29 April.

'The Time Warrior' (1973–1974), *Doctor Who*, television programme, BBC, 15 December – 5 January.

'Warriors of Kudlak – Part 2' (2007) *The Sarah Jane Adventures*, television programme, BBC, 22 October.

'Whatever Happened to Sarah Jane? – Part 2' (2007) *The Sarah Jane Adventures*, television programme, BBC, 5 November.

11

'Call the Celebrity': Voicing the Experience of Women and Ageing through the Distinctive Vocal Presence of Vanessa Redgrave

Ros Jennings and Eva Krainitzki

This chapter suggests that the BBC television drama, *Call the Midwife* (2012–), is a unique televisual timespace (May and Thrift, 2001) that provides opportunities for audiences to engage with a more complex understanding of ageing femininities than are usually available in popular television. Focusing on a specific period of production (Seasons 1–3), the chapter argues that central to the series' unique and fluid construction of age is Vanessa Redgrave's role as series narrator. In particular, the singularity of Redgrave's disembodied voice (incorporating intertextual elements of her controversial celebrity persona as well as the singularity of the sonic cadences of her theatrically trained and now postmenopausal voice) contributes to the series' distinctive, polysemically multi-layered representation of women and ageing. As the voice-over narrator in *Call the Midwife*, Redgrave's voice facilitates a rare example of female subjectivity that is built on a continuum of ages rather than firm or oppositional divisions between young and old.

This essay argues that, in the period under scrutiny, *Call the Midwife* disrupts many of the limited and negative representations of women and age by interventions that work to 'unfix' age and challenge many of the dominant ageist assumptions about older women that circulate in society. It does this in two important ways. First, it uses the technique of voice-over narration to explicitly link the immediate perspectives and experiences of the onscreen character Jenny Lee (who is a young nurse/ midwife just starting her career in the 1950s and played by Jessica Raine) with the very same events as introduced and summarised by her older self as offscreen narrator[1] – events that are mediated by memory, the filter of life experience and an extraordinary older female voice. Second,

Call the Midwife uses an intergenerational female ensemble cast to interrogate a wider age range of female subjectivities than is usually encountered in popular television. An innovative dimension of this is the skilful
construction of its oldest core character, Sister Monica Joan (Judy Parfitt).
In her 90s and suffering from dementia, Sister Monica Joan is represented through her age-(in)appropriate behaviour as existing on a fluid
spectrum of age. As will be explored, her characterisation also parallels
elements of Redgrave's own celebrity persona, embedding an additional
echo of Redgrave's disembodied presence within the televisual text. At
the same time, Sister Monica Joan's demented behaviour also mirrors
the dynamics of the series' voice-over narration (as her behaviour moves
from childish to wise crone within each episode), connecting young and
old, just as young and old Jenny are connected. The final part of the
discussion returns to the central role of Vanessa Redgrave's vocal presence in the series and analyses how her status as what we will show to be
a rather unusual kind of celebrity informs understandings of older age
and female identity in *Call the Midwife* as being powerful and authoritative. In moving towards the conclusion, the final section emphasises
the distinctiveness of the complex and positive timespace for women
and ageing and concentrates briefly on the third season's 'Christmas
Special' (broadcast 25 December 2014), which we argue is suggestive
of a transition to a new and less 'positive' phase for *Call the Midwife*.
With young Jenny Lee's departure at the end of the third season, the
pivotal connection between young Jenny and Mature Jenny is lost. As
the fourth season begins (January 2015), older Jenny's voice-over narrations become less 'authentic' and less authoritative. This becomes clear
when we analyse the framing flashback sequences of the third season's
'Christmas Special', where Redgrave's embodied presence typifies stereotypical ageist representations of older women, in contrast to the series'
portrayal of female ageing.

Ageing studies, old women and television

There is a level of agreement in humanities, social sciences and media
studies that ageism is part of contemporary society and that ageist
representations are a consequence (Cuddy et al., 2005). Although feminist analysis of television has a long tradition (Brunsdon et al.,1997),
and television is also often defined as a 'feminised' medium (Gray and
Lotz, 2012), the fact that it nevertheless 'substantially under-represents
women – and older women especially – seems a strangely contradictory
state of affairs' (Jermyn, 2013: 75).

As Marshall and Swinnen note, in the development of ageing studies scholarship, 'analyses of age, gender, and sexuality have evolved inter-sectionally from their conception' (2014: 157). Understandings of older age and ageing have not, however, been similarly integrated within women's studies and feminist scholarship (Browne, 1998; Calasanti, 2008; Calasanti and Slevin, 2006; Rosenthal, 1990; Woodward, 1995). For the most part, issues related to ageing and older women have not featured strongly within feminism, but recently this has begun to change as an ageing studies lens is slowly being incorporated (Jennings and Gardner, 2012), extending feminism's engagement with women and women's issues across the life course. The following exploration adopts a feminist ageing studies lens to explore the interconnections between older celebrity voice, women and ageing in *Call the Midwife*.

Whilst contemporary screen media now present more diverse images of older women than was previously the case (Tally, 2006; Vares, 2009), there is still a tendency to represent older women in relation to narratives of 'ageing as decline' or 'successful ageing'. Older women are consequently represented as either the object of a pathological gaze or, alternatively, as absent; they are erased and made invisible (Woodward, 2006) when their bodies do not conform to dominant notions of 'graceful agers' (Dolan and Tincknell, 2012: x–xi) or, the relatively new figure of the 'sexy oldie' (Vares, 2009). Within the field of ageing studies, binary constructions of ageing as 'progress-versus-decline' (Gullette, 2004) or of young versus old have been challenged, in recognition of the fact that 'one of the intractable problems of the discourse of age itself [is that] it pivots on the blunt binary of young and old, as if there were only two states of age' (Woodward, 1999: xvii). A more productive approach to emerge from ageing studies is the understanding of ageing as a continuum (Woodward, 1999) where conceptually we can be young and old – old and young – at the same time (Moglen, 2008; Segal, 2013). *Call the Midwife* succeeds in offering a more nuanced representation and conception of ageing than commonly encountered on contemporary television by approaching age as being diverse and fluid.

Older women in the timespace of *Call the Midwife*

The television series *Call the Midwife* is loosely based on former nurse and midwife Jennifer Worth's memoirs[2] and was first broadcast on UK televi-sion in 2012. Despite being scheduled in the peak family viewing slot at 8pm on a Sunday evening, the drama has been described by *Radio Times* reviewer Alison Graham as 'the most subversively feminist mainstream drama on television' (Graham, n.d.). Following the lives of two groups of women – a group of young nurses/midwives, at the early stages of their careers in community nursing, and a group of highly experienced Anglican nuns/nurses/midwives – the series is set in a fictional representation of the London's East End Borough of Poplar in the late 1950s.

Call the Midwife seems to offer a welcome alternative to the progress-versus-decline binary of ageing (Gullette, 2004), generating what Tincknell (2013) suggests is 'a broader canvas' of female ageing (2013: 770), sidestepping 'the contemporary media fixation with "cosmeceutical" ageing, offering instead a series of diverse and textured depictions of female maturity that contrast sharply with the conventional Hollywood template' (ibid.).

Call the Midwife's intergenerational female ensemble cast of nuns, nurses and midwives places a range of different ages at the narrative centre of the series. The diversity of age categories is extended further by the wider community of Poplar (grandmothers, mothers, children and babies) that are involved in the storylines. Three of the Nonnatus House nuns are older women and are aged between their late 50s and 90s: Sister Julienne (played by Jenny Agutter, born 1952), Sister Evangelina (Pam Ferris, born 1948) and Sister Monica Joan (Judy Parfitt, born 1935). Although Sister Monica Joan no longer practices as a midwife/nurse herself, the other two do, and all three are actively engaged within their community.

A review in *The F word* emphasises *Call the Midwife's* exploitation of women-only spaces and experiences – women giving birth, assisted by midwives, nuns, nurses and also midwives living together as a community in the convent – as establishing: 'a sense of sisterhood: This was a commune of independent women, living together and sharing their daily lives without the domination of any man' (Kenway, 2012). Similarly, Iona Sharma explains that *Call the Midwife* 'deftly and lightly engages with feminist ideas through the reality of women's lives, rather than through the abstract' (Sharma, 2013). The focus on service, community and women's friendships provides an alternative to more pervasive postfeminist media texts which proclaim feminism as superfluous or antiquated in an era when women's equality has supposedly been achieved (Hall and Rodriguez, 2003; Tasker and Negra, 2007).

Sharma (2013) suggests, as much feminist research has also suggested (Maynard and Purvis, 1994; Stanley and Wise, 1983), that *Call the Midwife* can be read as a feminist text by the act of telling women's stories. This chapter argues that the series also facilitates an important televisual engagement between feminism and understandings of ageing.

Ageing studies research has been interested in the concept of time and its relationship to understandings of age. In the twenty-first century, the fact that chronological time structures the everyday and imposes order and meaning is rarely questioned. In relation to the concept of age, however, chronological age or age from birth (calendar age) 'should be taken very cautiously if we want to take aging processes seriously, especially because chronological age is widely used in contemporary societies to regulate all kinds of processes with many consequences for the people concerned' (Baars and Visser, 2007: 2). Other models of time that were in existence before chronological time became (de facto) the only version of time – such as kairotic time where time is conceived of as cyclical; experiential or 'felt time' (Crowther et al., 2014: 2);[3] and Augustinian time, where time involves experiential integration of 'an interrelation of the past, present and future' (Baars, 2012: 151) – have proved instructive when approaching concepts of age. *Call the Midwife* constructs a palimpsest of time that incorporates kairotic time,[4] Augustinian time and the more usual everyday chronological time. As Jan Baars indicates: 'The understanding of time begins with the experience of change: we begin to notice (what becomes subsequently articulated as) "time"...when we experience change' (2012: 145). Notions of change are crucial to *Call the Midwife*. As each episode commences, Redgrave's voice-over narration as the older Jenny articulates recollections that frame each storyline for the younger Jenny. The dominant discourse is one of change and coming to terms with new experiences. As Simon Biggs explains, 'the past is used as source material from which to build a serviceable identity in the present' (2004: 50). Consequently, if we think of time as change, then the presumed exactness of chronometric time is not as stable as it is usually considered to be and, as a result, common sense compartmentalised categories such as young and old are not as crisp and contained as popularly conceptualised. Baars suggests that narratives 'creep in and remain hidden behind chronometric exactness' (2012: 143), and therefore overlap with time understood in the older Augustinian sense (which conceptualises time as 'lived time'). To understand the notion of 'lived time' it is necessary to think of it as a formation which simultaneously embraces 'the past, the present and the future' (ibid.). The utilisation of kairotic and Augustinian notions of time generates narrative timespaces (May and Thrift, 2001) that 'interrogate the multiple complexities of time and context, assist with ways to think about unthinking stereotypes of older age that focus on decline' (Jennings, forthcoming 2015). Such timespaces also contest notions of generations as chronologically distinct or discrete entities. For instance, although *Call the Midwife* is set at an important historical and cultural juncture where notions of youth culture and a generation gap were taking hold of the public imagination in the UK (Marwick, 1998) and despite the fact that fashion and popular music are explored as sites of difference by the young nurses, the overwhelming message of the series is to find points of connectivity between people. This is achieved through respecting diversities of identity within a framework of common human decency.

Sister Monica Joan's dementia also works to upset rigid notion of chronological temporal linearity. Her representation weaves an element of kairotic time into the narrative 'gifting a moment of grace, meaningful insights and knowing' (Crowther et al., 2014: 2) that works neither to deny the illness of dementia nor her vitality. Her dementia means that her presence and, more especially, her words merge to form an overlapping past and present suffused with elements of the mundane, the poetic, the mystical and the spiritual.[5] Equally, the visual style of the opening credits of each episode, where handwritten pages of what we come to believe is/are Jenny Worth's memoir/s are superimposed over each other and intercut with scenes of life in the East End of London in the 1950s, introduces a fluid concept of time from the outset.[6] The accompanying voice-over narration for each opening sequence and the visual techniques in the sequences outlined above construct time in a sophisticated way in *Call the Midwife* as being multi-layered.

As well as constituting a challenge to linear concepts of ageing in time, Sister Monica Joan, within the Christian framework of her vocation as a nun, emphasises the series' rather idealistic approach to feminism as a supportive sisterhood that can transcend the materialities of class, race, ethnicity and age.[7] Her characterisation and biography also provides an interesting diegetic parallel to that of the celebrity-infused vocal presence of Vanessa Redgrave as narrator of the series. As will be discussed, Redgrave is associated with acts of politicised rebellion and an unwillingness to conform to the expected behaviours that her privileged status as a member of the Redgrave acting 'aristocracy' affords her. Similarly, Sister Monica Joan is also portrayed as a rebel.[8] As a young woman, she gave up the comforts and entitlements of aristocratic life to serve the poor as a nun and nurse – becoming, at the turn of the twentieth century, one of the first women to qualify as a midwife.

Vanessa Redgrave's star persona and the cultural politics of celebrity

Redgrave certainly conforms to the notion of a star in Richard Dyer's sense, in that she embodies 'what it is to be a human being in contemporary society' (2004: 7) and more specifically a flawed one at that. Dyer states that the star phenomenon 'consists of everything that is publicly available about stars', including 'interviews, biographies and coverage in the press of the star's doings and "private" life' (2004: 2). Most importantly, a star's image is also 'what people say or write about him or her' (Dyer, 2004: 3), and an analysis of what is written about Vanessa Redgrave suggests that there are two dominant influences that combine to form her media presence.

First, there is a widespread reverence and admiration for her as an accomplished actress. Redgrave was born in 1937 and her family is often described as a dynasty of actors (Adler, 2012; Spoto, 2012): both her parents – Michael Redgrave and Rachel Kempson – were actors, a profession shared, too, by her grandfather Roy Redgrave, brother Corin Redgrave, sister Lynn Redgrave, her two daughters Joely and Natasha, and son-in-law Liam Neeson. Redgrave studied at London's Central School of Music and Drama and, after her film debut in *Behind the Mask* (Hurst, 1958), she became, in Morrison's words, 'one of Britain's, if not Hollywood's, most accomplished and daring stars' (2002: 23). At almost six feet tall, Redgrave has always been an imposing physical presence. In interviews she has been inclined to describe herself or be described as having little care for her appearance, but her consummate understanding of performance has enabled her 'to switch on her beauty almost at will' (Adler, 2011). She is described as a woman possessed of confidence, authority and, most importantly in the context of this chapter, someone who has aged successfully (Viner, 2002) and exudes life experience (Morrison, 2002). Lynn Barber likens her to a reigning matriarch; explaining that she 'almost feel[s] inclined to curtsy' (2006) when in her presence. James Morrison highlights her 'air of almost presidential confidence – a form of eminence that can only be grown into with age and experience' (2002: 23).

Second, there is her political activism which has been the source of much of Redgrave's celebrity. Concepts of stardom and celebrity are often used interchangeably in scholarship and the media (Drake and Miah, 2010), and certainly in Vanessa Redgrave's case, the boundaries of where her star persona ends and her celebrity persona begins are not clear. Redgrave, however, is a star 'with a voice' – both in terms of the easily recognisable and charismatic sound of her voice and also, figuratively, as a star with strong political opinions who is not afraid to express them. Her celebrity persona is encapsulated in Taylor's (2011) description of her as the 'grande dame who won't conform'.

The concept of celebrity can be understood 'as a discursive category' (Holmes and Redmond, 2006: 12). Redgrave's own celebrity status is especially contradictory and multifaceted. For many years, Redgrave was predominantly 'an individual who is first and foremost known for their public profile and media circulation rather than their skilled performances in a particular field' (Drake and Miah, 2010: 51). Renowned as a versatile and commanding performer on stage, on film and on television, Redgrave's celebrity status is complex, sometimes incongruous, and able to evoke extreme feelings. As Marina Hyde wrote in her blog: 'Your opinions about Vanessa will have calcified one way or another sometime during the early 70s – even if you weren't born until the 80s. Indeed, scientists recently discovered that being able to stomach Vanessa is now simply genetic, like tongue rolling or tasting PTC. Either you can do it, or you can't' (Hyde, 2011). Redgrave's multi-layered star persona thus combines the talents of an actress and the extra-cinematic presence of a politically active celebrity (Drake and Miah, 2010: 56). King argues that 'an actor is always a signifier with at least three intertwined referents: the private person, the fictive person or character, and the type under which these two dimensions of identity are categorically subsumed.... By contrast, the celebrity is semantically extracinematic and transmedial, even if appearing in a specific film' (King, 2010: 8).

Her championing of humanitarian causes has been a source of tension in her public life, seemingly damaging her popularity as an outstanding actress. Unlike other British actresses who emerged in the 1960s and built impressive reputations for their craft (for instance Dame Judi Dench[9] or Dame Maggie Smith), Redgrave is not recognised by the public and media as a 'national treasure'. Her image is arguably too controversial and too spikey. Her aura of grandeur contradicts both her humility and her championing of the downtrodden. In her analysis of the phenomenon of celebrity charity, Jo Littler argues that the endorsement of humanitarian causes can be used positively to create or maintain a certain celebrity's brand, to promote themselves or their product, maintaining their 'profile and topical currency' across the media (2008: 241). Redgrave's politics and her 'celebrity of caring' (Littler, 2008) stems from her profound political beliefs. Though her political beliefs undeniably stimulate her celebrity, they seem to harm her 'brand' rather than generate sympathetic interest. Hyde describes Redgrave as a 'celebrity angel of death' (Hyde, 2011), and even though Redgrave's political convictions conform to the same notions that Littler uses in relation to Angelina Jolie (i.e., they can be seen to align with '"real" and "intimate" life' (2008: 238)), Redgrave is seemingly the 'wrong type' of humanitarian activist to gain public and media respect. She has never conformed to the type of celebrity brand that can be considered either popular or sexy. More recently her political activism has also been subjected to ageist slurs. Hyde's review of Redgrave's attendance at a protest event fixated on what she referred to as Redgrave's 'grey cardigan of care' (Hyde, 2011), rather than her solidarity in the particular cause she was supporting. In the media, her earnestness and her obsessive desire to promote certain causes above all else[10] is seen as both excessive (Brown, 1995; Hyde, 2011) and negative.

Dyer has argued, however, that a star can embody contradictory elements: audiences 'cannot make media images mean anything they want to, but they can select from the complexity of the image the meanings and feelings, the variations, inflections and contradictions, that work for them' (2004: 4). Redgrave's complex celebrity and star persona is the culmination of a rich and contradictory tapestry of discourses, influences and behaviours. If, as Hilde Van den Bulck argues, ageing 'does not sit well with celebrity culture' (2014: 65) by virtue of its intrinsic worship of youth and beauty, Redgrave has nonetheless enjoyed life-long stardom. The public discourse surrounding Redgrave is as ambiguous as her own star persona, combining praise for her stage and screen performances with derisory comments on Redgrave's choice of political causes. Her life and career can be read through the lens of paradox; negotiating, as she does, the freedoms of privilege, talent and artistry, the sorrow of personal loss[11] and a steely commitment to humanitarian causes, radical politics and the determination to battle on behalf of the disenfranchised. Redgrave embodies these tensions and contradictions in her celebrity and star persona and expressively and symbolically in her voice. As stated above, she is a 'star with a voice', both dramatically and politically.

Vanessa Redgrave's distinctive aged voice

In Clarice Butkus' (2012) discussion of female voice-over narration, she suggests that in recent successful female-centred series such as *Sex and the City* (HBO, 1998–2004) and *Desperate Housewives* (ABC, 2004–2012), the narration and interior monologues used are 'stereotypically "feminine" – higher pitched and lilting' (Butkus, 2012: 186). Despite

being an older woman's voice, Redgrave's voice in *Call the Midwife* resonates more closely with the deeper registers that Butkus ascribes to the
female 'warrior' register (2012: 186); signifying a more active/activist
and possibly feminist presence. Voices have meanings related to age,
gender and place in society (Divita, 2012) and female vocal registers
are inflected by cultural understandings of the power relations between
women and men within a patriarchal society. The tonal quality of voices
also change over the course of an individual's life from childhood to deep
old age, and diminishing vocal frequency and lack of vocal intensity in
later life is frequently associated with dominant cultural and medical
narratives of decline (Divita, 2012; Prakup, 2012). In contemporary
Western youth-centred culture, an ageing voice is generally deemed *less*;
less vigorous, less attractive and therefore implying a lack of authority
(Divita, 2012).

Vanessa Redgrave's voice, however, strongly resists this definition
through the weight of her star persona and the quality of her voice
as an instrument of communication. The distinctive quality of her
vocal instrument is the consequence of genetic timbre, her training as
an actress and a lifetime of practicing her vocal skills as a performer.
Physiologically, vocal folds or vocal chords require training and exercise
to prevent deterioration of vocal quality (Prakup, 2012) and Redgrave's
60-year engagement with the practice of acting has ensured her
continued skilled delivery of vocal frequency, intensity, range, power
and quality.

Redgrave's voice is also made husky by her status as a life-long
smoker, a factor that has contributed to deepening her vocal register
and making her voice one of her key distinguishing features. In her late
70s, Redgrave's voice is still powerful and seemingly filled with emotion,
as described by one interviewer: 'You cannot see her but her voice fills
her small Chiswick flat. It is a loud voice, deep and sonorous, with a
tremolo effect that suggests barely controlled fury' (Walsh, 1998: 22). It
is this unique voice that narrates each opening and closing sequence of
a *Call the Midwife* episode.

Voicing Jenny Lee in *Call the Midwife*

The narrator is a well-researched concept within literary studies and
screen studies. The idea of the unreliability of narration has been particularly influential in relation to theorising the (unreliable) male narrator
in American independent film (Ferenz, 2005). For the female narrator,
the main focus has been the exploration of the tensions between the

expression of female subjectivity and the positioning of women within patriarchal culture (Hollinger, 1992). The dynamics between female voice-over narration and the viewer or the wider cultural meanings of the aged voice in voice-over narration remain under-explored.[12] Michael Chion's (1999) concept of *acousmêtre*, or the vocal presence of 'a special being, a kind of talking and acting shadow' (1999: 21), is a useful tool to approach Redgrave's vocal identity in the series. The expectation of seeing a not-yet-seen voice, that is, the moment of revelation, or as Chion describes the moment of 'de-acousmatization' (1999: 23), is evident in *Call the Midwife* from the start. The viewer almost expects a sudden close-up of the 'mature' Jenny writing her memoirs.[13] For those cognisant of Redgrave's celebrity, the knowledge that this brings is likely to add to their reading of her disembodied vocal presence.[14] For those aware of her star actress persona, the quality of her inimitable voice conveys superlative authoritative communication. As Brian Viner explains, '[a]s elegant as Redgrave is, it is her voice – soft, slow, precise – that transfixes' (2002: 8). For those completely unaware of Redgrave, her vocal ability to 'transfix' acts as a persuasive conduit to the intrinsic values of *Call the Midwife* that are set out in her voice-over narration that introduces and closes each episode.

The voice-over narration in *Call the Midwife* performs several textual and meta-textual functions. This device anchors the narrative on the protagonist, establishing the bridge to a timespace where the first-person narrative of the memoir, its handwritten pages depicted in the title sequence, and its screen adaption all converge. The address is to a female audience, as signalled by the female ensemble cast and the emphasis on women-focused plots. Most importantly in this context, the voice-over narration is crucial to suggesting the idea of ageing as a continuum in the series, more specifically, of being able to conceptualise the notion of being old and young at the same time.

Being old and young at the same time

Moglen introduced the idea of ageing as 'a multiple, ambiguous, and contradictory process, which provides us – continuously and simultaneously – with images of the past, present, lost, embodied, and imagined selves' (2008: 303–304). Against a binary concept of age identity as a past (of youth) and a present (of old age), and against the idea that 'the authentic, younger self that is trapped inside an unreal, decaying body' (Moglen, 2008: 302), *Call the Midwife* explores age in a holistic way that moves beyond the limitations of chronological compartmentalisation.

As suggested earlier, the style of the opening credits is deliberately multi-layered to embrace the concept that '[a]s we age, changing year on year, we also retain, in one manifestation or another, traces of all the selves we have been' (Segal, 2013: 4). In each episode from season 1–3, when the contemporary audience watches, they are pulled into the 1950s' timespace signalled by the *mise-en-scène* (fashions, cars, street furniture, etc.) and through the older Jenny's words, as narrated by Redgrave, they are implicated in the co-presence of kairotic, Augustinian and chronological times (young Jenny, older Jenny, the 1950s and the twenty-first century when they themselves are watching). In the first episode of the series, the black-and-white pages of Worth's handwritten memoirs and the photographs depicting 1950s London change from black and white into colour as we are drawn into the diegetic world of the episode.[15] Close-up shots from several different camera angles establish Jenny Lee as the protagonist and affirm the connection between the 'voiced' Jenny and the diegetic character. The camera alternates between a point-of-view shot where the camera is behind her head, and close-ups revealing her first reactions to East End London street life. As the first episode of *Call the Midwife* opens with a scene of two women fighting in the street, the viewer hears Jenny's opening voice-over (Redgrave):

> I must have been mad.
> I must have been mad. I could have been an air hostess.
> I could have been a model.
> I could have moved to Paris or been a concert pianist.
> I could have seen the world, been brave, followed my heart.
> But I didn't.
> I sidestepped love and set off for the East End of London,
> because I thought it would be easier.
> Madness was the only explanation.

At that point, the viewer understands that the 'I' in the handwritten pages is the 'I' who vocalises these recollections. Different recollections bookend each of the episodes, with Redgrave's ageing voice bringing this character-narrator's experiences to life. At this stage, young Jenny's inexperience and naivety are in stark contrast to the voice of experience that is narrating. Feeling unable to intervene in the fight, she turns away, helpless in this strange environment. As she turns away, one of the other midwives, an older nun who we later learn will be her colleague, Sister Evangelina, arrives at the scene and, with one powerful interjection, brings the violence to a halt. This type of confidence and authority comes from experience, which young Jenny Lee is still to gain. Tincknell accurately associates *Call the Midwife*'s presentation of older women as wise and authoritative with Redgrave's vocal presence:

> It is also the somewhat hoary device of a voice-over spoken by Vanessa Redgrave at the opening and close of each episode which foregrounds the ageing woman as cultural sage. Redgrave's calmly authoritative and decidedly 'cultured' tones, with their offering of little pockets of homespun wisdom pertaining to the events about to unfurl on screen, not only seem to secure the programme's truth claims, but also to affirm the 'feminine' values being articulated by it. (Tincknell, 2013: 781–782)

Vanessa Redgrave's voice is the reassuring core in a fluid timespace, and its connotations signal that young Jenny will, of course, become brave. In the process of this televisual narration, the naivety of the young Jenny, and the life experience of Redgrave and the older Jenny, are in confluence creating a situation where the audience can access the notion of Jenny as old and young at the same time.

The confidence of Redgrave's serene, measured voice suggests that identity integration is achieved along the life course. The younger Jenny is thus mediated by an older woman's experiences and, at the same time, the late life narrative of the older Jenny is invigorated. Each moment of voice-over narration presents an intergenerational coming together of the younger and the older self and in this process it is a memoir that is used as the device for Redgrave's vocal presence to create the memory bridge between young and old, past and present. This creates, as Segal indicates, a practice where 'old age no longer appears as simply a type of foreign country separated off from the rest of a life' (2013: 62).

2014   Christmas Special: 'Mature Jenny' revealed

In *Call the Midwife*'s 2014 'Christmas Special' Redgrave appears onscreen as the elderly Jennifer Worth ('Mature Jenny'). This moment of 'de-acousmatization' consists of a close-up of her hands, as she writes, not her memoirs, but a Christmas card. The moment of revelation is significant in terms of the representation of both Redgrave and the older woman. Here in a flashback ('Christmas, 2006'), the voice-over narration links the years 2006 and 1959 (when the episode is set). The choice of depicting Jenny writing Christmas cards rather than her memoirs is only the first element that destabilises the previously strong connection between the voice-over narration, young Jenny and the other characters in *Call the Midwife*. Following a close-up of Mature Jenny's ageing hands,[16] the moment of 'de-acousmatization' is one of disjuncture for the audience rather than the fulfilment of expectations. Accustomed to Mature Jenny's voice-over, intoning wisdom and personal experience through Redgrave's powerful ageing voice, the viewer encounters an image that stands in stark contrast with the disembodied voice. Jenny's first enunciation is of helplessness and disorganisation in line with one of the stereotypes of old age – she has misplaced a Christmas ornament and her husband comes to the rescue and helps looking for it. In contrast to the unusual, female-centred space the viewer has become accustomed to in *Call the Midwife*, the decision to represent Mature Jenny within the context of domesticity undermines previously age-positive ethos of *Call the Midwife*. Mature Jenny, complete in 'age-appropriate' attire, hair style and spectacles,[17] appears *against type* in terms of Redgrave's celebrity persona and against type in terms of young Jenny's characterisation throughout the series.

In contrast to the notion that ageing is a continuum, which Jenny's voice-over narration facilitates, as has been argued here, the portrayal of Mature Jenny and her husband Philip (Ronald Pickup) suggests a more static notion of ageing, where old is the binary opposite of young. As they both gaze nostalgically upon the many black-and-white photographs of the midwives of Nonnatus House that feature on the sideboard in their living room, including some that show Jenny as a young woman in the 1950s, they say almost longingly, 'We were so young'. Discussing Sister Monica Joan, they mention that she must have been over 80 at that point in time. The focus in this brief flashback on chronological age, and the binary construction of 'now' and 'then', as well as of young and old, signals a return to dominant ageist constructions of ageing and age which rely on fixed categories of old and young.

Conclusion

Seasons 1–3 of *Call the Midwife* are a rare example of a series that transcends what Woodward calls the 'blunt binary of young and old' (1999: xvii). In so doing, it provides multiple points of identity through the use of an intergenerational female ensemble cast and the creative manipulation of a fluid timespace that allows experiences to be co-present through kairotic notions of 'special moments' and Augustinian points of change over a continuum of the past and present. Redgrave's voice remains strong and authoritative despite approaching her eighth decade, her narration suggests both reliability and also a comfortable sense of identity integration along the life course. Her vocal characteristics mirror some of the series' welcome portrayals of a wide range of ageing female subjectivities. Most importantly, her voice-over serves to link the past and present of one of the series' central characters (Jenny) in a rare convergence of older and younger selves. Younger Jenny is thus mediated by an older woman's experiences and, at the same time, the late life narrative of the older Jenny is re-energised by younger Jenny's curiosity and passions. As the series moves from the December 2014 'Christmas Special' into Season 4, this earlier period of *Call the Midwife*'s production should be recognised and prized for its radical engagement with holistic understandings of ageing and female ageing in particular.

Notes

1. Vanessa Redgrave is cited in the cast list as 'Voice of Mature Jenny'.
2. The midwife who wrote the original books, about her experiences in the 1950s East End, the first of which gives the name to the BBC series, see *Call the Midwife: A True Story of the East End in the 1950s* (Worth, 2009).
3. Crowther et al. (2014) suggest that 'Kairos time emerges between past and future' (3).
4. It is interesting that birth which is one of the main threads of *Call the Midwife* is regarded as particularly significant for notions of kairotic time – see Crowther et al. (2014).
5. Her character profile on the BBC web page for *Call the Midwife* lists her interests as cake, astrology and knitting, in no particular order (see http://www.bbc.co.uk/programmes/profiles/5hM1j3fSQyShMly53k70jQx/sister-monica-joan).
6. The musical soundtrack encapsulates and underscores this by highlighting repetitive string sounds reminiscent of Buddy Holly's *It's Raining in My Heart* (Coral, 1959) fused with a traditional orchestral score.
7. These are all intersectional elements of female identities that are explored in the series.
8. Small acts of rebellion still continue in her old age by taking more than her fair share of cake.
9. See, for instance, the article in *The Telegraph* (Anon, 2008).
10. Higginbotham (2012) refers to her Academy Award acceptance speech in 1978 for her role in the film *Julia* (Zinneman, 1977) when she used it as an opportunity to make anti-Zionist comments that marked her as an anti-Semite for many years.
11. Within two years, 2009–2010, Vanessa Redgrave endured the loss of her daughter Natasha, her brother Corin and her sister Lynn (Teeman, 2013).
12. In terms of unreliable narration, *Notes on a Scandal* (Eyre, 2006) comes to mind as an example where the older female character voices a remarkably unreliable voice-over narration, challenging the stereotypes of the maternal,

grandmotherly older woman. See, for instance, Krainitzki's (2012) analysis of *Notes on a Scandal*.

13. Which is exactly how the physical presence of Redgrave is introduced in the Season Three 'Christmas Special'.

14. The strength of her bodiless presence is explored humorously in the *2013 Comic Relief* sketch, where the other members of the cast hear her voice and, looking up to where the voice is presumably coming from, address her as 'Vanessa Redgrave', rather than 'Jenny' (available at: http://youtu.be/3ePfiwLuNGg).

15. This mechanism is repeated in the opening of each episode.

16. A similar shot can be found in the opening scenes of *Notes on a Scandal*, where the protagonist Barbara (Dench) writes her diary. See Krainitzki (2012). See also Rona Murray's discussion of Agnès Varda's use of this motif in Chapter 5 of this collection.

17. Her agency further undermined by the gendered ageism underlying her portrayal as the stereotypical 'granny' (Coupland, 2013).

References

Adler, T. (2011) 'A Bisexual Father. A Marxist Mother. No Wonder the Redgrave Girls Wished They Had an Oxo Family Childhood', 9 May, *Daily Mail* online, available at http://www.dailymail.co.uk/femail/article-1385341/Vanessa-Redgraves-girls-Joely-Natasha-Richardson-wanted-Oxo-family-childhood.html [accessed 5 December 2014].

Adler, T. (2012) *The House of Redgrave: The Lives of a Theatrical Dynasty* (London: Aurum Press).

Anon (2008) 'The Treasures like Dame Helen Mirren and Dame Judi Dench Who Enrich Our Arts. Who in Britain Deserves to Be Called a National Treasure?', 19 July, *Telegraph* online, available at http://www.telegraph.co.uk/news/newstopics/nationaltreasures/2435900/The-treasures-like-Dame-Helen-Mirren-and-Dame-Judi-Dench-who-enrich-our-arts.html [accessed 5 March 2010].

Baars, J. (2012) 'Critical Turns of Aging, Narrative and Time', *International Journal of Ageing and Later Life*, 7(2), pp. 143–165.

Baars, J. and Visser, H. (2007) *Aging and Time: Multidisciplinary Perspectives* (New York: Baywood Publishing Company).

Barber, L. (2006) 'She's Got Issues', 19 March, *The Guardian* online, available at http://www.theguardian.com/stage/2006/mar/19/theatre2 [accessed 14 November 2014].

Biggs, S. (2004) 'Age, Gender, Narratives, and Masquerades', *Journal of Aging Studies*, 18, pp. 45–58.

Brown, G. (1995) 'And She's Off... Pouring Forth Her Views on War, Poverty and Injustice, Barely Pausing to Draw Breath (or to Answer a Question). Georgina Brown Goes the Distance with Vanessa Redgrave', *The Independent* online, 10 April, available at http://www.independent.co.uk/life-style/and-shes-off-1615057.html [accessed 10 November 2014].

Browne, C. V. (1998) *Women, Feminism, and Aging* (New York: Springer Publishing Company).

Brunsdon, C., D'Acci, J. and Spiegel, L. (1997) (eds) *Feminist Television Criticism: A Reader* (Oxford: Oxford University Press).

Butkus, C. M. (2012) 'Sound Warrior: Voice, Music and Power in Dark Angel', *Science Fiction Film and Television*, 5(2), pp. 179–199.

Calasanti, T. (2008) 'A Feminist Confronts Ageism', *Journal of Aging Studies*, 22, pp. 152–157.

Calasanti, T. M. and Slevin, K. F. (2006) (eds) *Age Matters: Realigning Feminist Thinking* (New York and London: Routledge).

Chion, M. (1999) *The Voice in Cinema* (New York and Chichester: Columbia University Press).

Coupland, J. (2013) 'The Granny: Public Representations and Creative Performance', *Pragmatics and Society*, 4(1), pp. 82–104.

Crowther, S., Smythe, E. and Spence, D. (2014) 'Kairos Time at the Moment of Birth', *Midwifery*, available from: doi: http://dx.doi.org/10.1016/j.midw.2014.11.005 [accessed 5 January 2015].

Cuddy, A. J., Norton, M. I. and Fiske, S. T. (2005) 'This Old Stereotype: The Pervasiveness and Persistence of the Elderly Stereotype', *Journal of Social Issues*, 61(2), pp. 267–285.

Divita, D. (2012) 'Online in Later Life: Age as a Chronological Fact and a Dynamic Social Category in an Internet Class for Retirees', *Journal of Sociolinguistics*, 16(5), pp. 585–612.

Dolan, J. and Tincknell, E. (2012) (eds) *Aging Femininities: Troubling Representations* (Newcastle upon Tyne: Cambridge Scholars Publishing).

Drake, P. and Miah, A. (2010) 'The Cultural Politics of Celebrity', *Cultural Politics*, 6(1), pp. 49–64.

Dyer, R. (2004) *Heavenly Bodies: Film Stars and Society*, 2nd edition (London andd New York: Routledge).

Ferenz, V. (2005) 'Fight Clubs, American Psychos and Mementos', *New Review of Film and Television Studies*, 3(2), pp. 133–159.

Graham, A. (n.d.) 'Call the Midwife Review Series 2 – Episode 5', *Radio Times*, available at http://www.radiotimes.com/episode/vbh8r/call-the-midwife – series-2 - -episode-5 [accessed 5 December 2014].

Gray, J. and Lotz, D. (2012) *Short Introductions: Television Studies* (Cambridge: Polity Press).

Gullette, M. M. (2004) *Aged by Culture* (Chicago and London: The University of Chicago Press).

Hall, E. J. and Rodriguez, M. S. (2003) 'The Myth of Postfeminism', *Gender & Society*, 17(6), pp. 878–902.

Higginbotham, A. (2012) '"Why Do I Work? I'm Mortgaged up to the Hilt": The World Decided Vanessa Redgrave Would Be One of the Greats Even before She Was Born. But She Had Ideas of Her Own, Too. The Actress and Activist Talks to Adam Higginbotham', 15 April, *The Sunday Telegraph*, available at: http://www.lexisnexis.com/uk/legal/ [accessed 10 November 2014].

Hollinger, K. (1992) 'Listening to the Female Voice in the Woman's Film', *Film Criticism*, 16(3), pp. 34–52.

Holmes, S. and Redmond, S. (2006) (eds) *Framing Celebrity: New Directions in Celebrity Culture* (London and New York: Routledge).

Hyde, M. (2011) 'Sadly, Vanessa Redgrave Is Another Celebrity Angel of Death', 1 September, *Lost in Showbiz blog, The Guardian*, available at http://www.theguardian.com/lifeandstyle/lostinshowbiz/2011/sep/01/vanessa-redgrave-celebrity-dale-farm [accessed 19 December 2014].

Jennings, R. (2015, forthcoming) '"Growing Old Disgracefully" – Notions of Subculture and Counter Culture Come of Age', *Age, Culture, Humanities*, no page.

Jennings, R. and Gardner, A. (2012) (eds) *'Rock On': Women, Ageing and Popular Music* (Farnham: Ashgate).

Jermyn, D. (2013) 'Past Their Prime Time?: Women, Ageing and Absence on British Factual Television', *Critical Studies in Television: The International Journal of Television Studies*, 8(1), pp. 73–90.

Kenway, E. (2012) '*Call the Midwife*: Another Kind of Nostalgia', *the F word*, available at http://www.thefword.org.uk/reviews/2012/06/call_the_midwif [accessed 20 June 2014].

King, B. (2010) 'Stardom, Celebrity, and the Money Form', *Velvet Light Trap: A Critical Journal of Film & Television*, 65, pp. 7–19.

Krainitzki, E. (2012) *Exploring the Hypervisibility Paradox: Older Lesbians in Contemporary Mainstream Cinema (1995–2009)* [Unpublished Doctoral Dissertation] (UK: University of Gloucestershire).

Littler, J. (2008) '"I Feel Your Pain": Cosmopolitan Charity and the Public Fashioning of the Celebrity Soul', *Social Semiotics*, 18(2), pp. 237–251.

Marshall, L. and Swinnen, A. (2014) '"Let's Do It Like Grown-Ups" a Filmic Ménage of Age, Gender, and Sexuality', in C. L. Harrington, D. D. Bielby and A. R. Bardo (eds) *Aging, Media, and Culture* (Lanham: Lexington Books), pp. 157–168.

Marwick, A. (1998) *The Sixties: Cultural Revolution in Britain, France, Italy, and the United States, c. 1958 – c.1974* (Oxford University Press: Oxford).

May, J. and Thrift, N. (2001) *Timespace: Geographies of Temporality* (London: Routledge).

Maynard, M. and Purvis, J. (1994) (eds) *Researching Women's Lives from a Feminist Perspective* (London: Taylor & Francis).

Moglen, H. (2008) 'Ageing and Transageing: Transgenerational Hauntings of the Self', *Studies in Gender and Sexuality*, 9, pp. 297–311.

Morrison, J. (2002) 'A Vanessa Redgrave Production...', 8 December, *Independent on Sunday*, available at http://www.lexisnexis.com/uk/legal/ [accessed 15 November 2014].

Prakup, B. (2012) 'Acoustic Measures If the Voices of Older Singers and Non-singers', *Journal of the Voice*, 26(3), pp. 341–350.

Rosenthal, E. R. (1990) (ed.) *Women, Aging and Ageism* (New York and London: Harrington Park Press).

Segal, L. (2013) *Out of Time: The Pleasures and Perils of Ageing* (London & New York: Verso).

Sharma, I. (2013) 'The Women They Are: Engaging with Feminist Ideas through Women's Different Battles', *the F word*, available at http://www.thefword.org.uk/reviews/2013/04/call_the_midwife_two [accessed 20 June 2014].

Spoto, D. (2012) *The Redgraves: A Family Epic* (New York: Crown).

Stanley, L. and Wise, S. (1983) *Breaking Out: Feminist Consciousness and Feminist Research* (London: Routledge & Kegan Paul).

Tally, M. (2006) '"She Doesn't Let Age Define Her": Sexuality and Motherhood in Recent "Middle-aged Chick Flicks"', *Sexuality & Culture*, 10(2), pp. 33–55.

Tasker, Y., and Negra, D. (2007) 'Introduction. Feminist Politics and Postfeminist Culture' in Y. Tasker and D. Negra (eds) *Interrogating Postfeminism: Gender and the Politics of Popular Culture* (Durham and London: Duke University Press), pp. 1–25.

Taylor, P. (2011) 'Vanessa Redgrave: A Grande Dame Who Won't Conform', 6 December, *The Independent* online, available at http://www.independent.co.uk/ arts-entertainment/theatre-dance/features/vanessa-redgrave-a-grande-dame-who-wont-conform-6272704.html [accessed 5 March 2014].

Teeman, T. (2013) 'My One Regret Is Leaving My Children to Work', 2 May, *The Times* online, available at http://www.lexisnexis.com/uk/legal [accessed 10 November 2014].

Tincknell, E. (2013) 'Dowagers, Debs, Nuns and Babies: The Politics of Nostalgia and the Older Woman in the British Sunday Night Television Serial', *Journal of British Cinema and Television*, 10(4), pp. 769–784.

Van den Bulck, H. (2014) 'Growing Old in Celebrity Culture', in C. L. Harrington, D. D. Bielby and A. R. Bardo (eds) *Aging, Media, and Culture* (Lanham: Lexington Books), pp. 65–76.

Vares, T. (2009) 'Reading the "Sexy Oldie": Gender, Age(ing) and Embodiment', *Sexualities*, 12(4), pp. 503–524.

Viner, B. (2002) 'Nothing Like a Dame; Vanessa Redgrave Is as Famous for Her Radical Politics as for Her Acting', 10 July, *The Independent*, available at http://www.lexisnexis.com/uk/legal [accessed 10 November 2014].

Walsh, J. (1998) 'Interview: Liberty, Equality, Severity; When It Comes to Human Rights Vanessa Redgrave Takes No Prisoners', 25 April, *The Independent*, available at http://www.lexisnexis.com/uk/legal/ [accessed 10 November 2014].

Woodward, K. (1995) 'Tribute to the Older Woman: Psychoanalysis, Feminism and Ageism', in M. Featherstone and A. Wernick (eds) *Images of Ageing: Cultural Representations of Later Life* (London and New York: Routledge), pp. 79–96.

Woodward, K. (1999) 'Introduction', in K. Woodward (ed.) *Figuring Age: Women, Bodies, Generations* (Bloomington and Indiana: Indiana University Press), pp. ix–xxix.

Woodward, K. (2006) 'Performing Age, Performing Gender', *NWSA Journal*, 18(1), pp. 162–189.

Worth, J. (2009) *Call the Midwife: A True Story of the East End in the 1950s* (London: Hachette).

Filmed

Behind the Mask. Directed by Desmond Hurst. UK, 1958.
Call the Midwife. Created by Heidi Thomas. UK: BBC, 2012–.
Desperate Housewives. Created by Marc Cherry. USA: ABC, 2004–2012.
Julia. Directed by Fred Zinnemann. USA, 1977.
Notes on a Scandal. Directed by Richard Eyre. US/UK, 2006.
Sex and the City. Created by Darren Star. US: HBO, 1998–2004.

Index

30 Rock (2006–13), 122

ageing
  and agency, 9, 10, 20, 26–9, 30, 32–3,
    35, 39, 84, 91, 92, 128–9, 130,
    134, 136, 138, 141, 143, 150, 153,
    171–2, 173, 178, 179, 180, 181, 191
  'appropriately'/'inappropriately',
    5, 7, 8, 12, 16, 17, 19, 35, 108,
    112–14, 115, 116, 117, 122, 127,
    153, 155, 156, 179, 191, *see also*
    ageing, 'well'; 'graceful agers'
  and class, 19, 39
  and ethnicity, 5, 16, 21, 59–62,
    67–9, 101–2, 109
  and fashion, 3, 7, 33, 127–8, 135–6,
    138, 139, 153–4
  as 'fight/battle', 18, 55, 136
  in film, 14, 29, 30–3, 43–55 *passim*,
    77–92 *passim*, 115, 128, 147, 149,
    150, 155–6, 157
  and heteronormativity, 6–7, 21, 103,
    112, 117, 118, 119, 122, 139, 171
  and illness, 43, 44, 51
  and the internet, 18, 43, 130, 153
  population, 13, 103
  and press/ magazines, 2, 18, 116,
    117–19, 153
  and sexuality, 1–2, 21, 25–6, 27, 30,
    33, 34, 35, 36, 38, 40, 68, 69, 72,
    73, 103, 108, 109, 117–18, 122,
    148, 150, 168, 171, 180
  in television, 13, 15, 128–43 *passim*,
    162–74 *passim*, 178–92 *passim*
  'well'/'successfully', 137, 146, 153,
    163, 169, 170, 173, 174, 180, 184,
    see also ageing, 'appropriately/
    inappropriately'; 'graceful ager'
  and 'wisdom', 37, 39, 47, 49, 55, 79,
    102, 103, 150, 190
ageism/age discrimination, 16, 17–19,
  20, 47, 49, 86, 114, 130, 132,
  167–8, 172, 179

agelessness, 37, 97, 101, 106, 107,
  109, 151, 163, 174
Agutter, Jenny, 181
Aldrich, Robert, 49
Alexander, Hilary, 154
All About Eve (1950), 44, 48, 49, 54
Along Came Polly (2004), 121
Alvarado, Manuel, 167
Amazing Grace (1974), 64, 68
Aniston, Jennifer, 6–7, 112–24
Ant and Dec, 12
anti-ageing products, 9, 18, 33–4, 136
Apfel, Iris, 3, 153
Apostrophes (1975–90), 82
As Time Goes By (1995–2002 & 2005),
  149
Asher, Jane, 173
audiences, 13, 19–21, 49, 62, 99,
  106–7, 123, 163, 164, 174, 188

Baars, Simon, 182
Badger, Clarence G., 29
Barber, Lynn, 184
Bardot, Brigitte, 8
Barnet, Marie-Claire, 92
Barnett, Vincent L., 28
Barry, David, 52
Barrymore, Drew, 122
Barthes, Roland, 81
Basinger, Jeanine, 54
Baxter, Anne, 48
Beauvoir, Simone de, 12, 81, 85
Behind the Mask (1958), 184
Berger, John, 135
Berridge, Susan, 6
Best Exotic Marigold Hotel, The (2011),
  147, 149–50, 157
Beugnet, Martine, 89, 90
Beyond the Forest (1949), 47
Bignell, Jonathan, 164
Bittar, Alexis, 3
Bizzle, Lethal, 152
Boarding House Blues (1948), 67, 68

Bonaparte, Eugénie, *see* France,
   Empress Eugénie of
Boorstin, Daniel, 13
Bourne, Sue, 7, 127–43
Bourseiller, Antoine, 82
Bow, Clara, 29, 30, 33
Break-up, The (2006), 121
Brooks, Jodi, 49
Bruce Almighty (2003), 121
Brunsdon, Charlotte, 114–15
Bryant, Charles, 35
Buerk, Michael, 13
Butkus, Clarice, 186–7

Calendar Girls (2003), 147
Call the Midwife (2012–present), 8,
   178–92
Canby, Vincent, 52
Carman, Emily, 28
Celebrity Studies, 4, 12, 14–17, 20–1,
   26, 40, 60, 81, 114, 115, 163–4
Céline, 3
Chapman, James, 167
Chenu, Alaine, 86
Cher, 16
Chion, Michel, 188
Chocolat (2000), 147
Chung, Alexa, 25
Cixous, Hélène, 85
Cléo de 5 à 7 (1962), 80, 87
Clooney, George, 25, 123
Cohen, Ari Seth, 130
Cohen, Larry, 43
Collins, Joan, 153
Connolly, Billy, 150
consumerism, 18, 33, 78, 89, 136, 137
Conway, Kelly, 86
Cooke, Rachel, 128
Coppola, Francis Ford, 82
corporeality, 13, 17, 18, 20, 43–54
   passim, 68, 71–2, 89–90, 101–2,
   103, 164, 174
Corrigan, Timothy, 88–9
cosmetic surgery 8, 18, 30, 46, 49,
   116, 117, 155, 156
Countryfile (1988–present), 13
Cowl, Jane, 48
Cranford (2007), 150, 156

Crawford, Joan, 49, 50
Crosland, Alan, 28
cultural stereotypes of ageing, 101,
   122, 129, 151, 154, 180
Cunningham, Chris, 97, 107, 109
Currie, Edwina, 11–12, 27
Curtis, Thomas Quinn, 51, 53
Curzon, Lord George Nathaniel, 26
Cutting Edge (1990–present), 127

Dancing with the Stars (2005–present),
   16
Dangerous (1935), 45
Daquerréotypes (1976), 88
Davies, Marion, 28
Davis, Bette, 5, 43–55
De Mille, Cecil B., 28
death, 8, 91–2, 100, 102, 143, 149,
   163–4, 169, 173–4
death/dying, 51, 143, 164
Debbouze, Jemel, 83–4, 84
deCordova, Richard, 27
Demetrakopoulos, Stephanie, 102
Demy, Jacques, 79, 82, 87, 91, 92
Demy, Mathieu, 92, 84, 85
Dench, Judi, 7, 16, 25, 146–58, 185
Deneuve, Catherine, 82, 85, 154
Desae, Tena, 157
Desperate Housewives (2004–12), 186
Diaz, Cameron, 119
Dicks, Terrance, 165
Didion, Joan, 3
Dietrich, Marlene, 39
Doctor Who (1963–89 & 2005–present),
   7, 8, 162, 163, 164, 167, 168, 171
Dolan, Josephine/Josie, 12, 16, 146
Downton Abbey (2010–present), 38,
   156
Driving Miss Daisy (1989), 53
Dukakis, Olympia, 121
Dunne, Irene, 28
Duponchelle, Valérie, 91
Dyer, Richard, 60, 81, 83, 121, 149,
   157, 184, 186

Easton, Nina, 43, 53
Eiso Trot (2014), 149
Ellis, Havelock, 37

Epstein, Julius, 50
Epstein, Philip, 50

Fairbanks, Douglas, 28, 36
Fairbanks Jnr, Douglas, 37
Fairbanks, Mary, 28, 36
Fairclough, Kirsty, 9, 18, 116, 136
Fatal Attraction (1987), 172
femininity, 5, 7, 16, 46, 49, 51, 52,
    53, 65, 84–6, 92, 136, 142, 148,
    153, 167, 169, 171, 172, 174,
    178
Feminist Gerontology, 12, 15, 20
Feminist Media Studies, 12, 14–16,
    20–1
Ferris, Pam, 181
Fisher, Eileen, 154
Fleetwood, Nicole, 61
Flirt and the Flapper (1930), 29, 36
Fonda, Jane, 78, 154, 156
Fowler, Marina, 38–9
France, Empress Eugénie of, 39
Franklin, Caryn, 128
Freeman, Hadley, 128
Freud, Sigmund, 36
Friends (1994–2004), 112–13, 120

Gaffney, John, 81, 85
Garde-Hansen, Joanne, 16, 155, 174
Gardner, Abigail, 16, 101
Garner, Ross, 172
generationalism, 14, 137, 170
gerontophobia, 79, 90, 91, 114, 141,
    146, 150
Gill, Ros, 137
'Girling', 35, 78, 151
Gish, Lillian, 51–2
Glyn, Elinor, 4–5, 25–40
Godard, Jean-Luc, 80, 83
Goldberg, Whoopi, 5, 59–74
Goldeneye (1995), 147
Goldwyn, Samuel, 31, 37, 40
Gone with the Wind (1936), 72
Gordon, Lady Lucy (Lucille) Duff, 39
Gorton, Kristyn, 16
Goude, Jean-Paul, 98, 107
'graceful ager' (Dolan and Tincknell),
    7, 19, 146, 148, 153, 180, *see also*

ageing, 'appropriately'/'inappropr
    iately'; ageing, 'well'
Graham, Alison, 181
Graham, Avril, 154
Graham, Judith, 141
Graham Norton Show, The, 151
Greco, Juliette, 81
Greer, Germaine, 12, 136, 139
Gullette, Margaret Morganroth, 12
Gunning, Tom, 32
Guzman, Maria, 103
Gwynne, Joel, 168

Haggins, Bambi, 68, 69
Hall, Jerry, 153
Hamad, Hannah, 7–8
Hanson, Michelle, 143
Hartnell, William, 169
Hathaway, Anne, 153–4
Hearst, William Randolph, 28
heat, 18
Heinich, Natelie, 81
Hellman, Lillian, 50
He's Just Not That Into You (2009), 121
Hills, Matt, 162
Hilmes, Diane, 81, 85
Hinchcliff, Sharon, 168
Holloway, Karla F.C., 102
Holmes, Su, 4, 17, 81, 113–14, 118
Horne, Lena, 60
Horrible Bosses (2011), 122
Horrible Bosses 2 (2014), 122
Hughes, Langston, 64, 67
Hurston, Zora Neale, 64
Hyde, Marina, 185

I'm a Celebrity...Get Me Out of Here
    (2002–present), 11
Iris (2001), 147, 150
It (1927 (novella)), 29, 33
It (1927(film)), 25, 30–2, 37
It's Complicated (2010), 147

Jacobs, Marc, 3
*Jacques Demy et Agnès Varda à propos de
    leurcouple, de leurs films*, 82
Jacquot de Nantes (1991), 82
James, Greg, 152

Jani, Abu, 154
Jennings, Ros, 8
Jensen, Joli, 164
Jermyn, Deborah, 4, 7, 11, 26, 33, 78, 115, 147, 156, 167, 170
Jezebel (1938), 45
Jolie, Angelina, 113, 119, 120
Jones, Grace, 6, 97–109
Jones, Steve, 164

Kreitzman, Sue, 128, 129–30, 132, 133–5, 138, 139–41, 142, 143

Ladies in Lavender (2004), 147, 150, 156
Lamare, Amy, 18
Landi, Elisa, 28, 36
Lange, Jessica, 3
Last of the Blonde Bombshells (2000), 149
Last Orders (2001), 147
Le Bonheur (1965), 82
Le Grand Journal (2004–present), 83–4
Le Pointe-Courte (1955), 79–80, 82, 87
LeBlanc, Matt, 112
Les glaneurs et la glaneuse (2000), 86, 89, 92
Les parapluies de Cherbourg (1964), 91
Les plages d'Agnès (2008), 79, 80, 86–7, 88, 92
Les veuves de Noirmouiter (2004), 92
Letter, The (1940), 44
Letts, Barry, 164, 167
Linen Press, 154
Little Foxes, The (1941), 50
Littler, Jo, 185
Lohan, Lindsay, 16
Longevity Through Exercise (2014), 132
L'Opéra-Mouffe (1958), 79, 90
L'Oreal, 148, 151
Loring, Hope, 29
Love's Blindness (1929), 38
Lucas, George, 82
L'une chante, l'autre pas (1977), 82
Lynne, Gillian, 128, 130, 132, 136, 137, 138, 139, 142, 143

Mabley, Jackie 'Moms', 5, 59–74
McConaughey, Matthew, 25

McDaniel, Hattie, 72
MacFadyen, Matthew, 151
Madonna, 16, 108, 174
Magritte, René, 87
Mamma Mia!: The Movie (2008), 147
Man and Maid (1922), 30
Man and the Moment, The (1915), 30
Manning, Katy, 167
Marrill, Gary, 48
Marshall, Barbara L., 132
Marshall, Leni, 180
Martin, Rosy, 157
menopause/ post-menopause, 12, 71, 73, 103, 108, 137, 150, 172, 173, 174
Miller, Norma, 66
Mirren, Helen, 7, 16, 21, 25, 148, 149, 151, 153
misogyny, 12, 13, 146, 173
Mitchell, Billy, 65
Moglen, Helene, 188
Mohindra, Anjhli, 173
Monroe, Marilyn, 25
Moody, Harry, 141
Moreno, Antonia, 31
Morin, Edgar, 45–6, 81, 83
Morrison, James, 184
Morrison, Jim, 82
Morse, Margaret, 30
Mosby, Aline, 47
Mother, The (2003), 147
Mrs Brown (1997), 147, 149, 150, 151
Mrs Henderson Presents (2005), 147, 149
Mrs Skeffington (1944), 44, 45–7, 50–3, 54
Mulshine, Molly, 3
Mum and Me (2008), 129
Murder with Mirrors (1984), 51
Murray, Rona, 6
My Street (2009), 129

NARS cosmetics, 3
Neeson, Liam, 184
Negra, Diane, 17, 113–14, 117, 118, 121, 123
neo-liberalism, 7, 19, 136, 168
Nicholson, Rebecca, 128

Nighy, Bill, 150, 157
Notes on a Scandal (2006), 147, 150, 156
Now Voyager (1942), 45

O'Day, Andrew, 164
Old Acquaintance (1943), 45
Old Maid, The (1939), 44, 50
Onassis, Jacqueline Kennedy, 39
O'Neill, Edward O., 99
O'Neill, Patrick, 164
Ono, Yoko, 154
O'Reilly, Miriam, 13

Paltrow, Gwyneth, 16
Parfitt, Judy, 179, 181
Parton, Dolly, 16
Patel, Dev, 157
Paulicelli, Eugenia, 140
Payment on Demand (1951), 47–8
Peau d'âne (1970), 91
Peck, Gregory, 82
perezhilton.com, 18
performance, 5, 6, 31–3, 36, 38, 39, 43–4, 45, 48, 49, 51, 59–60, 62, 63, 69, 71, 78, 86–92, 98, 100, 104–5, 121, 149, 184, 187, 190
Perry, Matthew, 112
Petrified Forest (1936), 44
Phillips, Arlene, 13
Philomena (2013), 147, 156
Pickford, Mary, 33
Pickup, Ronald, 191
Picture Perfect (1997), 121
Pilcher, Jeremy, 39
Piper, Billy, 169
Pitt, Brad, 7, 113, 117, 118, 119, 120, 121
Porter, Lynette, 173
post-feminism, 6, 8, 14, 17, 25, 33, 78, 112, 114–15, 119, 121, 123, 124, 137, 151, 152, 163, 168, 169–70, 171, 172, 174, 181, 190
Potter, Sally, 151
Pride and Prejudice (2005), 151, 156
Private Lives of Elizabeth and Essex (1939), 44
Project Runway (2004–present), 1

Quartet (2012), 147

Rage (2009), 151
Rahman, Momin, 132
Railton, Diane, 16, 153, 156
Rampling, Charlotte, 3
Randell, Karen, 4–5
Redgrave, Corin, 184
Redgrave, Joely, 184
Redgrave, Lynn, 184
Redgrave, Michael, 184
Redgrave, Natasha, 184
Redgrave, Roy, 184
Redgrave, Vanessa, 8, 148, 178–9, 182–92
rejuvenation, 141–2, 148, 149, 150, 156, 162, 163
Rivette, Jacques, 88–9
Riviere, Joan, 46
Robeson, Paul, 60
Rojek, Chris, 17
A Room With a View (1985), 147
Rosello, Mirelle, 90
Royster, Francesca, 98–9

Sans toit ni loi (1985), 80
Sarah Jane Adventures, The, 7, 162
Sartre, Jean-Paul, 81
Schwartz, Margaret, 164
Schwimmer, David, 120
Scorsese, Martin, 82
second-wave feminism, 114–15, 164, 165–6, 167, 170, 173
Sedgwick, Edie, 25
Segal, Lynn, 9, 190
Self, Daphne, 128, 130, 132, 137, 142
Sex and the City (1998–2004), 137, 186
Shakespeare in Love (1998), 147
Shanley, Lauren, 134
Sharma, Iona, 181
Shingler, Martin, 5
Shipping News, The (2001), 151
Simpson, Jessica, 119
Skyfall (2012), 147
Sladen, Elisabeth, 7–8, 162–74
Smith, Alison, 83

Smith, Maggie, 147, 148–9, 150, 156, 185
Smith, Meredith Etherington, 39
Smothers Brothers Comedy Hour (1967–70), 61–2
Smothers, Tom, 62, 68
Sojourner, Bridget, 120, 128, 130, 132, 135, 137, 138, 139, 141, 142, 143
Something's Gotta Give (2003), 147, 157
Song for Marion (2012), 147
Sontag, Susan, 12, 17, 50, 169
Spade, Kate, 3
Spielberg, Steven, 82
Stallings, LaMonda H., 69
Stanwyck, Barbara, 28
star image, 7, 8, 16–17, 25–6, 27, 29, 32, 36–9, 43, 45, 48, 49, 63, 64–6, 69–70, 78–9, 81–3, 86–7, 97, 112, 116, 117, 120–1, 123, 147, 148, 149, 153–7, 166–7, 170–1, 174, 179, 183–6, 188
Star, The (1952), 44, 48
Stepping Stones (1977), 167
Streep, Meryl, 25, 115
Street Porter, Janet, 27
Streisand, Barbara, 139, 154
Strictly Come Dancing (2004–present), 13, 16
Swanson, Gloria, 28, 33, 36
Swinnen, Aagje, 180
Switch, The (2010), 121

Takeda, Allison, 2
Tasker, Yvonne, 114
Tatty Devine, 134
Taylor, Paul, 185
temporality, 6, 7, 8, 73, 89, 103, 113–14, 117, 119, 121, 123, 171–2, 182–3, 188–90
Tennant, David, 169
Thalberg, Irving, 28
Theroux, Justin, 113, 117, 118
Three Weeks (1924), 25
Tincknell, Estella, 12, 146, 190
Troughton, Patrick, 169
Truffaut, François, 80
Trumpington, Baroness Jean, 128, 130, 132, 137, 138
Tulloch, John, 167

Turner, Graeme, 20
Twigg, Julia, 77, 90–1, 149
Twiggy, 153

Uhry, Alfred, 53
Upton, Kate, 25

Valentino, Rudolph, 28, 36
Van den Bulck, Hilde, 186
Varda, Agnès, 6, 77–96
Varda, Rosalie, 82, 85
Vaughan, Vince, 119, 121
Vidor, King, 47
View, The (1997–present), 70
Viler, Jean, 91
Vincendeau, Ginette, 8, 85
Viner, Brian, 188
visibility/ invisibility, 4, 5, 11, 12–21, 27–8, 30, 33, 38, 40, 49–50, 61, 77–8, 91, 92, 129, 130–2, 135–6, 143, 147, 157, 162, 180
von Arnim, Elizabeth, 50

Waller, Fats, 65
Warhol, Andy, 82
Watch on the Rhine (1943), 44
Watson, Paul, 16, 153, 156
Wearing, Sadie, 5, 16, 115, 116, 141, 148, 151, 163
Weedon, Alexis, 4–5, 28
Weidhase, Nathalie, 6, 16
Weinstein, Harvey, 147, 151
We're the Millers (2013), 121
West, Mae, 82
Whales of August, The (1987), 51–2, 54
Whatever Happened to Baby Jane? (1962), 44, 49–50, 54
Whelehan, Imelda, 168
whiteness, 101, 137
Whoopi Back to Broadway (2005), 70–3
Whoopi Direct from Broadway (1985), 70–3
Whoopi Goldberg Presents Moms Mabley, 60, 61–70, 73–4
Wicked Stepmother, (1989), 43, 53
Williams, Elsie, 63, 67–8, 69
Williams, Melanie, 7
Williams, Michael, 149
Williams, Rebecca, 122

Windsor, (Wallis Simpson) Duchess
  of, 39
Wissinger, Elizabeth, 140
Wood, Sam, 28
Woods, Jean, 128, 130, 132, 136, 137,
  142, 143
Woodward, Kathleen, 12, 46, 77, 114,
  142

Worth, Jennifer, 180, 183, 189, 190
Wynn, John, 38

youth/youthfulness, 33–4, 46, 52–3, 114,
  115–17, 123, 135, 142, 152, 169
Yves St Laurent, 98

Zoomer, 132

CPI Antony Rowe
Eastbourne, UK
January 18, 2019